Linda Elder has coauthored the fo...
Thinker's Guides with Richard Paul:

PRAISE FOR *LIBERATING THE MIND*

"How easy it is to see the corrosive effect of groupthink in others—over history or across borders. Linda Elder wants more from us. She wants us to comprehend, in ourselves and in our own time, just how much our fragile psyches are built of beliefs and opinions that have value only as signs of group membership."

—Ethan Watters, Author of *Crazy Like Us: The Globalization of the American Psyche*

"Human beings are, above all, social animals. On the whole, this is a good thing, but it can also lead to the kind of groupthink that poet William Blake called 'mind-forged manacles.' *Liberating the Mind* is a clarion call for independent thinking and critical analysis. Using compelling examples, Linda Elder illuminates the perils of sociocentric thought."

—Mark Pendergrast, author of *Victims of Memory* and other books

"Many people understand the drawbacks of egocentric thought. Less widely known, however, is the downside at the other extreme: 'sociocentric' thought. Yet, as Linda Elder shows so clearly, excessive group-orientation can dangerously deform our thoughts, our lives, our planet. Read *Liberating the Mind* and then reflect on how sociocentric thought (actually, a failure of thought) has influenced you and those around you. When it comes to counteracting this insidious process, there is nothing better than good, clean, honest, hard, serious and probing thought, and *Liberating the Mind* is a superb handbook for precisely this antidote."

—David P. Barash, professor of psychology, University of Washington, and author, most recently, of *Homo mysterious: evolutionary mysteries of human nature*

"*Liberating the Mind: Overcoming Sociocentric Thought*, by Linda Elder, provides a detailed and challenging review and examination of critical thinking, and serves as an effective guide toward careful and productive thought. Various patterns and pitfalls of common cognitive practices are evaluated. Abundant examples are given of human problems and failures resulting from actions based on self-centered and group-centered thinking. Dr. Elder's many quotations from notable thinkers provide interest and color . . . Linda Elder has done it again. Her latest contribution is a very worthwhile treatise on the importance of critical thinking. It will (and should) be widely distributed and read."

—Joseph Erwin, primatologist, editor and author of *Captivity and Behavior*

Liberating the Mind offers useful exercises to help readers think through their own preconceptions as well as those held by their families, religions, and societies. A practical tool for those looking to free their minds."

—Doug Merlino, author of *The Hustle*

FOREWORD

In *Liberating the Mind: Overcoming Sociocentric Thought and Egocentric Tendencies*, Linda Elder addresses the topic of sociocentrism, one of the two most serious obstacles to critical thinking and to developing a critical society. (The other, which she also discusses with insight, is egocentrism.) She lays out many of the crucial and all-pervasive ways that our socialization, our very human trait of being a member of a group, influences our thinking and our behavior; she details the skills, faculties of mind, and intellectual virtues that constitute our main ways to recognize and emancipate ourselves from the dysfunctionalities of that influence; and she heads us toward an ideal—the ideal of a critical society—that can be created only by the systematic, explicit, global, and disciplined cultivation of our rational selves.

It is unusual for a book on critical thinking to devote so much focused attention to the obstacles to thought. Writers on critical thinking often tend to bypass extensive discussion of obstacles in favor of treating the skills, and sometimes the dispositions, of critical thinking. But Elder argues persuasively that the influence of sociocentrism is so deeply rooted in being human that it permeates all aspects of our thinking skills and dispositions. What we take to be clear, accurate, and relevant depends, to a disturbing degree, on what the groups we belong to assume is clear, accurate, and relevant. Even critical thinking virtues, such as fairmindedness and intellectual empathy, can be tainted by sociocentrism: the points of view toward which we are fairminded and intellectually empathetic tend to be those sanctioned by the social mores we live within; points of view that are at odds with our sociocentrism tend not to receive such fair and empathetic treatment. Thus, what Elder analyzes is the dark side of being a social animal. And she illuminates key steps to take for us to emancipate ourselves from the dysfunctionalities it produces.

Her emphasis, though, is not on critical thinking in a vacuum, or even on fostering it for its own sake. Hers is not a rarefied or ivory-tower view of critical thinking and education. Valuable as she believes critical thinking to be in itself, even more valuable is the power it has to move us toward critical societies. For all its detailing of the dysfunctionalities of society, Elder's is at heart a visionary book. She lays out six of what she calls "the hallmarks of a critical society." These are factors such as the extent to which clear, accurate, relevant thinking is actually valued in the society, or the extent to which ethical reasoning and the intellectual virtues are fostered in public discourse and action. As she articulates these hallmarks, it becomes apparent how very far we are from anything like achieving a critical society. At the same time, her work on the elements, standards, and traits of critical thinking lays out the most fundamental means for seeing through the negative influences of our societies, and the means also perhaps of changing those societies.

— Gerald Nosich, author of *Learning to Think Things Through: A Guide to Critical Thinking across the Curriculum*

Graphic Design: Kathy Abney
Proofreading/Editing: Jon Kalagorgevich
Printing Oversight: Rachael Collins

Liberating the Mind:
Overcoming Sociocentric Thought and Egocentric Tendencies
by Linda Elder

Published by Rowman & Littlefield
An imprint of The Rowman & Littlefield Publishing Group, Inc.
4501 Forbes Boulevard, Suite 200, Lanham, Maryland 20706
www.rowman.com

In partnership with The Foundation for Critical Thinking
1-800-833-3645
www.criticalthinking.org

First paperback edition published in 2022.

Published in the United States of America

Library of Congress Cataloging-in-Publication Data Available
ISBN 978-1-5381-3762-8 (cloth)
ISBN 978-1-5381-7414-2 (paperback)
ISBN 978-1-5381-3763-5 (electronic)

LIBERATING THE MIND

OVERCOMING SOCIOCENTRIC THOUGHT AND EGOCENTRIC TENDENCIES

LINDA ELDER

FOREWORD BY GERALD NOSICH

FOUNDATION FOR CRITICAL THINKING
TOMALES, CALIFORNIA

The Foundation for Critical Thinking

The Rowman & Littlefield Publishing Group

DEDICATION

This book is dedicated to the life and memory of Richard Paul (1937-2015), whose seminal work in critical thinking is widely recognized. When Paul established the Center for Critical Thinking in 1980, his goal was to establish a permanent center of scholarship that would bring together, over the long run, scholars, educators, and citizens interested in pursuing a substantive conception of critical thinking—one relevant to thinking within all professions and academic disciplines, in all domains of human thought and life. Since establishing the Center, and later the Foundation for Critical Thinking, Paul worked indefatigably to help people understand the importance of critical thinking to the cultivation of fairminded critical societies. Paul's work and thought largely laid the groundwork for a bonafide field of critical thinking studies. Almost 40 years later, the message is the same: if we want to significantly improve the decisions we make in human societies, we must improve how we think about the decisions we make. Our thinking is the key, the tools of critical thinking, the fundamental answer.

Paul emphasized the importance of fairmindness and intellectual integrity in a rich conception of critical thinking, and was himself a living example of the essential human virtues. For every theoretical point laid down, Paul helped us work our way through real problems. From early on in Paul's work, keeping with the Socratic tradition, we see a commitment to understanding things as they are, conceptualizing reality in ways that make most sense given the evidence, and living in accordance with the ideas one professes. Paul argued for the most foundational and transformative ways of approaching thought, so as to gain the greatest leverage for most effectively dealing with issues and problems in every part of life.

As a long-time student of Paul, my work dovetails in such a way with Paul's thinking as to make our conceptual work united, if not virtually one. Hence, the underpinnings for this book have been laid over many years of my work with Richard Paul. For my own scholarship, I am indebted to him for the deep and enduring insights he illuminated in his early and mid-life writings. (All of his later work was written in coauthorship with me.) I am even more in his debt for the tremendous energy he personally dedicated to my learning and development throughout the 20 extraordinary years of our marriage. Before he became ill, Paul wrote the Afterword for this book; but he was taken from us before we were able to get this manuscript to publication. Its realization is a humble contribution to his memory.

CONTENTS

CONTENTS, continued

CONTENTS, continued

PREFACE
COMMANDING THE DARK SIDE WITHIN

This book has been written fundamentally to help bring the problems implicit in sociocentric thought more prominently into view in human life. It focuses on the types of influences groups tend to have on individual human thought, and on some of the significant problems that result from these influences. It is concerned with the dysfunctional patterns within which groups routinely operate, as well as the root causes of groupthink. In short, it is about the problem of sociocentricity in human life.

Sociocentrism, in brief, is the powerful propensity among humans to privilege their own and to control, or eliminate, those who go against the group. It is routinely found throughout human life in the tendency to be biased in favor of our own groups, to impose sanctions on those who go against the group, to unquestioningly submit to those in power, and to validate the beliefs of our respective groups.

Sociocentrism is a powerful force in every culture in the world. It is exemplified in widespread group selfishness, conformity, and myopia. It threatens the well-being of humans, other species, and the planet. Due to technological advances, the capacity of human groups to cause great suffering among themselves, as well as to other sentient creatures, is now unprecedented. Insofar as I understand, the magnitude of destruction to the planet at the hands of human groups in the last 150 years has been exponentially greater than anything seen in the previous history of *Homo sapiens*. This is due largely to speciescentrism, a form of sociocentrism in which humans see themselves as superior to other living creatures in terms of fundamental rights.

Pressing and complex problems deriving from sociocentric thought now abound in every important domain of life. Our only hope for dealing with these problems lies in our thinking. There is no other way. Yet, we as humans give very little attention to the thinking that leads to most of our problems. Until we do, we won't be able to emancipate our thinking from the shackles of social ideologies, rules, conventions, mores, taboos, groupthink, prejudice, bias, vested interest, selfishness, arrogance, closed mindedness, and hypocrisy. Until we do, we cannot hope to significantly reduce sociocentrically-caused human destructiveness.

To my mind, we are in need of an integrated, intuitive, substantive conception of sociocentric thought. To date, what has been written about sociocentricity has often been written under the label "ethnocentricity" or the term "groupthink"; the research that illuminates it is often scattered and disorganized. Consequently, no adequate theory has been developed that makes full sense of why and how sociocentricity occurs in human cultures. No integrated theory has been articulated that illuminates root tendencies in human thought and their interrelationships. For instance, little has been written about the relationship between native egocentric and sociocentric thought—about how these two sets of tendencies influence, and are influenced by, one another. Further, the complex interplay between sociocentric thought, egocentric thought, and rational thought has been little explored in the developing theory of the human mind.

Root causes of problems in human thought can be largely understood in terms of these two sets of cognitive tendencies, both of which are "natural" and "comfortable" to the human mind: 1) egocentrism, or narrowminded, selfish thought, and 2) sociocentrism, or narrowminded, "groupish" thought. Both are briefly dealt with in this book. Again, the primary focus is on sociocentrism; but because egocentric and sociocentric propensities are best understood in relationship with one another, these irrational tendencies are approached as an interactive pair.

Finally, let us not forget the human potential for fairminded thought and rational living. I believe that we humans are capable of gaining significant command of our egocentric and sociocentric tendencies if: 1) we understand them deeply, and 2) we actively work to diminish their power in our lives.[1]

In this book, I argue that each of us is a mixture of reasonability, selfishness, and what I term "groupishness." We routinely engage in all three ways of thinking (often every day). The best hope for our survival and the well-being of the planet lies in cultivating our capacities for fairmindedness and criticality, diminishing thereby the power of our native egocentric and sociocentric tendencies.

If we are ever to thrive as a species, we must embrace new ways of thinking. We must ask new questions, pursue new purposes, create new ideas. We must begin with new assumptions and look at things from new perspectives. And we need all of these new ways of thinking to be based in *critical thought*—not selfishness, arrogance, or groupthink.

For instance, when we grasp the intimate connection between thinking and behavior, we understand that our actions are caused by our thinking. When we

---

1   It is important to point out, before going further, that there are many ways to conceptualize the mind, some better than others. The concepts of sociocentric, egocentric, and rational thought are well rooted in scholarship focused on understanding human behavior. The ways in which I have developed these ideas are in keeping with educated uses of words and can be easily exemplified by a careful study of human behavior. But the human mind is complex and, in the final analysis, can only be imperfectly understood, and then often only through analogies and metaphors.

understand the role that thinking plays in our lives, we begin to take command of the thinking that is controlling us. We can change the thinking that causes us to behave in irrational ways. We can replace unreasonable, illogical, self-centered, or group-centered thought with reasonable, logical, ethical thought.

We can work toward the cultivation of critical societies—societies in which fairminded, critical thought is the rule rather than the exception. We can create cultures in which people routinely enter and empathize with alternative viewpoints, within and among cultures. We can develop societies in which people regularly look for and correct mistakes in their thinking, and in which people expect the same high standards of themselves that they expect of others. We can follow the example of Socrates; we can try to *live the examined life*, even within complex political structures.

The ideas in this book are largely conceptual, rather than empirical, in nature. I have tried to use intuitive examples to support a given conceptual point. But this is not a guide to experimental studies on humans as social animals. Many excellent studies have been conducted that illuminate our understanding of human thought and behavior. Some of these studies have been referenced herein. But this book is primarily constitutive of theory, not enumerative of scientific fact. When you come across a point that seems counterintuitive, it might help to formulate your own examples before you decide whether to accept or reject the idea for which I am arguing. I have at all times tried to adhere to what I consider paradigm cases and examples.

Where I do refer to empirical studies, some will wish I had used more current studies. Where I quote from important thinkers from the past, some will wish I had quoted from important thinkers of today. I have tried to keep this book brief while supporting the conceptual points implicit in a substantive conception of sociocentric thought, critically analyzed and assessed. These points could certainly be further developed with additional examples. Many of the conceptual points might perhaps have been supported by better examples.

Moreover, a number of my examples may be considered controversial. This is a natural implication of the concepts with which I am dealing, since examples meant to illuminate sociocentric thought will focus on critiquing the received views of human societies (either past or present). If you have accepted uncritically an established cultural practice, and someone is critical of that practice, your natural tendency will be to negate or feel offended by their critique. This is true for us all as humans, *precisely because we are sociocentric*. Ironically, then, our very sociocentrism may keep us from internalizing the idea of sociocentrism itself (because by negating the idea, we can avoid facing our own irrational tendencies within our respective groups). In the final analysis, it is for you to judge whether the theory I have developed and the assertions I have made are sound and worthy of your serious attention.

Because there are many complexities in human thought generally and sociocentric thought more specifically, I have been unable to deal with all the theoretical relationships between and among the concepts introduced in this book. My hope has been to develop scaffolding that helps us more deeply comprehend groupthink and group selfishness—to better understand how human thought becomes dysfunctional in human groups, and how we can intervene in our thought to create, in the long run, more just and free societies.

I should point out that two of the primary terms used in this book— egocentricity and sociocentricity—are often used in various ways that may differ from my use herein. For instance, some might argue that egocentric and sociocentric thought are important or have been important for human survival. These people tend to look at human behavior from an evolutionary perspective. My concern is not so much with what may have helped humans survive tens of thousands or more years ago, but rather *what we need to do to survive and thrive today and into the future.* Thus, I view egocentric and sociocentric thought as inherently problematic, naturally-occurring phenomena in human thought. The labels we use for these realities and their evolutionary roots are not nearly as important as that we come to terms with them, and that we explicitly intervene in them wherever they rear their ugly heads.

In short, the world is in desperate need of a better way of living that can only come to fruition through better ways of thinking. Sociocentric thought along with egocentric thought, in my view, together represent a formidable twin-barrier to reasonability and the cultivation of fairminded critical societies. Hence the need for this book, and for open minds to read it.

ACKNOWLEDGMENTS

I wish to acknowledge the excellent feedback on this book given to me by Gerald Nosich and Rush Cosgrove. This work has been significantly improved as a result of their comments and suggestions. To Gerald especially, I express my appreciation for giving his considerable time to this project. I wish also to acknowledge, posthumously, Richard Paul's willingness to allow me to use some of the material in this book from our other writings, most especially in the section on ethical reasoning.

Notwithstanding these acknowledgements, I lay claim to any theoretical mistakes made and all controversial examples used. I have been justly warned by my colleagues, and have not always taken their good advice.

LIBERATING
THE MIND

CHAPTER ONE
THE PROBLEM OF SOCIOCENTRISM

As humans, we are all born *centered in ourselves.* We feel directly and unavoidably our own pain and frustration, our own joy and pleasure. We largely see the world from a narrow, self-serving perspective. But we humans are also social animals. We must interact with others to survive as beings in the world. In interacting with others in groups, we form complex belief systems. These belief systems often reflect a variety of forms of intellectual blindness as well as intellectual insights. In living a human life, we develop worldviews that are a mixture of self-serving, group-serving, and rational thought.

Our social groups not only provide us with ways and means of surviving; they also impose on us relatively narrow ways of looking at the world, and they powerfully influence our thoughts and actions.

Our intrinsic narrowness of perspective, focused on our own needs and wants, merges with our group views as we are increasingly socialized and conditioned, over time, to see the world not only from our own point of view, but from the perspectives of our groups: family, gender, peers, colleagues, ethnic group, nationality, religion, profession, and indeed any groups in which we are members. Thus, we come to see the world as Japanese, American, Turkish, Korean, or Chinese persons. We see it as Christians, Jews, Muslims, Buddhists, Hindus, Agnostics, or Atheists. We see it as teachers, entrepreneurs, lawyers, doctors, judges, prosecutors, or police officers. We see it as women, men, people of a certain age, heterosexuals, homosexuals, people of a certain ethnic group, and so on.

Sociocentric thought is the native human tendency to see the world from narrow, biased, group-centered perspectives—to operate within the world through subjective and partial group beliefs, group influences, group rules, and group interests. It seems intimately connected with the human "need" for validation—the

> Conventional people are roused to fury by departures from convention, largely because they regard such departures as a criticism of themselves. … Where the environment is stupid or prejudiced or cruel, it is a sign of merit to be out of harmony with it. … Galileo and Kepler had "dangerous thoughts" … and so have the most intelligent men of our day.
>
> — *Bertrand Russell, 1930*

innate need to be accepted and esteemed by others.

This mentality can be seen, for instance, in a powerful social force pervasive in many powerful countries today: nationalism—or, in other words,

> *our country is the best. We have the best government, legal system, schools, cars, and cities. We are the most sophisticated and charming, talented, and inventive. To demonstrate our superiority, we need to have the best weapons, be the first to go to the moon, have the most sophisticated satellite systems, surveillance systems, and rockets. You are either for us or against us. You are either on our side, or on the side of our enemies.*

Our social groups not only provide us with ways and means of surviving; they also impose on us relatively narrow ways of looking at the world.

Sociocentrism, as a way of thinking, contrasts with that of the emancipated human mind (the mind that thinks beyond narrow group interests to the rights and needs of all humans, as well as other sentient species). The first is intellectually dysfunctional but common; the second is a high and challenging ideal, largely unrealized in human groups. The first entails prejudices and delusions in favor of group interests and desires; the second requires openmindedness, intellectual autonomy, and intellectual empathy. The first comes naturally to the mind; the second must be cultivated.

Starting at a very young age, humans begin fitting themselves into groups. They do so not by their own choice, but out of instinct, and primarily in order to survive. Young children lack the skills to critique the beliefs thrust upon them by these various groups—to determine group practices that make sense to accept, to identify those that need modification, and to abandon those that should be rejected. Thus, from a very young age, humans for the most part uncritically accept the beliefs of family, school, religion, peers—indeed any group in which they become members. Then they spend their lives largely defending and building on views they have uncritically accepted as children. As we age, we don't *naturally* become less sociocentric, just perhaps more sophisticated in our sociocentrism.

Test the Idea

Think of one group you were thrust into as a child that influenced your thinking (this might be your "family"). Complete these statements:

1. I would describe this group in the following ways . . .
2. Some beliefs I probably uncritically accepted from this group are . . .
3. Some problems I see with these beliefs are . . .
4. It makes sense to replace these beliefs with the following beliefs . . .

Of course, many of the beliefs given to us through group membership make perfect sense to accept; many of them help us survive. But many are based in dangerous ideologies. And we don't inherently distinguish the one from the other.

Test the Idea

Distinguish between the reasonable and unreasonable ideas within one group you belong to. Complete these statements:

1. Some beliefs in this group that seem to make perfect sense, objectively speaking, are ...
2. Some beliefs in this group that cause problems are...
3. I believe that these beliefs need to be replaced with the following, more rational, beliefs ...

Jean Piaget, an eminent twentieth-century developmental psychologist and philosopher, conducted numerous studies to better understand the ways in which children specifically, and people more generally, perceive reality; he was interested in the psychological and intellectual processes implicit in human thought. Through his studies, he uncovered sociocentricity as a common, universal phenomenon in children. For instance, he documented the fact that even young children routinely display the belief that their group is best. Consider this passage from Piaget's study for UNESCO (Campbell, 1976), a dialogue between an interviewer and three children from three different countries, about the causes of war. These dialogues illuminate the problem of nationalism:

Michael M. (9 years, 6 months old): Have you heard of such people as foreigners? *Yes, the French, the Americans, the Russians, the English ...* Quite right. Are there differences between all these people? *Oh, yes, they don't speak the same language.* And what else? *I don't know.* What do you think of the French, for instance? *The French are very serious, they don't worry about anything, an' it's dirty there.* And what do you think of the Russians? *They're bad, they're always wanting to make war.* And what's your opinion of the English? *I don't know ... they're nice ...* Now look, how did you come to know all you've told me? *I don't know ... I've heard it ... that's what people say.*

Maurice D. (8 years, 3 months old): If you didn't have any nationality and you were given a free choice of nationality, which would you choose? *Swiss nationality.* Why? *Because I was born in Switzerland.* Now look, do you think the French and Swiss are equally nice, or the one nicer or less nice than the other? *The Swiss are nicer.* Why? *The French are always nasty.* Who is more intelligent, the Swiss or the French, or do you think they're just the same? *The Swiss are more intelligent.* Why? *Because they learn French quickly.* If I asked a French boy to choose any nationality he liked, what country do you think he'd choose? *He'd choose France.* Why? *Because he was born in France.* And what would he say about who's the nicer? Would he think the Swiss and French equally nice, or one better than the other? *He'd say the French are nicer.* Why? *Because he was born in France.* And who would he think more intelligent? *The French.* Why? *He'd say the French want to learn quicker than the Swiss.* Now you and the French boy don't really give the same answer. Who do you think answered best? *I did.* Why? *Because Switzerland is always better.*

Marina T. (7 years, 9 months old): If you were born without any nationality and you were given a free choice, what nationality would you choose? *Italian.* Why? *Because it's my country. I like it better than Argentina where my father works, because Argentina isn't my country.* Are Italians just the same, or more, or less intelligent than the Argentineans? What do you think? *The Italians are more intelligent.* Why? *I can see people I live with, they're Italians.* If I were to give a child from Argentina a free choice of nationality, what do you think he would choose? *He'd want to stay an Argentinean.* Why? *Because that's his country.* And if I were to ask him who is more intelligent, the Argentineans or the Italians, what do you think he would answer? *He'd say Argentineans.* Why? *Because there wasn't any war.* Now who was really right in the choice he made and what he said, the Argentinean child, you, or both? *I was right.* Why? *Because I chose Italy.*

One can easily see that the children in these interviews have been indoctrinated into the beliefs, with accompanying ideologies, of their respective nations and cultures. These children cannot articulate why they think their countries are better than others, but they have no doubt that they are. Seeing one's group as superior to other groups is both natural to the human mind and encouraged by the cultures in which we live, and it has grave consequences which will be explored presently.

Sociocentricity operates at the unconscious level of thought; it is not explicitly recognized by the mind, yet it guides much human behavior.[2] Only to the extent that each of us takes command of this hidden part of our nature can we begin to extricate ourselves from dogmatic and dangerous group ideologies, from irrational group rules, taboos, and conventions, and from group righteousness, all of which undermine the cultivation of critical societies.

This picture illuminates the fact that human social thought and behavior can be harnessed for good; Martin Luther King, Jr. exemplified extraordinary courage and leadership in bringing people together, peacefully, to work towards the realization of the most basic of civil rights.

Photo and caption taken from: https://commons.wikimedia.org/wiki/File:Martin_Luther_King_Jr_St_Paul_Campus_U_MN.jpg

---

2   In other words, humans do not inherently recognize sociocentricity in their own thought. It should be pointed out, however, that people often do notice it in others.

Test the Idea

Think of some ways in which children in our culture are indoctrinated into group ideologies (e.g., that "our country is the best," that learning means doing what the teacher says, that everyone must stand and say the pledge of allegiance when told to do so). Complete these statements:

1. From a very young age, children in our country are indoctrinated into the following beliefs ...
2. In schools, children are often indoctrinated into the following beliefs ...
3. These types of beliefs cause the following significant problems for children and people in our country ...

SOCIOCENTRIC THOUGHT SHOULD BE DISTINGUISHED FROM SOCIOLOGICAL THOUGHT

There are many situations in which people need to work together as a cohesive unit. For this to happen, some level of agreement is necessary. *That* people function in groups is not the problem; this is only natural. But *how* they function in groups often is a problem—whether and to what extent blind obedience is required or expected, whether and to what extent reasoned dissent is allowed and encouraged, etc. These realities determine, to a large degree, the extent to which any group can be said to be reasonable or rational.

Thus it is important to distinguish *dysfunctional* group-centered thought and behavior from that which is either productive and useful, or neutral. Healthy groups can and do exist (though every group can potentially fall prey to groupthink, prejudice, bias, distortion in thought, and so on). Many advocacy groups have well-reasoned goals and processes for reaching those goals. Many families function as rational entities, concerned not only with the well-being of family members but also with the well-being of those outside the family. In short, many groups function so as to nurture group members, while at the same time being concerned with the rights and needs of those outside the group.

Test the Idea

Think of some group in which people work together toward positive change or toward the advancement of at least some aspect(s) of fairminded critical societies. Complete these statements:

1. One group I believe brings about positive change in the world is ...
2. The good that this group is working to bring about can be described as follows ...
3. If more people took this group's ideas seriously and acted on them, things could improve in the following ways ...

Yet the extent to which any particular group can be said to be sociocentric is a matter of degree. Just as people are a mixture of the reasonable and the unreasonable, so are groups. Group members may, for instance, function reasonably well as a group, with each member taking into account the concerns of all other group members, while at the same time ruthlessly pursing vested interests which harm those outside the group. Many businesses exemplify this phenomenon. Take, for example, the marketing department of a successful tobacco company. The marketing "team" may work effectively together, showing concern and empathy for one another's viewpoints. They may spend time together on weekends enjoying one another's company and that of their families. They make exchange gifts at Christmas and sympathize with one another through personal difficulties. They may, in short, function reasonably and empathically within the group in terms of interpersonal relationships, while at the same time creating marketing strategies that play a key role in the deaths of millions of gullible people who become addicted to cigarettes (not to mention the millions of people who don't necessarily die from smoking cigarettes, but suffer other negative effects associated with it). Similarly, people focused on environmental advocacy may work together to advance the health of ecological systems while, alas, simultaneously forming "in-groups" that lead to back-biting and/or other forms of group pathologies. An organization focused on helping animals may be unwilling to work with other groups that have the same goals, because it sees its approach and philosophy as "superior" or wants more money for its group.

In sum, humans are naturally *social*; and though, to some extent, they will always be *sociocentric*, they need not be primarily so. Social behavior is a problem only when it causes problems, objectively speaking. Because groups tend to assume their own thought and behavior to be reasonable, they often have difficulty recognizing their own unreasonable perspectives, viewpoints, inferences, and conceptions.

Test the Idea

Think of some behavior that a group you belong to sees as reasonable, but which you think is dysfunctional (or you might choose a group you belonged to in the past). Complete these statements:

1. I would describe this group in the following ways . . .
2. The beliefs this group perceives as reasonable, but which I see as unreasonable, are . . .
3. I think these beliefs are unreasonable because they lead to the following types of behavior . . .
4. If I were to mention my views to the group, I think its members would react to my views as follows . . .

Those who aspire to critical thinking recognize that any group to which they belong may or may not pursue reasonable goals, and may or may not work together in ways that take into account the views of all relevant parties. They seek to participate only in those groups that have fairminded purposes and healthy systems of communication. They avoid dysfunctional groups where possible. They look for potential contradictions in the ways they themselves treat in-group and out-group members, and they naturally work to avoid such contradictions in the pursuit of intellectual integrity.

HUMANS ARE INFLUENCED BY GROUPS WITHIN GROUPS

Because humans are intrinsically social creatures, we form groups for almost every imaginable purpose. Any given person will belong to numerous groups in a lifetime. These groups will each have their own sets of social rules, expectations, and taboos. Many groups will overlap with others; some will operate more independently. Some people will be more autonomous, allying themselves with fewer groups. And each of us, whether we like it or not, belongs to a broader culture or society that imposes rules on its members.

To put this another way, everyone is part of a number of groups, each of which has its own influence and many of which influence one another. Any given individual is usually influenced first by the family, each member of which has in turn been influenced by the groups he or she has been a member of. Then, as we go through life, the groups we become members of (either voluntarily or involuntarily), with their various ideologies and belief systems, influence our thought and actions in many ways.

A typical pattern of group influence begins with family, wherein the views of the family are thrust upon the child—views on "the family," on marital relations, sibling relations, intimacy, parenting, sexuality, health and well-being, and so forth. If the family is religious, the child is likely expected to uncritically accept the religious beliefs of the family. When the child goes to school, the views of teachers are inculcated into the mind of the child. At the same time, peers can have significant influence on the child's developing mind. As the child moves through childhood and adolescence, there are many influencing parties—teachers and peers, neighbors and clergy, and still the parents and siblings—each having varying degrees of sway at different ages. Religion, sports, TV (and other media), extracurricular activities, and other agencies contend for the child's attention. The young adult may attend college and be carried along by various crowds in various directions, then move into the world of work, and of professions with their varied influences. Add to all of these the many cultural ideologies

In most instances, the mind can find ways to justify itself—even when engaging in highly unethical acts.

trickling down through each group and manifested, again, in media sources like TV, newspapers, radio, and the internet.

Given these many group influences, from birth throughout life, one can hardly imagine what one's life or views would be, or would have been, without them. Importantly, these influences cause us to form ideas and assumptions almost before we have the benefit of conscious reasoning, and certainly before we have developed critical capacities for discerning what to accept and what to reject. When we do develop these capacities, to the extent that we do, we still are often overly influenced by groups and cultures—by groups within groups that affect the way we think and live.

When significant contradictions arise between and among groups to which we belong, we often (if not typically) compartmentalize, rather than resolve the contradictions. Take, for example, the wealthy college student whose parents have taught him not to socialize with people of lower economic status. Let's imagine that this student has uncritically accepted the view of his parents—that people of a lower economic class are "beneath" him. Then, while attending college, he is thrown into a social group comprised of people from differing economic levels, and befriends someone less wealthy than his family. In so doing, he has two choices: he rejects (either in the long- or short-run) his parent's views as narrow and dogmatic, or he makes an exception in this particular case (again, either short- or long-term). Very likely he will do the latter, having been indoctrinated into his parents' views before he could reasonably critique the validity of these beliefs. This is a common way of dealing with contradictions in the mind— maintain the original beliefs while making an exception.

Critical thinkers recognize that they have been influenced by all of the groups in which they have been members. They examine their beliefs to understand how, and to what extent, these beliefs have been guided by group assumptions and ideologies. They understand that the differing agendas and convictions of the groups to which they belong often conflict with one another. They try, whenever possible, to deal directly and forthrightly with these conflicts and contradictions. Insofar as possible, they join only those groups that function with a critical spirit. Recognizing that all groups may fall prey to irrational thought, they are ever on the lookout to tease apart the reasonable from the unreasonable views and actions within a given group.

Test the Idea

Make a list of the groups you believe have had the strongest impact on your thinking. Complete these statements for each group:

1. This group has influenced my thinking in the following ways …
2. The following ideas within this group seem incompatible with one another …
3. I would now question the following beliefs I "received" from this group …

After answering these questions for each group, write out whether and to what extent the beliefs of each group are "compatible" with one another.

PRIMARY FORMS OF SOCIOCENTRIC THOUGHT

Sociocentric thought may be categorized into at least four distinct forms. These forms function, and are manifest, in complex relationships with one another; all are destructive, and they are seen throughout human life in potentially all domains.[3] We may summarize these tendencies as follows:[4]

1. *Groupishness*[5] *(or group selfishness)*—the tendency of groups to seek the most for the in-group without regard for the rights and needs of others, in order to advance the group's vested interests. Groupishness is almost certainly a primary tendency in sociocentric thinking, a foundational driving force behind it (probably connected to survival in our evolutionary past). Everyone in the group is privileged; everyone outside the group is denied group privileges and/ or seen as a potential threat.

2. *Group validation*—the tendency on the part of groups to believe their way to be the right way, and their views to be the correct views; the tendency to reinforce one another in these beliefs; the inclination to validate the group's views, however dysfunctional or illogical. These may be long-held or newly-established views, but in either case, they are perceived by the group to be true and in keeping with the group's interests. This tendency informs the world view from which everyone outside the group is seen and understood, and by which

---

3 Remember that the term "sociocentric thought" is being reserved for those group beliefs that cause harm or are likely to cause harm. Group thought that is reasonable, useful, or helpful would not fall into this category. In my view, it is important to see sociocentric thought as destructive because the mind will find a variety of ways to rationalize it. By recognizing it as irrational, we are better able to identify it in our thinking and take command of it.

4 Also see Appendix B for "the logic of" each form.

5 By groupishness we mean group selfishness. This term refers to group pursuit of its interests without sufficient regard for the rights and needs of those outside the group; its counterpart is selfishness, which refers to individual pursuit of one's interests without sufficient regard for the rights and needs of others. We might use the term "group selfishness" for our intended meaning here; but it seems rather to be an oxymoron. How can a group be selfish, given the root word "self," which refers to the individual? The term "groupish" seems a better fit for the purpose. Note that this use of the term "groupish" differs from the way in which evolutionary biologists use the same term. Their use generally refers to the fact that members of a group are aware of their group membership and are aware that there are others (like them) in the group.

everything that happens outside the group is judged. It leads to the problem of *in-group* thinking and behavior—everyone inside the group thinking within a collective logic, and everyone outside the group being judged according to the standards and beliefs of the in-group.

3. *Group control*—the tendency on the part of groups to ensure that group members behave in accordance with group expectations. This logic guides the intricate inner workings of the group, largely through enforcement, ostracism, and punishment in connection with group customs, conventions, rules, taboos, mores, and laws. Group control can also take the form of "recruitment" through propaganda and other forms of manipulation. It is often sophisticated and camouflaged.

4. *Group conformity*—a byproduct of the fact that to survive, people must figure out how to fit themselves into the groups they are thrust into, or that they voluntarily choose to join. They must conform to the rules and laws set down by those in control. Dissenters are punished in numerous ways. Group control and group conformity are two sides of the same coin—each presupposes the other.

These four sociocentric tendencies interrelate and overlap in a multiplicity of ways, and thus should be understood as four parts of an interconnected puzzle. Some of their interrelationships will be discussed presently.

These pathological forms of thought largely lie at the unconscious level. It isn't that people are aware of these tendencies and consciously choose to go along with them. Rather, these dispositions are, at least to some extent, hidden by self-deception, rationalization, and other native mechanisms of the mind that keep us from seeing and facing the truth in our thoughts and actions. The mind tells itself one thing on the surface (e.g., we are being fair to all involved), when in fact it is acting upon a different thought entirely (e.g., we are mainly concerned with our own interests). In most instances, the mind can find ways to justify itself—even when engaging in highly unethical acts.[6,7]

Test the Idea

A good way to test your understanding of an idea is to articulate it in your own words. Before reading further, write down each of these main forms of sociocentric thought (groupishness, group validation, group control, and group conformity):

1. Articulate the meaning of each one in your own words.
2. Come up with one or two examples of each from your own experience.

---

6   See the section on egocentrism for further discussion on this topic.

7   It should be pointed out that there are many circumstances where rational behavior might be confused with sociocentric behavior. For instance, group members may well validate among themselves views that are reasonable. And groups should expect group members to behave in ethical ways. There may also be many other conditions under which it would make sense for an individual to conform to group expectations (e.g. to keep from being tortured, or to contribute to the well-being of the planet).

A primary form of pathology in groupishness is its disregard for the rights of those in the "out-group."

Let us now look more closely at these four sociological dispositions and consider some cases that exemplify them.

THE LOGIC OF GROUPISHNESS

Groupishness, as I am using the term, refers to the native human tendency to pursue group agendas without concern for the rights and needs of those outside the group. This innate human tendency leads group members to see "outsiders" as either falling in with their interests, or working against them. The group functions as a cohesive unit working toward its goals, which, again, in itself isn't problematic; a primary form of pathology in groupishness lies in its disregard for the rights of those in the "out-group."

In speaking of the relationship between vested interests and group customs, sociologist William Graham Sumner (1906; 1940) wrote:

People in mass have never made or kept up a custom in order to hurt their own interests. They have made innumerable errors as to what their interests were and how to satisfy them, but they have always aimed to serve their interests as well as they could. (p. 58)

Much of the pollution caused by humans can be traced to groupishness.

The essence of groupishness is this: that which is perceived to be in the interest of one's group is considered good; that which goes against the perceived interests of one's group is to be avoided, denounced, or attacked. Take, for instance, the problem of industrial pollution. For as long as industrial giants have existed, many have failed to take responsibility for the pollution they generate. They have been unwilling to purchase and install devices which would reduce this pollution (often citing expense). At the same time, many of these companies have enjoyed tremendous profits. Is it the case that they don't

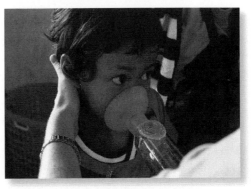

Pollution is increasingly linked to common diseases that affect the lungs and airways.

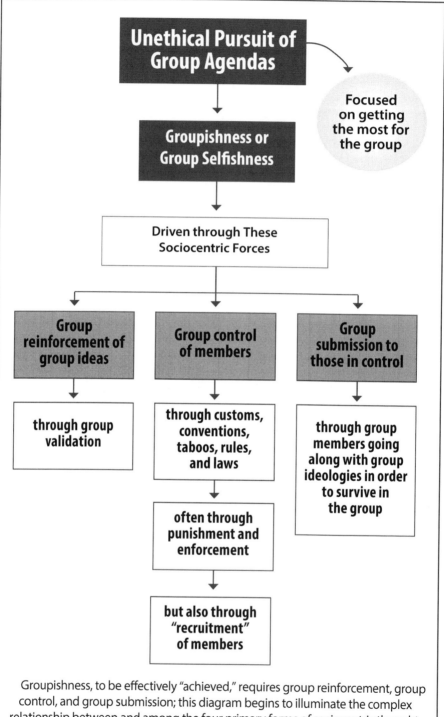

Groupishness, to be effectively "achieved," requires group reinforcement, group control, and group submission; this diagram begins to illuminate the complex relationship between and among the four primary forms of sociocentric thought.

realize they are causing pollution? Or is it that they deceive themselves into thinking that as long their profits are realized "legally," *they are automatically realized ethically?* Perhaps they tell themselves that the amount of pollution they cause isn't nearly as much as the pollution caused by some other companies, or that the pollution doesn't lead to serious health or environmental problems, or they can't afford to make the changes asked of them. All these are reasons used to justify this type of unethical behavior. But the real reason is greed—as much as possible for "our group," whatever the cost to others. The reasons given are masks behind which companies hide—rationalizations that enable them to avoid facing

the truth themselves, and to hide the truth from others outside their "in-group."

The pursuit of vested interest is common in the corporate world; it is also common in the professions. Consider the following example of a potential conflict of interest, seen in child psychiatry, with important implications for the increasing number of children being diagnosed with "bipolar disorder." The phenomenon exemplified here is that of researchers being paid by medical companies which develop

Even very young children are now given a multitude of medications, some of which interact with one another; these drug prescriptions are frequently driven by pharmaceutical companies working in connection with influential psychiatrists who are motivated by the financially gain they enjoy from the relationship.

products to "solve" the problems researchers "uncover." It is unfortunately part of the much larger issue of vested interest potentially influencing medical decision-making (thereby causing errors in human judgment):

> *A world-renowned Harvard child psychologist whose work has helped fuel an explosion in the use of powerful antipsychotic medicines in children earned at least $1.6 million in consulting fees from drug makers from 2000-2007 but for years did not report much of this income to university officials, according to information given to Congressional investigators. ... Dr. Biederman is one of the most influential researchers in child psychiatry. ... Although many of his studies are small and often financed by drug makers, his work helped to fuel a controversial 40-fold increase from 1994 to 2003 in the diagnosis of pediatric bipolar disorder, which [has led to] a rapid rise in the use of antipsychotic medicines in children ... it is far from clear that the medications improve children's lives, experts say. ... In the last 25 years, drug and device makers have displaced the federal government as the primary sources of research financing, and industry support is vital to many university research programs. But as corporate research executives recruit the brightest scientists, their brethren in*

marketing departments have discovered that some of these same scientists can be terrific pitchmen. … Many researchers strongly disagree over what bipolar looks like in youngsters, and some now fear the definition has been expanded unnecessarily, due in part to the Harvard group. … Dr. E. Fuller Torrey, executive director of the Stanley Medical Research Institute, which finances psychiatric studies, [contends]: "In the area of child psychiatry in particular, we know much less than we should, and we desperately need research that is not influenced by industry money." (New York Times, *June 8, 2008*)

Pesticide misuse can cause numerous health problems and often results from groupishness and vested interest.

If it is in researchers' financial interests to conduct studies focused on whether a behavioral problem exists for which medicine can be prescribed—a medicine developed by the company funding the research—it is only reasonable to question whether and to what extent such studies can be considered unbiased. Note that though selfish interest is at play in examples such as these, the bigger problem is that many researchers *collectively* validate these practices.

Consider another example in the field of agriculture. For decades, the primary form of vegetable farming has been large-crop farming with mass use of chemical pesticides. In the meantime, scientists have become increasingly aware of the myriad problems caused by overuse of pesticides. Two of the most significant of these problems include ecological destruction and human-disease escalation (caused by pesticide exposure through ingestion and inhalation). For many years, eminent scientists worldwide have spoken out against these destructive practices. And yet the problem largely remains. By ignoring compelling information, by failing to think through logical implications, and by covering up important evidence, agriculturalists violate some of the very ideals they purport to advance. It seems reasonable to link this failure to the problem of vested interest—the simple fact that farming with pesticides is cheaper than farming without them. The bottom line is more money for farmers, with little or no regard for the health and well-being of those affected by the pesticides.[8]

Examples of the pursuit of group vested interest, and its consequences, can be found in every part of human life—in business and personal life, in professional disciplines and organizations, in religious programs, in schools, indeed everywhere humans gather together in groups. Groups use their vested interests to validate their irrational, group-serving views. It leads to a vast array of problems, including social stratification, poverty, hunger, group bullying, terrorism, genocide, torture,

8   One might argue that not using pesticides drives up the price of food, and therefore has negative implications for the poor and disadvantaged. Though this may be true, governments, if willing, can find ways to deal with this problem. Instead, governmental leaders are often connected with agricultural farming in ways that do not serve the public interest.

and any number of other unethical actions committed by groups against other people or groups.[9]

By implication, groupishness often *damages people outside the privileged group* while protecting and privileging people within the group. Those inside the group win; those outside the group lose.[10]

Those who aspire to critical thinking realize that groupishness is a natural problem in human thought and human life. They are always on the lookout for groupishness in any group to which they belong. They realize they have a choice between doing only what is in the group's interest, and taking into account what is in the interest of all relevant persons and creatures. They attempt at all times to do what is best for all, not merely what is in the interest of "their" group.

Test the Idea

See if you can come up with three or four examples of your own which illuminate the problem of groupishness. Then, be on the lookout for examples of groupishness in the daily news.

THE LOGIC OF GROUP VALIDATION

Groups tend to see their way as the right way and their views as the correct views, even when they haven't thought seriously about either. Group members implicitly tend to validate one another's views, reinforcing group beliefs deeply held, beliefs perceived to be in the group's interests, or beliefs the group just happens to believe are true. Thus, group validation may be connected with groupishness, but is often simply connected with maintaining existing group beliefs.

> Groups tend to see their way as the right way and their views as the correct views, even when they haven't thought seriously about either.

We see this phenomenon throughout human life in every domain. For instance, it is commonly exhibited by sports players and fans— "our team is the most victorious," "our athletes are the biggest and most talented," "our cheerleaders are the sexiest," "our pitchers are the best," "our quarterback is the greatest," "our uniforms are the most colorful," "our team has the nicest facilities and biggest stadiums," and so on. We line up behind our team, and we

---

9 Again, it is important to understand that whether and to what extent a group is engaging in groupishness must be determined case by case, using unbiased reasoning and evidence.

10 Of course, the extent to which someone is "inside of" or "outside of" a group may be a matter of degree. For instance, because of stratification that exists within groups, every larger group has potentially a number of smaller groups within it. Some of those smaller groups will get more of the "goodies" within the group than others. Thus, the larger group might pursue the goals of the entire group while at the same time privileging certain smaller groups of people within the larger group. This phenomenon is seen quite plainly within countries that seek to get resources for the larger population in the country ("more for our country"), but which dole out those resources lopsidedly, giving more to the ruling class or wealthy than to the people at large.

cheer and root for our team. We can't stand the other team. We always want the other team to lose; we always need to win. When we win, we played the best; when they win, the referees were biased in favor of their team. The way in which people refer to the team they support as "us" and "we" is telling. "We" missed the field goal. The referees gave "us" a bum deal.[11]

This may seem a trivial example, but it helps us recognize the phenomenon of group validation in a common human activity. Unfortunately, this form of sociocentric thought isn't at all confined to the trivial.

Theoreticians have conceptualized the problem of group validation in different but often overlapping ways. In his article (Oct. 2008) on "mob mentality," Laurence Gonzales targets a term psychologists call "groupness ... the tendency of various animals, including humans, to form in-groups. When the

People often cheer for "their team" without the least sense that if they lived in another place, they may "despise" this same team, and "root" for an opposing team.

in-group encounters individuals from outside the group, the default response is hostile. People protect their group from outsiders and from outside influences. ... If a group invests a lot of effort in a goal and succeeds, its boundaries become stronger, and it tends to become even more hostile to outside influences. This may not be overt hostility. It may simply be a subtle and unconscious tendency to reject anything from another group" (p. 28).

People often have no sense of how their views are enmeshed in cultural beliefs passed down through generations over time.

Sumner (1906; 1940) describes "folkways" as the socially perceived "right" ways to satisfy all interests according to group norms and traditions. He says that in every society:

There is a right way to catch game, to win a wife, to make one's self appear ... to treat comrades or strangers, to behave when a child is born. ... The "right" way is the way which ancestors used and which has been handed down. The tradition is its

---

11 If you tend to believe that this way of thinking makes perfect sense, you might ask yourself whether you would feel the same way about "your team" if you backed a different team, say in a different city or at a different college or university. If so, doesn't this demonstrate that you would support any team with which you identified? Wouldn't you be caught up in the "our group is the best" mentality, no matter what group you supported? Consider a study focused on perception, in which two psychologists showed football game films to students at Dartmouth and Princeton. Students were instructed to be "completely objective" and note each infraction of the rules and which team was responsible. Princeton students saw *twice* as many infractions by Dartmouth as Dartmouth students saw (Hastorf & Cantril, 1954). The same was not true of the Dartmouth students, who may have been less sociocentric, at least in this regard.

own warrant. It is not held subject to verification by experience. ... In the folkways, whatever is, is right. (p. 28)

John Stuart Mill (1859; 1997), in *On Liberty*, points out that all countries throughout history have tended to hold their views uncritically, while perceiving such views to be *prima facie* correct. He says that, when deciding on rules and laws to be followed,

No two ages and scarcely any two countries, have decided it alike; and the decision of one age or country is a wonder to another. Yet the people of any given age and country no more suspect any difficulty in it, than if it were a subject on which mankind had always been agreed. The rules which obtain among themselves appear to them self-evident and self-justifying. This all but universal illusion is one of the examples of the magical influence of custom ... (p. 45)

In human societies, children are systematically indoctrinated into the beliefs of their culture and expected to *accept those beliefs without question*, i.e., to take them on blind faith. Children are taught to see the customs and taboos of the society as the *right way to live*, rather than as some ways to live among many possibilities.

People often don't know why they believe what they do. They haven't objectively examined their thoughts. They haven't considered other ways of looking at the beliefs they have been expected to accept uncritically. They have little or no sense of how their views are enmeshed in cultural beliefs passed down through generations over time. They cannot see that these views are largely arbitrary, based more in "the way we have always done things" than in well-reasoned perspectives. Trapped in narrow present-day views, people often lack the knowledge that can be gained through a broader historical perspective. They don't see that there is frequently a more reasonable way of looking at issues, ideas, and situations than that which their culture expects or requires. At the same time, they often fiercely defend their beliefs (i.e., the beliefs of the group) as evidently reasonable.

In studying how children understand and relate to rules, Piaget (1962) uncovered the roots of this problem. He noted that children pass through the following three stages of development:

Stage one—the child, being fundamentally egocentric, does not see rules as obligatory, and basically does what feels good. Rules, when followed, are unconsciously received.

Stage two—rules are considered sacred and untouchable, emanating from adults and lasting forever.

Stage three—rules are considered the result of mutual consent. The child believes that to be loyal one must "respect" the laws. Laws can be altered if you can enlist general opinion on your side. (p. 28)

Piaget considers the "collective rule," the belief that everyone must follow the rules, to be initially external to the child. But over time, the child begins to see the rules as freely chosen, a product of mutual consent and an "autonomous conscience." In other words, the child uncritically accepts the rules and laws of society, and yet sees them as independently chosen. This phenomenon is evident in adult thinking as well. Many rules of society are accepted without question, blindly, yet people believe they have come to their beliefs through their own good reasoning. Though they uncritically adhere to societal customs and taboos, still they see themselves as autonomous thinkers.

In 1993, Richard Paul, a preeminent authority on critical thinking, was one of the earliest philosophers to detail the connection between sociocentric thought and prejudice. He says:

> Traditional research into the nature of prejudice has these seven basic flaws:
> 1) Researchers tend to approach prejudice as an aberration, something abnormal or atypical, something outside the normal mechanisms of thought, desire and action ... 2) They tend to emphasize the dysfunctional nature of prejudice. To ignore the many advantages in power, wealth, status, and peace of mind that come from prejudiced states of mind. 3) They tend to focus on negative prejudices, "prejudices-against," and assume that positive prejudices, "prejudices-for", are independent of negative ones and largely benign. 4) They play down or ignore prejudices against belief systems and ideologies, as though prejudices were only against people as such. 5) They fail to emphasize how prejudice is embedded in the pervasive problem of everyday human irrationality. 6) They tend to focus on the content of prejudices, rather than on the mode of thinking generating them. 7) They fail to recognize that significant prejudice reduction requires long-term strategies for developing fair and openminded persons in fair and openminded societies. (pp. 229-230)

The problems Paul illuminates are directly linked to the human propensity to validate group beliefs. All such propensities are steeped in prejudicial thinking, in the rich sense of the term Paul elaborates. All humans are naturally prejudiced toward their group's beliefs; they naturally prejudge situations and events according to what they already believe, and to what their group believes.

Those who think critically are keenly aware of the fact that there are many problems caused by group validation in human life. They are on the lookout for this tendency in the groups in which they are members, and in the groups that would have them as members. Whenever they detect such tendencies in their own thought, they attempt to intervene in their thinking to avoid accepting group beliefs that fail the test of reasonability. When feasible, they point out this problem to the group and attempt to influence the group toward a more reasonable, openminded view.

Test the Idea

See if you can come up with three or four examples of your own which illuminate the problem of group validation. Elaborate your examples in written form. Then, be on the lookout for examples of group validation.

Many Group-Validated Beliefs Are Dangerous

Those who hold creationist views exemplify the problem of group validation. Devout creationists are frequently Christian fundamentalists who take the Bible literally, beginning with the six days of creation referred to in Genesis. Incredibly, many such persons believe the earth was formed in six 24-hour days, and that a supernatural being created people during those six days. Creationists argue that their view of the earth should be taught alongside, or instead of, evolution, which they reject as an explanation of the diversity and complexity of life on Earth. To create the appearance of legitimacy, creationists have developed the concept of "creation science," a term which implies that their theory is scientific in nature when, in fact, it is clearly theological. Mainstream scientists naturally reject this theory.

People can hold their religious views either critically or uncritically. Those who hold their religious views critically are open to alternative ways of looking at religion, and are comfortable with metaphor; those who hold their religious views uncritically are locked into literal ways of looking at religion, and continually seek to validate their group's religious views. Too often, religious beliefs are held in the same uncritical way that creationists explain how the earth, and life on Earth, began.

Similar to the claims of creationists, the claims of astrologers are validated within certain groups of people, but of course rejected by the scientific community. Though most adults have taken many science classes in school, many fail to scientifically assess the claims of astrologers. In fact, many students, and even teachers, believe that astrology provides accurate personality descriptions and valuable advice. Noted astrologers earn sizeable incomes as consultants. To many, the personality descriptions based on horoscopes seem to fit. As people read the descriptions of personality traits attributed to those born under their "sun sign," they examine themselves and find that they have many of the traits depicted. But

they don't look to see if descriptions associated with other signs of the Zodiac might fit them equally well.

Scientists agree that the positions of the sun, moon, and possibly even some nearby planets affect living organisms—but not in the ways claimed by astrologers. Carefully controlled studies of predictions based on astrological theories have consistently yielded negative results. Yet, many people continue to validate one another in these beliefs that "feel right" to the group.

Many harmful folkways have existed throughout human history, and can only occur through the mechanism of group validation.

Many harmful folkways have existed throughout human history, and can only occur through the mechanism of group validation. For instance, foot binding was a custom practiced in China on young girls and women for a thousand years, beginning in the tenth century and ending in the first half of twentieth century. This practice, extremely painful in itself, rendered women unable to walk except very slowly. It led to the appearance of smaller feet, and it caused women to sway when they walked, which was considered erotic. It was a sign of wealth and privilege when families could afford to bind their girls' feet—publicly displaying that

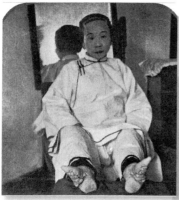

Left: a high caste lady's dainty "lily feet," showing deformation (the shoe was worn on the great toe only), circa 1900

Below: x-ray of bound feet, China

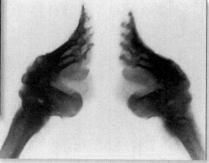

The "baptism by fire" of "Old Believer" leader Avvakum in 1682.

these girls need never work. That a culture of millions of people could have supported this painful tradition shows the power of groupthink.

Given the history (and absurdity) of many human beliefs, it is clear that there is hardly a belief that groups wouldn't, under certain conditions, validate. The term "porn addict," as understood by the Westside Family Church in Lenexa, Kansas, exemplifies this point (*New York Times*, May 3, 2010). The church's leader, Crystal Renaud, offers a group for women who see themselves as addicted to pornography. Her view is shared by the XXX Church (this XXX is not a typo; the XXX Church is a non-profit Christian organization that aims to help those who "struggle" with pornography "addiction"), which can be found on the internet and offers speakers for anti-pornography events. The views of Renaud and the XXX Church diverge "from secular sexual theory by treating masturbation and arousal as sins rather than elements of healthy sexuality. Emphasis is on recovering 'sexual purity,' in which thoughts of sex outside marriage are illicit." The XXX Church offers a test online so that anyone interested can learn whether they are addicted; the church's 30-day online workshop "sells 100 copies a month, at $99 each," according to its youth pastor. Such views are apparently lucrative, but they are steeped in Puritanical ideologies, not substantiated by reasoned thought. Those who join this group collectively validate and allow themselves to be swept along by absurd group beliefs.

> There is hardly a belief that groups wouldn't, under certain conditions, validate.

Witch-hunts represent a pathological mode of in-group thought which resulted in tens of thousands of tortures and executions during the fifteenth through the eighteenth centuries, and which is still found in some countries today. Legal codes of punishment for sorcery and witchcraft can be found in the earliest extant legal precepts of Egypt and Babylonia.

A modern day form of witch-hunt in the United States after the Second World War was that of McCarthyism, in which thousands of Americans were accused of being communists or of sympathizing with communists. Though then-Senator Joseph McCarthy led the charge in these investigations, he was supported by a vast number of leaders in Washington, D.C., as well as much of the American public. Those hunted by the McCarthy machine became the subjects of pernicious government investigations based on flimsy or nonexistent evidence; they were

A propaganda comic book published in 1947 by the Catechetical Society, Educational Society, warning of the dangers of a communist takeover.

AMERICANS.....
DON'T PATRONIZE REDS!!!

YOU CAN DRIVE THE REDS OUT OF TELEVISION, RADIO AND HOLLYWOOD . . . . .

THIS TRACT WILL TELL YOU HOW.

W H Y WE M U S T DRIVE THEM OUT:

1) The REDS have made our Screen, Radio and TV Moscow's most effective Fifth Column in America . . . have been the chief financial support of Communist propaganda in America . . . 2) OUR OWN FILMS, made by RED Producers, Writers, Directors, and STARS,are being used by Moscow in ASIA, Africa, the Balkans and throughout Europe to create hatred of America . . . 4) RIGHT NOW films are being made to craftily glorify MARXISM, UNESCO and ONE-WORLDISM . . . and via your TV Set they are being piped into your Living Room—and are poisoning the minds of your children under your very eyes ! ! !

So REMEMBER — If you patronize a Film made by RED Producers, Writers, Stars and STUDIOS you are aiding and abetting COMMUNISM . . . . . every time you permit REDS to come into your Living Room VIA YOUR TV SET you are helping MOSCOW and the INTERNATIONALISTS to destroy America ! ! !

AMERICA UNDER COMMUNISM!

Typical U.S. anticommunist literature of the 1950s, specifically addressing the entertainment industry.

interrogated before government and private-industry panels, agencies, and committees under the direction of McCarthy. Those who participated in the McCarthy "anti-communist" investigations systematically ignored evidence and failed to examine the assumptions at the foundations of their thinking—for instance, that if people read a book by Karl Marx, or if they believed that college faculty should be allowed to give their personal views in class, they were on the side of communism and were hence a threat to the U.S. government.

Government employees, educators, union activists, and people in the entertainment industry were primary targets. Many of those questioned were imprisoned and/or suffered the loss of career and, hence, livelihood. Fittingly, McCarthyism is a term now used to describe the making of accusations of disloyalty, subversion, or treason without proper regard for evidence.

And even though Americans generally feel they learned their lessons from the McCarthy era, it seems we move from one form of "witch hunt" to another. Consider the "birther movement," which insists that former President Barack Obama was not born in America, despite the fact that the state of Hawaii has produced his birth certificate. Consider the problem of false allegations of sexual harassment or abuse. Consider the treatment of many undocumented immigrants in the U.S.

In her book *Message from an Unknown Chinese Mother: Stories of Loss and Love* (2011), writer and broadcaster Xinran focuses on the deplorable fact that in China, baby girls are often killed at birth, due to the government's one-child ruling (which began in 1979). Families engage in this practice because of the traditional Chinese belief that boys are superior to girls. Families that don't kill their daughters might raise them to a certain age, then abandon them. This case further illuminates the problem of group validation (the Chinese people validating one another in the view that males are superior to females) and some of its sad implications.

> Even though Americans generally feel they learned their lessons from the McCarthy era, it seems we move from one form of "witch hunt" to another.

These examples are just a few of the almost unlimited number we could draw from throughout history (or even on a given day in the news)—of groups protecting and validating beliefs not based in sound reasoning, of groups adhering to beliefs handed down through group folkways, of groups unwilling to be moved by the evidence before their very eyes, etc.[12] Of course, these groups *are* moved by ideologies that substitute for reason and evidence.

Critical thinkers recognize that groups often validate absurd beliefs that lead to suffering, either for humans or other feeling creatures. Critical thinkers do not allow themselves to get swept along by mass hysteria. They examine issues for themselves and attempt always to make decisions based on sound reasoning, adhering to intellectual standards such as accuracy, relevance, logicalness, and fairness.

THE LOGIC OF GROUP CONTROL; THE LOGIC OF CONFORMITY

Now let us consider two additional predominant tendencies of sociocentric thought: 1) group control of its members, and 2) people conforming or submitting to the controlling forces within the group. These two sets of tendencies are best understood in relationship with one another.

> The phenomenon of group conformity entails successfully fitting into the groups to which one belongs.

Group conformity entails successfully fitting into the groups to which one belongs—one's family, clubs, gender, peer groups, school, university, religion, country, and so forth. It largely means learning the rules, taboos, customs, laws, and regulations of the group and molding oneself so as to survive within it—to be accepted and retained as a group member.

A common form of group control involves manipulating people to go along with "the party line" set by the group. This is often done through propaganda and can be understood as "recruiting" people into the group. It is frequently used in so-called democracies when people cannot be directly controlled by those in power. A good example of this occurred in 2004, when he people of California voted, through Proposition 66 on whether to amend the "Three Strikes" law (which sends people to prison for life when they are convicted of three felonies, however minor). Days prior to the vote, the overwhelming majority of people were in favor of amending the law. Then wealthy businessmen, supported by the governor of California (as well as governors from several other states), financed a huge scare campaign, paying for large numbers of television and radio ads

---

12 This phenomenon is supported by empirical evidence. For instance, one important study by Lord, Ross, and Lepper (1979) found that people tend to look at evidence that supports their view far more favorably than evidence that goes against their view. In this study, subjects who supported or opposed capital punishment were exposed to two purported studies, one seemingly confirming and the other seemingly disconfirming their existing beliefs about whether the death penalty has a deterring effect. As might be expected, both groups rated as more convincing the results of studies that confirmed their own views.

which erroneously asserted that if this law were amended, tens of thousands of murderers and rapists would be let loose on the streets. The people were effectively manipulated. The law was not amended. Thus, in the state of California, there are still people in prison for life for such crimes as stealing a videotape (as their "third strike"). To control the people in this case, those in power had to "recruit" them through propaganda and lies.

> Social rules should lead to the advancement of critical societies. They should be guided by ethics, rather than unjustifiable social conventions and practices.

Again, it only stands to reason that there will be social expectations within every group; as social animals, people have to get along, to coexist. But the extent to which one is accepted in human societies is often determined by whether, and to what extent, one goes along with unreasonable or dysfunctional group ideologies, not reasonable group norms.

Social rules should lead to the advancement of critical societies. They should be guided by ethics, rather than unjustifiable social conventions and practices. However, because even otherwise insightful people frequently confuse social rules with ethics, ethical principles are often violated in today's societies. Thus, group expectations frequently seem reasonable, when in fact they violate people's rights. (See the section on ethics for examples.)

Critical thinkers do not follow along passively with the crowd. They think through issues on their own, taking into account the relevant evidence, using reasoned judgment. They embody intellectual autonomy. They do not allow themselves to be manipulated by authority figures or charismatic leaders. They do not control or manipulate others unreasonably.[13]

Groups Impose Ideologies on Group Members

John Stuart Mill (1859; 1997) wrote extensively about the problem of group imposition on the individual. He aptly noted that, though most every group in every historical period has created its own social rules and customs, these social conventions are typically seen by the group as perfectly correct and self-evidently good. In his words:

> *The effect of custom, in preventing any misgiving respecting the rules of conduct which mankind impose on one another, is all the more complete because the subject is one on which it is not generally considered necessary that reasons should be given, either by one person to others or each to himself. ... The practical principle which guides [people] to their opinions*

---

13 At times, it is necessary to "control" or "manipulate" people for their own well-being, such as when a parent prohibits a child from running into the street in front of a car, or when a parent uses "rewards and consequences" to positively shape a child's behavior. But we must always make sure our behavior is based in fairmindedness, and that the actual well-being of the people being controlled or manipulated, rather than selfishness, groupishness, or some other irrational agenda.

on the regulation of human conduct, is the feeling in each person's mind that everybody should be required to act as he, and those with whom he sympathizes, would like them to act. (p. 45)

As Mill points out, people frequently impose rules on others without seeing themselves as obliged to even give reasons for these rules. Mill sees the prevailing principle for human conduct in modern societies as something like this: *Everyone should be required to act as I, and other people who agree with me, would have them act.* People tend to assume their group's norms to be inherently ethical, and they expect everyone to behave in accordance with these norms. Naturally, people are not consciously aware of these assumptions. They wouldn't admit to them, even to themselves.

In addition to the fact that people tend not to recognize the pervasive role that customs play in their lives, people tend not to understand the pervasive role that ideologies play in their thought and conduct. Ideologies, or human belief systems, often lead people to conjure up images, negative or positive, of all kind of controversial ideas, like impurity, sinful living, perversion, patriotism, free markets, democracy, and the good life.

Ideologies thrust upon us lead us to think in particular ways about marriage, the family, intimacy, cooperation, ethics, religion, education—indeed, potentially any complex concept. At one point most people in the U.S. believed in this notion: *spare the rod, spoil the child.* In recent decades, a more enlightened view has begun to prevail. Similarly, it is now commonly believed that students should undergo weeks of "standardized testing" to prove some level of "proficiency" before moving to the "next grade," and that this level of "proficiency" is intimately connected with becoming an educated person. This view, however, cannot be substantiated.

The imposition of group ideologies on group members is antithetical to critical thinking and *intrinsically damaging to people inside the group.* Because human cultures do not actively work against sociocentric group control, and instead tend to encourage it, children are injured by society from the very beginning of their lives. For the most part, children are not encouraged to understand their minds, to cultivate their minds, to grapple with the problematics in native human thought, or to see through capriciously-imposed group control. There is, then, a sense in which *society is abusive to the developing child.* The child needs and wants to grow, to develop intellectually, but societies typically won't allow this unless to a limited degree. Societies instead impose subjective, often unethical, rules

> The practical principle which guides [people] to their opinions on the regulation of human conduct, is the feeling in each person's mind that everybody should be required to act as he, and those with whom he sympathizes, would like them to act.
>
> — *John Stuart Mill*

and customs on the mind of the growing child.[14] From almost the beginning of life, the child is continually molded into prefabricated shapes designed by society through the following types of messages:

> *You can wear these types of clothing, but not these other types. You cannot remove your clothes in public (unless you are a man, and then you cannot remove your pants). You must sit in your seat in class. You must stay in a line when walking down the hallway at school. You must stand for the pledge of allegiance. You must not burp at the table. You can take these "medications," but not these "drugs." You must go to church on Sunday morning and Sunday evening. You cannot be in the park after 10 p.m. You must make enough money to function in a complex economic system. But if you cannot make enough money to support yourself, you cannot live on the streets.*

Critical thinkers recognize that groups continually bombard them with messages about how to behave and how not to behave. Critical thinkers resist group messages based in narrow ideologies rather than good reasoning. They also seek to identify, within their own minds, ideologies they have implicitly (and, hence, uncritically) accepted. Because of the hidden nature of these beliefs, they recognize the difficulties in doing this.

It is easy to identify group-imposed ideologies. For instance, public nudity is something that many people automatically see as unethical. But what if there were health benefits of nudity? In the introduction to the book *Among the Nudists* (Merrill & Merrill, 1931; 1933), John Langdon-Davies foresees a future in which all reasonable governments will insist on the removal of clothes, "on the grounds of public morality and health." (p. ix) Authors Merrill and Merrill (1931; 1933), in discussing the German nudist movement "Nacktkultur" (literally, "culture of nakedness"), say that this movement "stressed the need of the human organism, particularly of the glandular and nervous systems, for sun- and air-baths, and the superiority of exercises taken unclad, to sports or gymnastics practiced with even the scantiest athletic costumes" (p. 9).

Most people have not and could not consider the possible health benefits of nudity, because they have been indoctrinated into the view that nudity is shameful and disgusting. In discussing this idea in a critical-thinking presentation to teachers once, one participant became visibly upset. He objected: "If you are nude in public in front of me, you violate my rights." When I asked him which right he was referring to, he said, "My right not to see you without clothes on." But in fact he could not offer a reasoned argument for his view. It was clear from his objection that he had never thought deeply about his views on nudity, about where they

---

14 There is a caveat to this in that although sociocentric societies damage the mind of the child, people in such societies "grow up" to damage others through influence, indoctrination, and domination. In other words, the intellectually damaged child eventually becomes the adult who is likely to impose unreasonable ideologies on his or her own children, as well as on others in the culture.

came from, or about how these views differed from other cultural views that might be as reasonable as (or, dare we say, more reasonable than) those of his culture. He couldn't fathom the idea that he had uncritically absorbed his puritanical view of nudity from (likely) his parents, church, school, and larger culture; he could not imagine any other way of looking at it.

These images illuminate the fact that different cultures may view nudity very differently.

In mainstream western cultures, men can go shirtless, while women must wear a top.

In other cultures, women can be seen topless in public.

People at Nambassa Festival in 1978. Nambassa was a series of festivals held between 1976 and 1981 on large farms in New Zealand. They were music, arts, and alternatives festivals that focused on love, peace, and respect for the earth's resources. Nudity was commonplace at these gatherings, as it was in the U.S. counterculture of the 1970s, showing that at various times in history, nudity may be allowed, while at other times it is made illegal.

Test the Idea

Think of some examples of beliefs, coming from group ideologies, that have been imposed on you (and that you have not already focused on thus far in working through this book). These are beliefs your culture or group expects you to accept unquestioningly. What are some implications of people uncritically accepting these beliefs?

People Tend to Blindly Conform to Group Rules and Groupthink

As I have said, living a human life entails membership in a variety of human groups. This typically includes groups such as nations, cultures, professions, religions, families, and peer groups. We find ourselves participating in groups even before we are aware of ourselves as living beings. We find ourselves as part of one or more groups in virtually every setting. What is more, every group to which we belong has some social definition of itself and some usually unspoken "rules" that guide the behavior of all members. Each group to which we belong imposes some level of conformity on us as a condition of acceptance. This includes a set of beliefs, behaviors, and taboos.

All of us, to varying degrees, uncritically accept as right and correct whatever ways of acting and believing are fostered in the social groups to which we belong. This becomes clear to us if we reflect on what happens when, say, adolescents join an urban street gang. When they do so, they identify themselves with:

- a name that defines who and what they are,
- a way of talking,
- a set of friends and enemies,
- gang rituals in which they must participate,
- expected behaviors involving fellow gang members,
- expected behaviors when around the enemies of the gang,
- a hierarchy of power within the gang,
- a way of dressing,
- social requirements to which every gang member must conform,
- a set of taboos—forbidden acts that every gang member must studiously avoid under threat of punishment.

> Each group to which we belong imposes some level of conformity on us as a condition of acceptance.

What we tend not to see is that these same principles, or slightly revised versions of them, are implicit in *most* group behavior, and are hence in no way confined to gang membership or "the masses." For instance, consider college faculty as a group. They have names or labels, such as "professor," "assistant professor," "instructor," and so on, each of which designates rank. When referring to ideas within their disciplines, they often speak with one another using specialized language that only they understand (and often write books for one another using this same type of specialized language). They invite one another to special parties and dinner engagements, and they exclude people not in their special "club." They might invite a select group of graduate-level students, or students considered "gifted," or in some other way considered "special" and therefore deserving of their attention. There is usually a hierarchy that everyone in the group recognizes and "respects," often having to do with "rank" or seniority. Those with more prestige (for instance, those who are highly published) might be viewed as deserving special attention, or they might be frowned upon as having too much status or "celebrity" outside the group (i.e., they are objects of professional jealousy). These faculty have a code of dress, often entailing a casual but "professional" look. Any number of taboos might be implicit in the group code, such as having too many publications, too few publications, or publications of the wrong sort; fraternizing too much with students; not being open enough to students (being considered "cold"); or teaching in any number of ways considered unorthodox within the group.

Test the Idea

Think of some group to which you belong, or have belonged, in the past. See if you can articulate the following for this group:

1. the name that defines who and what they are,
2. a way of talking,
3. a set of friends and "enemies" (or "out-group" persons),
4. rituals in which group members must participate,
5. expected behavior involving fellow members,
6. expected behavior when around the "enemies" of the group (or the "out-group"),
7. the hierarchy of power within the group,
8. the approved way of dressing,
9. social requirements to which every member must conform,
10. the group's taboos—forbidden acts that every member must studiously avoid under threat of punishment.

For most people, blind conformity to group restrictions is automatic and unreflective. Most people effortlessly conform without recognizing their conformity. They internalize group norms and beliefs, take on the group identity, and act as they are expected to act—without the least sense that what they are doing might reasonably be questioned. Sumner (1906; 1940) articulates the point well:

> *Whether the masses will think certain things wrong, cruel, base, unjust, and disgusting; whether they will regard certain projects as sensible, ridiculous, or fantastic, and will give attention to certain topics, depends on the convictions and feelings which at the time are dominant in the mores. (p. 114)*

> For most people, blind conformity to group restrictions is automatic and unreflective.

Historian Howard Zinn (2003) exemplifies the problem of blind conformity through nationalism, which is, in the main, achieved through manipulation of the masses. Consider how people collectively beat the drums to war, lining up behind those in power:

> *As always, in a situation of war or near-war, the air becomes filled with*

patriotic cries for unity against the enemy. What is supposed to be an opposition party declares its loyalty to the president. The major voices in the media, supposed to be independent of government, join the fray. Immediately after President Bush declared "war on terrorism" and told Congress, "Either you are with us or you are with the terrorists," television anchorman Dan Rather ... spoke. He said, "George Bush is the president. He makes the decisions, and, you know, as just one American, if he wants me to line up, just tell me where." Speaking again to a national television audience, Rather said about Bush: "He is our commander in chief. He's the man now. And we need unity. We need steadiness." (p. xiii)

Test the Idea

To what extent do you see nationalism as a problem in human societies today? Give examples that illuminate this problem. Look in the news for examples. Look particularly at your own country, which may be more difficult than finding the problem of nationalism in other countries. (What countries do we consider "our friends"? What countries do we consider "our enemies"? How do we decide who our friends and enemies are, as a country? How do we treat each one? Do we base our treatment of other countries on ethics, or on some ulterior motive?)

Again, conformity of thought, emotion, and action is not restricted to the masses, the lowly, or the poor. It is characteristic of people in general, independent of their role in society, independent of status and prestige, independent of years of schooling. It is in all likelihood as true of college professors and their presidents as it is of students and custodians, as true of senators and chief executives as it is of construction and assembly-line workers. Conformity of thought and behavior (or group submission) is the rule for humans; independence is the exception. If we, the people, are to cultivate fairminded critical societies, critique of mores and ideological convictions must become commonplace throughout the world.

In his classic text *The Power Elite*, C. Wright Mills (1956) examines the thinking and behavior of the powerful in America. He exemplifies groupthink as common among chief executives:

When it is asked of the top corporate men: "But didn't they have to have something to get up there?" The answer is, "Yes, they did." By definition, they had "what it takes." The real question accordingly is: the sound judgment, as gauged by the men of sound judgment who select them. The fit survive, and fitness means, not formal competence—there probably is no such thing for top executive positions—but conformity with the criteria of those who have already succeeded. To be compatible with the top men is to act like them, to look like them, to think like them: to be of and for them—or at least to display oneself to them in such a way as to create that impression. (p. 141)

In this example we see conformity coupled with validation of the group's beliefs and standards—however arbitrary, superficial, or absurd—as primary criteria for success at the executive levels of management. These standards are validated within the group, and thus determine the extent to which given persons will survive in the power structure as well as how "successful" they will become. Critical thinkers learn to recognize and systematically critique these practices.

In his autobiography *The Summing Up*, Somerset Maugham (1938) reveals how he came to see the sociocentric (uncritical) manner in which most people hold their religious beliefs, and how he consequently came to reject his own. He came to see that people conform to the beliefs of their country or religion without any sense that they are doing so. He says:

> To be compatible with the top men is to act like them, to look like them, to think like them: to be of and for them—or at least to display oneself to them in such a way as to create that impression.
>
> — *C. Wright Mills*

> ... *when I went to Germany I discovered that the Germans were just as proud of being German as I was proud of being English. I heard them say that the English did not understand music and that Shakespeare was only appreciated in Germany. They spoke of the English as a nation of shopkeepers and had no doubt in their minds that as artists, men of science and philosophers they were greatly superior. It shook me. And now at High Mass in Heidelberg I could not but notice that the students, who filled the church to its doors, seemed very devout. They had, indeed, all the appearance of*

Cultural practices that seem "unique"—and make us feel "different" and "special"—are often found in various forms throughout different cultures and historical periods, as these pictures reveal.

believing in their religion as sincerely as I believed in mine. It was queer that they could, for of course I knew that theirs was false and mine was true. …
It struck me that I might very well have been born in South Germany, and then I should naturally have been brought up as a Catholic. I found it very hard that thus through no fault of my own I should have been condemned to everlasting torment. My ingenious nature revolted at the injustice. The next step was easy: I came to the conclusion that it could not matter a row of pins what one believed; God could not condemn people just because they were Spaniards or Hottentots. … The whole horrible structure … tumbled down like a house of cards. (pp. 248–249)

Test the Idea

Articulate Somerset Maugham's point in your own words and think through some important implications of it. In other words, give it a reasonable interpretation and then ask, "if people took this line of reasoning seriously, how might they act differently?"

Because people tend to hold fast to deeply-held beliefs, especially those instilled through powerful group influences, this autobiographical example from Maugham's writings illuminates an ability quite rare—to reject such beliefs unreservedly.

In sum, group conformity in human life—the counterpart to group control—is so common as to be nearly undetectable by individuals engaging in it. People tend to automatically accept and follow the mainstream view. This phenomenon is connected with the largely unconscious need to feel accepted—to be validated within the group. Very few people are autonomous thinkers, since true independence of thought is so little valued in human cultures.

> Very few people are autonomous thinkers, since true independence of thought is so little valued in human cultures.

Conversely, conformity can be seen in almost every part of human life, from the way we wear our hair to the way we dress, from the food we eat to the cars we drive, and from the technological gadgets we purchase to the music we listen to. When, for instance, any new cell phone or music device is released onto the market, people flock to the store to get it before their friends have a chance to. People will often stand in line for hours to purchase some new electronic plaything, in case the store should run out before they get theirs. People spend $50 on a haircut because their friends pay the same, not because the cut is any better than the one they could get for $20. They wear clothing that fits the styles popular among their peers and in their culture. All of this is conformity to (might we say dysfunctional?) group values.

People are so busy conforming to group codes and conventions, while at the same time having no real sense of doing so, that the negative implications of group influence go largely unnoticed. For instance, the sheer amount of frivolous toys produced and sold in "developed" societies creates enormous strain on the earth's resources.

Furthermore, hundreds of thousands of rules and laws are thrust upon us when we enter life as humans, most of which are created by humans functioning within the twin logics of group control and group conformity. The critical thinker examines not the many thousands of mores and rules in a given culture, but the fundamental beliefs and assumptions upon which they are based.

People will race to get the "latest and best" gadget, with no sense that they are entrenched in sociocentric ideologies, sometimes even trampling others in the process.

Test the Idea

Now that you have a basic idea of group control and group conformity, articulate three or four examples of each which illuminate these problems. Then find examples of both in the news, a book, or an essay. Consider some examples in which people are "recruited" by those in control through effective propaganda.

Group Conformity Is Often Dangerous

Group conformity is often very dangerous. Because people don't see themselves conforming when they are, in fact, highly submissive to group beliefs, those who hold persuasive and literal power in the group can easily move the majority to do what is against their interests or those of other sentient creatures.

Take human sacrifice. For thousands of years, various human cultures have engaged in this horrific practice, primarily for religious purposes. Most people have gone along with this custom, believing it to be required or desired by their gods. Slaves were often chosen by the ruling group to be sacrificed. As long as people in these groups submitted to the dominating ideology, as handed down by the ruling class, the practice continued.

Female genital cutting, or female genital mutilation,[15] is a similarly ghastly practice; it deprives girls and women of the right to determine for themselves how their bodies are treated. It denies them the right to enjoy healthy sexuality through the full retention of their sexual organs.[16] This tradition, practiced mainly in Northern Africa and the Middle East, has been handed down through generations and continues primarily due to social pressure. The 2010 *Population Reference Bureau* reports that:

> *… an estimated 100 million to 140 million girls and women worldwide have undergone female genital mutilation/cutting (FGM/C), and more than 3 million girls are at risk for cutting each year on the African continent alone. FGM/C is generally performed on girls between ages 4 and 12, although it is practiced in some cultures as early as a few days after birth or as late as just prior to marriage.*

This folkway is considered essential to the proper raising of a girl, and preparatory to adulthood as well as marriage. Female genital cutting is connected with what is considered appropriate sexual behavior, namely, maintaining virginity before marriage and fidelity during marriage. It is associated with the notion of female cleanliness and beauty through the removal of body parts considered "male" or "unclean."

> People don't see themselves conforming when they are, in fact, highly submissive to group beliefs.

Of course, there is some opposition to this barbaric practice. The World Health Organization, the United Nations, and Amnesty International are strongly against it. This custom would almost certainly cease if all women in practicing countries simply refused to subject their daughters to it. The fact that so many women go along with this gruesome custom, when it denies both them and their daughters a fundamental human right, illuminates the power of group conformity.

The American war in Vietnam also provides a stunning case of dangerous conformity. For more than a decade, the American people supported this horrific war that was opposed by enlightened people across the world. Swept up in the zeal to stop "communism," at the behest of our leaders, the vast majority of Americans failed to question the roots of the war, the reasons for the war, or the implications of the war. Their view was mostly this: what our government tells us to believe, we believe; if we are asked to support war, there must be good reasons

---

15 It should be noted that many women and girls who undergo this procedure will fiercely defend their right to do this, just as many Chinese women were horrified when no longer required to bind their feet. Indeed, people may defend any common practice they have participated in but which is revealed as irrational or unreasonable. This fact exemplifies how deeply people can be, and are, indoctrinated into belief systems that are harmful, or which deprive them of some basic right. The fact that these people would defend irrational practices (in the name of doing what seems right to them, or behaving in accord with their beliefs) does not make them intellectually autonomous thinkers or reasonable persons.

16 Female genital cutting (FGC), also known as female genital mutilation (FGM), female circumcision, or female genital mutilation/cutting (FGM/C), is any procedure involving the partial or total removal of the external female genitalia or other injury to the female genital organs. The term is almost exclusively used to describe traditional or religious procedures on a minor, which requires the parents' consent because of the age of the girl.

to support it. Submitting to "authority" figures, assuming the U.S. government to be inherently right as our "leader," uncritically accepting the propaganda fed to the American people through media—all exemplify sociocentric conformity. In his book *War Crimes in Vietnam*, Bertrand Russell (1967) gives these estimates regarding the results of the war:

> ... *160,000 dead by mid 1963; 700,000 tortured and maimed; 400,000 imprisoned; 31,000 raped; 3,000 disemboweled with livers cut out while alive; 4,000 burned alive; 1,000 temples destroyed; 46 villages attacked with poisonous chemicals; 16,000 [concentration] camps existing or under construction. (p. 59)*

A refugee camp in Ukhia, Cox's Bazar, Bangladesh, is inhabited by Rohingya refugees that fled from ethnic and religious persecution in neighboring Myanmar. It is estimated that more than 24,000 Rohingya were killed by the Myanmar military and local Buddhists since "clearance operations" started in 2017. Ethnic wars directly result from dangerous group ideologies.

Photo and caption taken from https://en.wikipedia.org/wiki/ Rohingya_refugees_in_Bangladesh, September 3, 2019

Remembering that the war was to continue until 1975, the numbers reflecting tortures, murders, and false imprisonment grew well beyond these already staggering figures.

Russell (1967) illuminates the role often played by media in advancing the agendas of those in power. In referring to the Vietnam War and how mainstream media systematically fed the views of the government to the masses, Russell says:

> ... *although some newspapers were prepared to publish isolated pieces of horrifying information, they had no intention of forming a coherent picture of the war from these reports and every intention of preventing others from doing so. The informed press knew that there was something seriously wrong about the war, but restricted themselves to pedestrian comments and peripheral criticisms ... Repeatedly the press gets away with such disgraceful behavior through the helplessness of the public. ... As the war in Vietnam escalated, slowly and steadily, the* New York Times *came under increasing pressure not to print articles which exposed the lies and distortions of the American Government. An important suppression of vital information occurred as early as March 1962, for example, when the* New York Times *(as well as every other major American daily newspaper) declined to publish an article sent over the wires of the Associated Press by Mr. Malcolm Brown, later a recipient of the Pulitzer Prize in journalism for his reporting from Vietnam. (pp. 30-31)*

Dominating groups often create special rules for themselves, and other people (denied these same privileges) usually don't object. They conform to the status quo because they don't detect these special rules. On February 23, 2006, the *New*

York Times highlighted a report by Human Rights First; the report stated that five months was the longest sentence for any member of the American military linked to torture-related deaths of a detainee in Iraq or Afghanistan. "In only 12 of 34 cases has anyone been punished for the confirmed or suspected killings, said the group. ... Beyond those cases, in almost half of 98 known detainee deaths since 2002, the cause was never announced or was reported as undetermined." The report also documented the fact that "In dozens of cases ... grossly inadequate reporting, investigation and follow-through have left no one at all responsible for homicides and other unexplained deaths." In Baghdad, a victim's son said, "Justice wasn't done in our father's case by the U.S. forces, because if he was a criminal, they should have interrogated him fairly and not tortured him barbarically and then killed him." His father, who was suspected of "supporting the anti-American insurgency, died in 2003 when an Army interrogator covered him in a sleeping bag, sat on his chest and put his hand over his mouth." He had been detained when he appeared at an American base to seek the release of his four sons. His interrogator, originally charged with murder, was convicted of negligent homicide in a military trial and was reprimanded without jail time. If the average person in the United States committed murder in these same ways (outside the special rules of war), he would be convicted of murder under U.S. law, and would most likely serve life in prison or receive the death penalty. But the military often has special rules for its members, as is seen in this and many similar cases.

Group control and group conformity are implicit in *social stratification*. According to Plotnicov and Tuden (1970), since virtually all modern societies today are complex, characteristics of stratification presumably can be found in every such society. Each entails social groups that:

1. are ranked hierarchically;
2. maintain relatively permanent positions in the hierarchy;
3. have differential control of the sources of power, primarily economic and political;
4. are separated by invidious cultural distinctions that also serve to maintain social distances between the groups; and
5. are articulated by an overarching ideology which provides a rationale for the established hierarchical arrangements. (pp. 4–5)

Given this phenomenon, we should be able to identify, for any group in our society, where approximately it stands in the hierarchy of power, how the sources of power and control are determined and arranged, how the distinctions that indicate status are formulated, how social distances are maintained between the groups, and what overarching ideology provides the rationale for the group's perspective.

Test the Idea

Do you think that some people in your culture have more power than others? If so, complete these statements:

1. It seems to me that the groups with the most power in my country are … I think this because … These groups are (or are not) mainly economic or political (explain).

2. Those with the most power separate themselves from those with less power in the following ways …

3. The ideologies (or beliefs) that those in power use to maintain their power are … (consider, for instance, the wealthy. Do they tend to have more power in your country? If so, how?)

Dissenters Are Frequently Punished

Because people are expected to go along with mainstream views, dissenters, or those who simply do not live in accordance with conventional traditions, are often treated harshly in today's societies. A *New York Times* article (August 12, 2010) highlights a case in Iran in which Sakineh Mohammadi Ashtiani was charged with adultery and sentenced to death by stoning. Among other things, the article mentions the fact that one of her attorneys, Mohammad Mostafaei, was summoned by authorities to appear for interrogation. Another of her lawyers "fled Iran … after his office was ransacked and members of his family were arrested, and he is now seeking asylum in Norway. Mr. Mostafaei has taken on dozens of controversial cases, and has urged Iran's judiciary to ban stoning, juvenile executions and the imprisonment of political dissidents." In this case, the woman charged with adultery violated the sacred norms of society, not any objective standard of ethics. Her attorneys were willing to risk perhaps even their lives to work toward a more fair society. The Iranian government has made it clear that they will punish such dissention.

One of the most well-known dissenters in history is Socrates (c. 470–399 BCE), who was put to death by the state for "corrupting" the young by teaching them to think critically about traditions and customs, and for presumably not believing in the gods sanctioned by the "city." Galileo advanced the notion, put forth by Copernicus, that the sun (rather than the earth) was the center of the universe, which got him in trouble with authorities (1615). He was warned to abandon his view, which he did in order to save his skin. Later he defended his views (1632) in his most famous work, *Dialogue Concerning the Two Chief World Systems*. Consequently, he was tried by the Inquisition, found suspect of heresy, forced to recant, and spent the rest of his life under house arrest.

When Charles Darwin introduced his conception of evolution, "it was everywhere met with ridicule and abuse" (Macdonald, 1931; 1972, p. vii). In the

70 years between when Darwin published his first book and Macdonald wrote his important work, *Fifty Years of Free Thought*,

> the whole scientific world accepted [Darwin's] conclusion, and his theory of evolution is taught in every school worthy of the name. Amongst the intelligent people of the world it is almost as well established as the once heretical doctrine that the earth is round. It is well to take a look at the story of privation and suffering of the early apostles of freedom and science who at great risk and through dire privations went up and down the world seeking to emancipate the human mind. (p. vii)

> The truly autonomous thinker is rare, and penalties for independent thinking can be stiff.

Emotionally charged issues often lead people to stereotype dissenters, however sound the reasoning or justifiable the actions of those dissenting. The reader may recall the case of Dr. Jack Kevorkian, dubbed "Dr. Death" by mass media, who fought for the rights of the suffering to end their own lives in dignity. He argued that medical doctors have an ethical responsibility to assist terminally ill patients in ending their lives, should these patients choose to do so; he argued for euthanasia as a basic human right. Jack Lessenberry, a prominent Michigan journalist for the *Detroit Metro Times*, wrote, "Jack Kevorkian … was a major force for good in this society. He forced us to pay attention to one of the biggest elephants in the room: the fact that today vast numbers of people are alive who would rather be dead, who have lives not worth living" (*New York Times*, June 4, 2011). Though the debate continues as to whether euthanasia should be legalized, Kevorkian's advocacy for the right of people to end their lives impacted how people think of euthanasia. Further, Kevorkian's actions "helped spur the growth of hospice care in the U.S. and made physicians more sympathetic to those in severe pain and more willing to prescribe medication to relieve it" (*New York Times*, June 4, 2011). Still, Kevorkian spent eight years in prison for assisting one patient in ending her life. Because his perspective offended the mainstream, he was punished.

Dissenters can be found (and punished) in potentially any area of human life. Because of his views on Israel, Pulitzer Prize-winning playwright Tony Kushner was briefly kept from receiving an honorary degree from the Board of Trustees of the City University of New York. Kushner has criticized Israel's actions in the West Bank and Gaza. According to the *Press Democrat* (June 4, 2011), one trustee of the board, Jeffrey Wiesenfeld, denounced Kushner's views, branding him "'a Jewish anti-Semite' and a 'kapo,' a term for Jews who worked for the Nazis in concentration camps." In response, Kushner told graduates of John Jay College of Criminal Justice, "they, too, must engage with society's thorniest issues and urged them to 'find the human in yourself by finding the citizen in yourself, the activist, the hero in yourself.'"

Edward Snowden, former agent of the National Security Agency, was charged by President Obama with violating the Espionage Act for releasing this information: that the U.S. government systematically gathers information on potentially every person in the world through its secret technologies, that it can keep this information indefinitely, and that it can use this information at will in any way it chooses. Snowden fled from his home and job in Hawaii, and and was granted asylum in Russia; because of the inordinate power the U.S. "enjoys" in today's political climate, precious few countries even considered coming to Snowden's aid (even though these countries themselves have been victims of U.S. spying practices). Still, though some have questioned Snowden's motives and methods for disseminating the information he uncovered, his actions (and the actions of other similar whistleblowers) are celebrated by many of those concerned with the preservation of human rights across the world. At great risk to himself, recognizing that life as he knew it would be over, Snowden uncovered egregious, unlawful, and unethical actions on the part of the U.S. government.

Implications of increasingly harsh sex laws in the United States illuminate how people who violate sexual customs are treated in the society. In Petaluma, California (*Press Democrat*, October 21, 2010), a former high-school coach was charged with annoying and molesting a team member while serving as coach. Chief Deputy District Attorney Tashawn Sanders said the man's conduct "was motivated 'by unnatural or abnormal sexual interest in a person under 18 years old.'" This statement seems to imply a definitive cutoff point, at which being sexually interested in someone under that specific age should be considered perverted or disgusting. The problem is that such a cutoff point, wherever it is, must be arbitrary. There is no holy book of ages at which people should be allowed to engage in sexual relations, though societies act as if such a book exists. The history of sexuality shows that all ages of people have engaged in all manner of sexual behavior with one another. A little over 50 years ago, for instance, it was common for girls aged 12 to be married to men much older than themselves (in the United States). I don't mean to argue for marriage at so young an age, but only to show how norms change, and how when they do, attitudes of people change accordingly.

Sexual norms considered acceptable by one group at one point in time may well be considered perverted and pathological in another. Even in the United States today, the age of consent varies from 16 to 18. In many other countries, the age of consent is much lower. For instance, in Italy, Hungary, Peru, and Puerto Rico, the age of consent is 14. In South Korea, the age is 13. In some countries it is even lower.[17]

Sexual behavior considered criminal in one country might be considered a healthy norm in other countries. *What is often missed is whether, and to what extent, actual harm is done during the sexual experiences.* Further, what is often ignored is the harm caused, not by people of different ages engaging in consensual

---

17   This information was taken from www.ageofconsent.net and www.ageofconsent.us.

sex, but by puritanical beliefs that imply a "right" way to look at sexuality and its many complexities.

In 2004, Jonathan Johnson was convicted of engaging in unlawful sex with several teenage girls when he was between 18 and 20 years of age. A jury convicted Johnson of 41 felonies involving sexual contact with girls between ages of 13 and 16. Regardless of the girls' sexual consent, state law prohibits adults from having sex with minors. Johnson was sentenced to almost 200 years in prison (*Press Democrat*, July 14, 2008).[18] According to the *Press Democrat* (February 6, 2004), "During the trial and again in court Friday, his attorney [Chris Andrian] said the sentence was an unfair punishment for a young man who acted wrongly but not violently in pursuing sexual acts with partners who were willing, if unsophisticated, teenage girls. Chris Andrian said 'These are the same sentences that people get if they cut off your head with a machete, or if they lie in wait and kill your children.'" The mother of one of the teens who had sex with Johnson said, "You took my daughter, who was a virgin and innocent, and you violated her." During his six-week trial, prosecutors characterized Johnson as a sexual predator and said he used his position as wrestling coach to prey on girls who looked up to him. Assuming that all the sexual encounters between Johnson and these girls were consensual (he was not convicted of force in any of the cases), both the conviction and sentencing show a barbaric "justice" system steeped in Puritanical[19] ideology. The idea that teen girls are either not sexual,[20] that they shouldn't be sexual, or that they should not be allowed to decide the conditions under which to have sex is based simply in social beliefs, not objective truth.

A special issue of *The Economist* (August 8, 2009) highlights what it terms "America's unjust sex laws." A number of examples are offered of ways in which people have suffered because "America has pioneered the harsh punishment of sex offenders." In one example, a 17-year-old girl was asked to perform oral sex on a male student in class who was just shy of his 16th birthday. The girl was arrested. She was told by her public defender to plead guilty. Unaware of the implications of doing so, she complied. She was sentenced to five years on probation. "Not being the most

> ...many people dissent from mainstream view on sexuality; however they tend to do so privately, rather than publicly.

---

18 Upon appeal Johnson's sentence was later reduced to 18 years "instead of the 190-year term he was serving" (*Press Democrat*, August 17, 2009); this is still an appalling long sentence given the context and behavior he engaged in.

19 In a number of places in this book, I use the term "Puritanical" in reference to sexual mores, customs, or taboos. By Puritanical I mean viewing sexuality in excessively rigid and narrow terms, at the root of which is the biblical view of sexuality as designed for procreation, and as inherently "dirty" when engaged in for reasons of pleasure or outside of marriage. Traditional Puritanical beliefs entailed viewing sexual behavior such as masturbation, homosexuality, anal sex, and oral sex as perverted and prurient. Today, Puritanism in reference to sexuality may entail these traditional views, as well as other sexual taboos prevalent in a given culture. It is this use to which I refer in this book.

20 See the McKinsey studies on sexuality.

organized of people, she failed to meet all the conditions, such as checking in regularly with her probation officer. For a series of technical violations, she was incarcerated for more than a year." Now her personal information is on a public sex registry in Georgia, a website that "describes itself as a list of people who have 'been convicted of a criminal offence against a victim who is a minor or any dangerous sexual offence.'" As a result of what can appropriately be compared with the experiences of the girl in *The Scarlet Letter*, "she sees people whispering, and parents pulling their children indoors when she walks by" (p. 21).

All three of these examples on sexuality (taken from a behemoth number of similar cases) highlight not only the problem of unnecessarily harsh laws, but also the fact that many people in Puritanical cultures dissent from mainstream view on sexuality; however they tend to do so privately, rather than publicly. They hold beliefs about sexuality that would and do get them into trouble with the law. Though they may not publicly dissent, their behavior *implies* dissenting beliefs. They refuse to conform to group beliefs, and that refusal results in (often harsh) punishment. They probably rarely discuss their views on sexuality, since talking about different ways of viewing sexuality can get one into trouble, even in "democratic" countries.

In sum, the truly autonomous thinker is rare, and penalties for independent thinking can be stiff. Because people are taught to uncritically conform to group ideologies as children, the habit of acquiescing is ingrained in us by the time we reach adulthood. In uncritical societies, the idea of going against the rules is considered unpatriotic, anarchic, and irresponsible. Those who do are branded rebellious, undemocratic, dangerous, or heretical.[21]

Critical thinkers realize that human societies tend to punish those who publicly go against mainstream views. Critical thinkers are willing to stand alone in their beliefs and in fact become comfortable holding views that differ, often dramatically, from those of others. People must decide for themselves the price they are willing to pay to publicly dissent against the views of society when it might be dangerous to do so. But in the privacy of their own minds, they give the widest possible play to reason.

In critical societies, people are encouraged to dissent, to say what they believe, and to discuss and debate in good faith. They value the importance of dissent and expect dissent as a matter of course.

---

21 Some people see themselves as rebellious when doing such things as smoking cigarettes, or tattooing or piercing their body parts. But these acts are often sociocentric in nature; people do these things to "be like" other "rebellious" people, or to be validated by them.

Test the Idea

Think of your own examples of dissenters, or those who go against (or have gone against) mainstream views. What are some important consequences of their actions? See if you can find examples in the newspaper or another news source or book.

GROUPISHNESS, GROUP VALIDATION, GROUP CONTROL, AND GROUP CONFORMITY INTERCONNECT AND INTERACT

Though *groupishness, group validation, group control,* and *group conformity* each has a unique logic, these phenomena often interact in complex ways. From a sociocentric perspective, for the group to "successfully" achieve its goals and agendas, the group seeks cohesion. Group members continually reinforce (validate) a shared set of beliefs among themselves. The majority of people in the group submit (conform) to the collective will of the group. When too much dissent is allowed within the group—when differing subgroups hold conflicting philosophies and perspectives—the larger group cannot pursue its (groupish) objectives as effectively. Thus the group, concerned fundamentally with achieving what it perceives to be in its vested interests, requires conformity from its group members and affirmation of group ideologies. Dissent is discouraged or forbidden. Militant groups, which exact blind allegiance and obedience from their members, offer a paradigm case of this point. Again, in groups where direct force is frowned upon, group members are frequently "recruited" (controlled) through manipulation.

> The patriotic bias is a recognized perversion of thought and judgment against which our education should guard us.
>
> — *William Graham Sumner*

In understanding the relationship between groupishness, group validation, group control, and group conformity, there are countless examples we might draw upon. For one such example, consider how the "Tea Party" groups work with the oil industry to advance the notion that global warming either doesn't exist, or is not caused by human actions. This idea conveniently fits the vested interests of the oil industry, which has financially backed "Tea Party" candidates for congressional races. According to the *New York Times* (Oct. 21, 2010), the views of Tea Party candidates "align with those of the fossil fuel industries, which have for decades waged a concerted campaign to raise doubts about the science of global warming and to undermine policies to address them. ... The oil, coal and utility industries have collectively spent $500 million just since the beginning of 2009 to lobby against legislation to address climate change and to defeat candidates … that support it."

Groupishness and group validation are easily seen in this example. But what about group control and submission? The fossil-fuel industries supporting Tea Party candidates, according to the *New York Times* article, "have created and lavishly financed institutes to produce anti-global warming studies, paid for rallies and Web sites to question the science, and generated scores of economic analyses that purport to show that policies to reduce emissions of climate-altering gases will have a devastating effect on jobs and the overall economy."

All this propaganda is aimed at controlling the way people think about global warming and climate change, leading them to believe that humans aren't responsible for these problems (and therefore don't need to do anything about them). Those seeking office under the Tea Party flag are interested in power and control. The fossil-fuel industry is interested in money, more money, power, and control. Working together through disseminating incorrect or distorted information, they manipulate and control the way people think about climate change. If they are effective, people are recruited to their cause; these people reject the idea of climate change and support the candidates who have manipulated them.

The view that climate change is not a growing problem is sometimes coupled with the religious notion that the earth, and its resources, were designed by God to be enjoyed by his people and exploited for their own ends. This idea is used by many Tea Party candidates as part of their manipulative propaganda; apparently, it often works. In response to the issue of global warming, Norman Dennison (*New York Times*, Oct. 21, 2010), founder of the Corydon Tea Party, said, "It's a flat-out lie. … I read the Bible. … He made this earth for us to utilize." Lisa Deaton, a small-business owner who started We the People Indiana, a Tea Party affiliate, said, "They're trying to use global warming against the people. … It takes away our liberty. … Being a strong Christian I cannot help but believe the Lord placed a lot of minerals in our country and it's not there to destroy us."

We see in this example:

1. groupishness—unbridled pursuit of vested interests,

2. group validation—group members validating the primary views of the group,

3. group control (or recruitment) through manipulation and distortion of the truth, and

4. group conformity to those in power.

For another example, consider the treatment of women in Afghanistan. According to the *New York Times* (September 21, 2010), "in a land [Afghanistan] where sons are more highly valued, since in the tribal culture usually only they can inherit the father's wealth and pass down a name, families without boys are the objects of pity and contempt. Even a made up son increases the family's standing." Such made-up sons are actually young girls who dress as boys; they are called "bacha posh" in Dari, which literally means "dressed up as a boy." Couple this with the way in which women are often treated in Afghan culture—given in childhood by their families to be married, abused by their husbands and their husbands' families, unable to go out in public without being accompanied by a male family member—and you find a paradigm example of group-vested interest, group validation, group domination, and group submission working together and feeding into one another. Afghan men, who ultimately have almost all the power, have a vested interest in maintaining the view that males are superior to females.

Nazia, a 16-year-old Afghan woman, was attacked and injured by her 40-year-old husband. Theirs was an arranged marriage, in which Nazia said she was "afraid" [to refuse the marriage] and "had no choice."

Photo and caption taken from https://www.af.mil/News/Article-Display/Article/124496/abused-afghan-woman-to-receive-plastic-surgery/

Men and women collectively validate these views. Women conform to the control of men, following these pathological customs.

According to a *New York Times* article (November 8, 2010), "The choices for Afghan women are extraordinarily restricted: Their family is their fate. There is little chance for education, little choice about whom a woman marries, no choice at all about her role in her own house. Her primary job is to serve her husband's family. Outside that world, she is an outcast. 'If you run away from home, you may be raped or put in jail and then sent home and then what will happen to you?' asked Rachel Reid, a researcher for Human Rights Watch. … Returned runaways are often shot or stabbed in honor killings because families fear they have spent time unchaperoned with a man. Women and girls are still stoned to death."

In Afghan culture, men are the dominating group, but women also play a role in domination when they abuse their daughters-in-law or sisters-in-law, or when they condone their husbands or sons in doing so. The victims, often young married women, must submit to the domination or suffer the consequences, which can mean being murdered by their own families.[22] Women who abuse other women were likely abused themselves. Collectively, the dominating group

---

22 Note that though the men have most of the control in such a culture as this, they too have been indoctrinated into the ideologies of the culture. And though they enjoy far greater benefits in the culture than do the women, they also miss out on many essential dimensions of a healthy intimate marital relationship. For instance, in such a culture, men would likely seldom confide in their wives, would never be able to exhibit even mild forms of affection publicly, would rarely discuss how to raise their children, and would have impoverished sexual relationships. It is the culture at large that carries on the dysfunctional traditions, both men and women buying into it, with only a relatively few dissenters who become marginalized and are punished accordingly.

validates these unethical, pernicious ways of thinking and behaving. The victims have little choice but to submit or kill themselves. Through group validation, this tradition is carried on, generation after generation.

Critical thinkers seek to understand the relationships between groupishness, group validation, group control, and group conformity. They recognize that such understanding is required both for emancipating their own minds and for freeing the human species. They look for these phenomena, in their various forms and interrelationships, in every group in which they are members.

Test the Idea

Be on the lookout for examples that illuminate any of the four forms of sociocentric thought—groupishness, group validation, group control (or recruitment), and group conformity. As you look for examples, note that where you find one of these forms, you will often find one or more of the others. Look for interrelationships between and among them.

SOME HISTORICAL NOTES ON SOCIOCENTRIC THINKING

The idea of sociocentric thinking is not new. Throughout history, many important thinkers from diverse fields of study have commented on the problem of sociocentric thought. Numerous books, articles, and research studies have illuminated some of its many manifestations using a variety of organizing terms. Social phenomena, and hence, to some degree, sociocentric phenomena, are studied in sociology, psychology, anthropology, archeology, political science, history, literature, and other academic disciplines. Classic psychological and sociological studies have, for many years, revealed the pernicious nature of groupthink. (Some are included as examples later in this book.) Hence, it may be helpful here to consider some historical roots of sociocentric thought. This section is brief, being primarily intended to elucidate the fact that the problem of sociocentric thought has been a concern of enlightened people throughout history (however few their number, relatively speaking).

We can find traces of insights about sociocentric thought throughout human history, dating back to not only the earliest writings but, indeed, to some of the earliest artistic renderings. These have illustrated human and animal woes resulting from human behavior throughout the past 2,400 years or more. In Plato's *Apology*, Socrates (469–399 BCE), argues with the Senate to spare his life

Letter on a clay tablet sent by the high-priest Lu'enna to the king of Lagash. It tells the king of his son's death in combat. The script is cuneiform, the date ca. 2400 BCE.

when he is accused of believing in false gods and corrupting the youth. In his plea before the court (according to Plato) Socrates says:

> At first, I have to reply to the older charges and to my first accusers, and then I will go on to the later ones. For I have had many accusers, who accuse me of old, and their false charges have continued during many years; and I am more afraid of them than of Anytus and his associates, who are dangerous, too, in their own way. But far more dangerous are these, who began when you were children, and took possession of your minds with their falsehoods. (Plato, 1960, p. 448)

As we see, the last line in this passage is directly linked to the problem of inculcation and indoctrination, a common feature of sociocentric societies.

Half a century later, in writing about virtue and what it means to live a virtuous life, Aristotle (384–322 BCE) says:

> … the mass of men present an absolutely slavish appearance, choosing the life of brute beasts, but they meet with consideration because so many persons in authority share the tastes of Sardanapalus. Cultivated and practical people, on the other hand, identify happiness with honour, as honour is the general end of political life. (p. 64)

It is helpful to note that Sardanapalus was "the most luxurious"[23] Assyrian monarch. In this passage, Aristotle illuminates the problem of the masses slavishly following the practices of their leaders. And he implies that "cultivated and practical people" would not mindlessly follow either their leaders, or the masses.

In articulating some essentials of the Sceptics philosophy, Diogenes Laertius (ca. 3rd century BCE) points out the largely arbitrary nature of group beliefs:

> The fifth mode is derived from customs, laws, and belief in myths, compacts between nations and dogmatic assumptions … the same thing is regarded by some as just and by others as unjust, or as good by some and bad by others. Persians think it not unnatural for a man to marry his daughter; to Greeks it is unlawful. The Massageta, according to Eudoxus in the first book of his Voyage round the World, have their wives in common; the Greeks have not. The Cilicians used to delight in piracy; not so the Greeks. Different people believe in different gods; some in providence, others not. In burying their dead, the Egyptians embalm them; the Romans burn them; the Paeonians throw them in lakes. As to what is true, then, let suspension of judgement be our practice. (Smith, 1956, p. 176)

Laertius' solution, seen in the last line, is not satisfactory given that we must use judgment in reasoning through ethical issues, and indeed through any complex issue. But in terms of cultural *preferences*, groups should be allowed those preferences without outside intervention, as Laertius aptly points out.

---

23 See editor's footnote, Smith, 1956, p. 65, footnote 90.

Greek historian Polybius (ca. 204-122 BCE) perceives sociocentric thought to be so deeply ingrained in the views of the "multitude" as to require superstition to keep them in line. Note, of course, that this justification is itself encased in groupthink (the notion that leaders are justified in manipulating people through superstition):

> ... It is a course which perhaps would not have been necessary had it been possible to form a state composed of wise men, but as every multitude is fickle, full of lawless desires, unreasoned passion, and violent anger, the multitude must be held in by invisible terrors and suchlike pageantry. (Smith, 1956, p. 204)

One may well wonder whether, and to what degree, superstition is still used to manipulate the masses.

During the 13th century, Franciscan philosopher Roger Bacon wrote his views for the "benefit" of the pope (after coming under surveillance for sharing his scientific thinking with others). Bacon contends, in *Opus Majus*, that there are four causes of human ignorance:

> First, the example of frail and unsuitable authority ... Second, the influence of custom. Third, the opinion of the unlearned crowd ... Fourth, the concealment of one's ignorance in a display of apparent wisdom. From these four plagues, of which the fourth is the worst, spring all human evils. (Russell, 1945, p. 464)

Several centuries later, in *Novum Organum* (1620), Francis Bacon developed his conception of *Idols of the Mind*, to which he believed all humans fall prey. One of these idols, the *Idol of the Cave*, refers in part to the prejudiced ways in which people tend to view the world—in accordance with cultural or social ideologies.

In 1906, William Graham Sumner (1906; 1940) introduced the concept of ethnocentrism, a term often used synonymously with sociocentrism: [24]

> Ethnocentrism is the technical name for this view of thinking in which one's own group is the center of everything, and all others are scaled and rated with reference to it. ... Each group nourishes its own pride and vanity, boasts itself superior, exacts its own divines, and looks with contempt on outsiders. Each group thinks its own folkways the only right ones, and if it

---

24 The terms "ethnocentrism" and "sociocentrism" are often used interchangeably. However, it might be useful to distinguish the two terms in the following way. The term "sociocentrism" entails the roots "socio" and "centrism," together meaning centered on the group. The term "ethnocentrism" entails "ethno" and "centrism," most directly meaning centered on one's ethnicity or ethnic group. Looked at in this way, sociocentrism can be conceived as a much broader concept, encompassing all pathological groupthink (a group being defined as two or more people). On this view, ethnocentrism becomes a subset of sociocentric thought. It can roughly be defined as sociocentric thought (entailing any or all of its manifestations) within a group of people who share cultural, racial, religious, or linguistic traditions.

observes that other groups have other folkways, these excite its scorn. (p. 13)

Around the middle of the 20th century, with the rise of postmodernism and scientific thinking, researchers and professionals within the social disciplines began studying social behavior more systematically. For instance, social psychologist Kurt Lewin began using empirical methods to study group dynamics in the 1940s. His work (1947) revealed that groups often lack objective standards for determining whether a group has achieved its goals. In 1961, group therapist Wilfred Bion stressed the potential detrimental effects of group cohesion. He described how the efficiency of working groups is often compromised by shared assumptions that tend to preserve the group, rather than contribute to the work at hand. In a meta-analysis focused on cohesive group influence, Dorwin Cartwright and Alvin Zander (1968) concluded:

> *Other things being equal, as cohesiveness increases there is an increase in a group's capacity to retain members and in the degree of participation by members in group activities. The greater a group's cohesiveness the more power it has to bring about conformity to its norms and to gain acceptance of its goals and assignment to tasks and roles ... highly cohesive groups provide a source of security for members which serves to reduce anxiety and to heighten self-esteem. (p. 105)*

Note that group cohesiveness can lead to good or ill, depending on the extent to which such cohesiveness is steeped in pathological groupthink or, instead, in rational thought. In the 1950s, social psychologist Solomon Asch conducted a series of experiments that exposed how easily people will succumb to peer pressure, despite the facts before their very eyes. In these experiments, Asch showed subjects a screen depicting one line on the left and three comparison lines on the right. One of the comparison lines was the same as the line on the left. The other two comparison lines were clearly different in length. The goal was for the subject to figure out which line on the right matched that on the left. In each case, the experimental subject was brought into a room with six confederates, all of whom had been told to give the same wrong answer. (It must be noted here that the correct answer was quite obvious). After hearing six "wrong" answers, 75% of the naïve subjects succumbed to peer pressure and gave the same wrong answer, often after showing signs of confusion and even dismay (Asch, 1963).

In 1952, William Whyte, Jr. introduced the concept of *Groupthink* in Fortune magazine. He conceptualized groupthink as rationalized conformity, contending that group values are not only expedient, but implicitly right and good, showing a blurring of the distinctions between and among productivity, ethics, and social customs.

Two decades later, psychologist Irving L. Janis (1972) picked up the term "groupthink," but conceptualized it in a far more helpful way, first by clearly connecting it with dysfunctionality in group thought. He refers to groupthink as:

... a mode of thinking that people engage in when they are deeply involved in a cohesive in-group, when the members' strivings for unanimity override their motivation to realistically appraise alternative courses of action. "Groupthink" is a term of the same order as the words in the newspeak vocabulary George Orwell presents in his dismaying 1984—a vocabulary with terms such as "doublethink" and "crimethink." By putting groupthink with those Orwellian words ... groupthink takes on an invidious connotation. The invidiousness is intentional: Groupthink refers to a deterioration of mental efficiency, reality testing, and moral judgment that results from in-group pressures. (p. 9)

Janis (1972) reveals a number of patterns of thought implicit in what he calls "the groupthink syndrome," including:

1. an illusion of group invulnerability.

2. unquestioned belief in the group's inherent morality (or ethics).

3. collective efforts to rationalize the group's position (which causes a failure to examine their assumptions.)

4. stereotyping views of enemy leaders as evil.

5. self-censorship of deviations from group consensus.

6. direct pressure on any group member who suggests strong arguments against the group's stereotypes, illusions or commitments. (pp. 174-175)

Though Janis's analysis is well conceived, there has been little further conceptual development of groupthink as a system of understanding since the 1970s. Still, principal thinkers, from a number of subjects and fields, and from a variety of perspectives, continue to illuminate our understanding of sociocentric thought. For instance, French philosopher and social theorist Michel Foucault (1978) details sexual codes as prescribed by social customs:

Up to the end of the eighteenth century, three major explicit codes—apart from the customary regularities and constraints of opinion—governed sexual practices: canonical law, the Christian pastoral, and civil law. They determined, each in its own way, the division between licit and illicit. The marital obligation, the ability to fulfill it, the manner in which one complied with it, the requirements and violences in which one complied with it, the useless or unwarranted caresses for which it was a pretext, its fecundity or the way one went about making it sterile ... its frequency or infrequency, and so on. It was this domain that was especially saturated with prescriptions. The sex of husband and wife was beset by rules and recommendations. (p. 36)

German Sociologist George Simmel (1971), in *On Individual and Social Forms*, points out the restrictive nature of social pressures in human societies during the 1700s:

> *The inadequacy of the socially sanctioned forms of life in the eighteenth century, compared with the material and intellectual productivity of the period, struck the consciousness of individuals as an unbearable restriction of their energies. Those restrictive forms included the privileges of the higher estates as well as the despotic control of commerce; the still powerful survivals of the guild system as well as the intolerant pressure of the church; the corvee expected from the peasant population as well as paternalism in the life of the state ... (p. 218)*

One of the earliest uses of the term "sociocentricity" is found in the work of Richard Paul. In his book, *Critical Thinking: What Every Person Needs to Survive in a Rapidly Changing World*, Paul (1993; 2012) connects sociocentric thought with taboos, prejudice, blind allegiance to authority, and guilt. Paul understands that the development of intellectual character requires the ability to clearly distinguish between social "requirements" and what can be ethically justified in a given set of circumstances:

> *Egocentric minds and sociocentric societies are permanent breeding grounds for prejudice ... When people act in accordance with the injunctions and taboos of the group to which they belong they naturally feel righteous. They receive much praise in moral terms, and may even be treated as moral leaders, if they speak or act in a way that impresses the group. For this reason, few people distinguish moral or religious conformity or demagoguery from genuine moral integrity. Group norms are typically articulated in the language of morality and a socialized person inwardly experiences some sense of shame or guilt in violating a social taboo, and anger or moral outrage at others who do so. In other words, what commonly seems to be the inner voice of conscience is often nothing more than the internalized voice of social authority, the voice of our parents, our teachers, and our "superiors" speaking within us. Genuine moral integrity requires what might be called "intellectual character" and this requires rational assent, for moral decisions require thought discrimination between what is merely socially permitted and what is genuinely morally justified.*

As we see from these brief historical notes, the problem of sociocentric thought has, to a greater or lesser degree, been the concern of a cadre of progressive thinkers throughout time. Our understanding of this problem and its complexities has deepened significantly in the last 50-100 years. In the past several decades, with the growth of specialization in academic disciplines, many studies have been conducted in various fields to illuminate how people behave in groups, how people in groups influence one another, how people collectively deceive themselves, and so on. Insights from these studies, as they are revealed, need to be integrated into a cohesive dynamic theory of sociocentric thought that is conceptually rich and, hence, can, more effectively over time, lead people to develop as intellectually autonomous thinkers.

Concepts in Natural Languages That Imply Sociocentric Thinking or Its Opposite

Words that emphasize acting in accordance with the prevailing standards, attitudes, practices, etc., of a society or a group		Words that imply habitual activity or behavior transmitted from one generation to another	
Conformity	Subordination	Customs	Folkways
Compliance	Acquiescence	Traditions	Etiquette
Submission	Obedience	Mores	Conventions

Words that imply that certain behaviors *are not allowed* in a culture or group		Words that imply that certain behaviors *are expected* in a culture or group	
Taboos	Ban	Authorize	Authority
Prohibit	Unauthorized	Allow	Society
Illicit	Illegitimate	Sanction	Socialize
Forbid	Disobedient	Permit	

Terms that illuminate the problem of groups expecting their members to uncritically accept their views		Phrases that illuminate or characterize the *opposite* of sociocentric thought
Indoctrinate	Brainwash	Fairminded Critical Societies
Inculcate	Proselytize	Rational Societies
Instill		Reasoned Dissent
		Dialogical Reasoning
		Dialectical Reasoning
		Strong-Sense Critical Thinking
		Intellectual Autonomy

Phrases that imply that some groups see themselves as "better" than others	Additional terms or phrases that illuminate the problem of sociocentric thought	
Group Conceit	Chauvinism	Ethocentricity
Group Self-Glorification	Group Bigotry	Group
Group Favoritism	Fanatical	Selfishess
Undue Group Esteem	Patriotism	Vested Interest
	Group Partiality	Group
	Group Allegiance	Intolerance
	Groupthink	Groupishess
	In-Group Deception	

Test the Idea

Using a good thesaurus, see if you can add words to the categories in the table above.

CHAPTER TWO
MANIFESTATIONS OF SOCIOCENTRIC
THOUGHT IN HUMAN SOCIETIES

Examples of sociocentric thought can be found in virtually every part of human life where people gather in groups. Let us now consider some of the powerful manifestations of sociocentric thought. (There are many others.)

MASS MEDIA SHAPE AND
ARE SHAPED BY SOCIOCENTRIC THINKING

One of the most influential forms of sociocentric thought is found in media bias and propaganda. In any given country, the mass media and press tend to describe world events in terms that presuppose the correctness of the country's dominant ideologies. For instance, language is often used ideologically by the press. In so doing, the media violate the basic meanings of the terms themselves (see example, p. 109).

Those in mass media often forward a sociocentric agenda because they are naturally a part of the culture within which they function, and they therefore have, like others in that culture, been indoctrinated into its mainstream views.

For example, the mass media routinely validate the view that one's own country is "right" or ethical in its dealings in the world. This cultivates one-sided nationalistic thinking. The basic idea is that as largely sociocentric thinkers, all of us tend to think of our nation and the groups to which we belong in mostly favorable terms. It follows, therefore, that the media will present in mostly unfavorable terms those nations and groups that significantly oppose "us."

When we look critically at the mainstream mass media of a given country, it is easy to document how they present important world events in biased ways. For instance, the mainstream news media are biased in favor of their country's political "allies" and prejudiced against its "enemies." The media therefore present events that regard the countries of allies in the most favorable light possible, highlighting positive events while downplaying negative ones. As for its enemies, the opposite treatment can be expected. Thus, positive events in the countries of one's enemies are either ignored or given little attention, while

> One of the most influential forms of sociocentric thought is found in media bias and propaganda.

negative events are highlighted or distorted. The ability of a person to identify this bias in action and mentally rewrite the article or representation more objectively (as one is reading it) is an important critical-thinking ability.

For example, because Israel has historically been an ally of the United States, the U.S. media has tended to ignore or give minor attention to mistreatment of Palestinians by the Israelis. On the other hand, because Fidel Castro of Cuba has been, until only recently, considered an "enemy" of the United States, mainstream news writers have historically taken advantage of every opportunity to present Castro and Cuba in a negative light, ignoring most achievements of the Cuban government and its people (e.g., in the areas of universal education, literacy rates, and medical care).[25] Of course, if the doors of Cuba continue to open to U.S. commerce, our treatment of Cuba in the mainstream news will trend towards positive aspects of Cuba, and our "hatred" of Cuba will likely turn to friendship. Over time, this is especially likely if the U.S. can again gain economic control of Cuba. News reporters would likely soon forget their negative stories of the past as our "friendship" with Cuba solidified.

Another primary reason why those in the mainstream media distort reality in presenting "news" can only be understood in terms of its ultimate purpose—profit. To "sell" the news, the media industry must make it "palatable" to their "consumers." Otherwise people won't "buy" it. To make it palatable, they must present a sugar-coated version of the truth, or in any case, the version most people want to hear. When reporters are indoctrinated into the same unrealistic picture of life and what goes on within it (as is everyone else in the culture), the next step of telling people stories they want to hear is almost automatic.[26]

In illuminating the problems that now permeate journalism and the media world, including the role that profit plays in the news "served" to the American people. Leonard Downie, Jr. and Robert Kaiser (2002), of the *Washington Post*, say:

> *Most newspapers, television networks and local television and radio stations now belong to giant, publicly owned corporations far removed from the communities they serve. They face the unrelenting quarterly profit pressures from Wall Street now typical of American capitalism ... Americans would rather be entertained than informed ... The temptation to push serious news aside in favor of glitz and melodrama has too often been irresistible. A national infatuation with celebrities, both encouraged and exploited by news media, has had a profound influence on journalism.*

Those who reason from a critical perspective recognize the pervasiveness of media bias and propaganda in human societies. They recognize that news reporters in every country have been indoctrinated into the ideologies of their

---

25 For further discussion of the problem of media bias as a sociocentric force, see Richard Paul and Linda Elder (2006), *The Thinker's Guide for Conscientious Citizens on How to Detect Media Bias & Propaganda*. Dillon Beach: Foundation for Critical Thinking Press.

26 I have been referring here to those in the mainstream media, and pointing out general problems that are easily exemplified with a critical reading of the news. Reporters themselves will naturally fall on a continuum in terms of the extent to which they conform uncritically to mainstream views.

culture, and that this indoctrination may play a significant role in their reporting. Those who see through media bias understand that the primary purpose of news outlets is not to present unbiased stories of events, but to make money. Critical thinkers take these realities into account when critiquing the mainstream news. They seek alternative credible news sources to gain understanding of differing perspectives on important issues.

Test the Idea

Look for examples of media bias in the news that come from sociocentric thought. Newspapers are a good place to start. Select one issue in international news; to what extent do you see evidence of prejudice in favor of the "home" country, and prejudice against those countries we see as our "enemies"?

UNBRIDLED GLOBAL CAPITALISM IS A POWERFUL SOCIOCENTRIC FORCE IN HUMAN LIFE

Capitalism[27] is the predominant economic force on the planet. Almost all humans and other sentient creatures now experience implications of capitalism. Even countries with socialist governments are intertwined with capitalism. In his book *A Theory of Global Capitalism*, William Robinson (2004) argues that we are now living in a new economic system of global capitalism, the theory of which he details:

> Globalization is the underlying structural dynamic that drives social, political, economic, and cultural-ideological processes around the world in the twenty-first century. … Global capitalism has generated new social dependencies around the world. Billions of people who may have been at the margins of the system or entirely outside of it have now been brought squarely within its confines. The maintenance of the system is very much a life-and-death matter for millions, indeed billions, of people who, willingly or otherwise, have developed a stake in it. (p. xv)

Though capitalism has its strengths, the many negative implications that result from *unrestrained* capitalism are largely passed over or played down in today's mainstream western cultures and beyond. In developed countries, people tend to assume capitalism

…the many negative implications that have resulted from *unrestrained* capitalism are largely passed over or played down.

---

27 It might be useful to point out that the term "capitalism" has largely been replaced by the term "free-market economy." However, since a truly free market doesn't exist, this latter term is largely a politically-generated euphemism for capitalism.

is the best economic system; those who argue for public ownership and cooperative management of the means of production, through what are frequently stereotyped as "socialist" programs, are often marginalized and even demonized. People in capitalist countries generally fail to see capitalism as one choice among several viable economic systems. Born into capitalistic societies, they tend to uncritically accept capitalistic ideology.

Street child, Bangladesh.

And capitalism represents a tremendously powerful sociocentric force in human life today.

One problem with capitalism, according to Robinson, is that it naturally expands. "In order to survive, capitalism requires constant access to new sources of cheap labor, land, raw materials … and markets" (p. 3). In his concluding chapter on the contradictions of capitalism, Robinson (2004) points to some of its far-reaching problems:

> … as capitalism produces vast amounts of wealth, it also generates … social polarization and crisis … workers produce more goods and services than they are actually able to purchase with their wages … at some point capitalists as a group … are left with more goods and services produced by their workers than they are able to market. … This is the point at which economic recession typically sets in. … The polarization of world income, downward mobility, and declining purchasing power among broad swaths of humanity make it impossible for the world's majority to consume all the goods being churned out by the global economy … two processes germane to capitalist development have intensified through globalization. One is the secular process by which the spread of capitalism uproots precapitalist classes such as peasantries and converts them into members of the working class. The accelerated incursion of capitalist production into the countryside around the world in the second half of the twentieth century uprooted hundreds of millions of peasants and threw them into the capitalist labor market, often as unemployed or underemployed workers. (pp. 147–149)

One implication of unbridled capitalism is the growing disparity between the rich and the poor, not only in the United States, but across the world. The Center on Budget and Policy Priorities (June 25, 2010) reports: "The gaps in after-tax income between the richest 1 percent of Americans and the middle and poorest fifths of the country more than tripled between 1979 and 2007. … [T]he new data suggest greater income concentration at the top of the income scale than at any time since 1928." The United Nations reports that "around the world more than 2.5 billion men, women and children live in grinding poverty on less than

$2 a day. Such extreme poverty results in chronic hunger and malnutrition, preventable diseases such as malaria, measles and tuberculosis, environmental degradation, low literacy rates and countless other social, public health, economic and political problems."[28] According to the United Nations Development Report (1999), "Global inequalities in income and living standards have reached grotesque proportions."[29] The report goes on to say:

> *The richest countries, such as the United States, have 20 percent of the world's people but 86 percent of its income ... 82 percent of its exports and 74 percent of its telephone lines. The 20 percent living in the poorest countries, such as Ethiopia and Laos, have about 1 percent of each. The three richest officers of Microsoft—Bill Gates, Paul Allen and Steve Ballmer— have more assets, nearly $140 billion, than the combined gross national product of the 43 least-developed countries and their 600 million people.*
>
> *When the market goes too far in dominating social and political outcomes, the opportunities and rewards of globalization spread unequally and inequitably— concentrating power and wealth in a select group of people, nations and corporations, marginalizing the others.*

Around the world more than 2.5 billion men, women and children live in grinding poverty on less than $2 a day.

— *United Nations*

> *The challenge is ... to provide enough space for human, community and environmental resources to ensure that globalization works for people, not just for profits.*
>
> *One result of globalization is that the road to wealth—the control of production, patents and technology—is increasingly dominated by a few countries and companies ... this monopoly of power is cutting poorer nations off from a share of the economic pie and, often, from decent health care and education.*

Approximately 150 years ago, in a private letter, President Abraham Lincoln (1864) predicted that the wealth of the U.S. would increasingly fall into the hands of a few; in essence, he anticipated the term "überwealthy," now in almost common use. He could see powerful and unethical forces, emerging through capitalistic thought during his lifetime, and hence predicted what has in fact come true.

> *I see in the near future a crisis approaching that unnerves me and causes me to tremble for the safety of my country ... corporations have been enthroned and an era of corruption in high places will follow, and the money of the*

---

28 Taken from the website of the United Nations, http://www.un.org/works/sub2.asp?lang=en&s=17 December 19, 2010.

29 The United Nations Human Development Report, found at http://hdr.undp.org/en/reports/global/ hdr1999/

country will endeavor to prolong its reign by working upon the prejudices of the people until all wealth is aggregated in a few hands. … I feel at this moment more anxiety for the safety of my country than ever before, even in the midst of war.

Given the increasing gap between the rich and poor, and the consequent inordinate power now in the hands of the wealthiest few, Lincoln's fears, again, have been realized. In his book *Free Lunch: How the Wealthiest Americans Enrich Themselves at Government Expense (and Stick You with the Bill)*, David Cay Johnston (2007) writes:

> *In the past quarter century or so our government has enacted new rules that have created not only free markets, but rigged ones. These rules have weakened and even destroyed consumer protections while increasing the power of the already powerful. … The rich and their lobbyists have taken firm control of the levers of power in Washington and the state capitals while remaking the rules in their own interests … For more than a quarter century now our government has been adopting rules that tilt the playing field in favor of the rich, the powerful, and the politically connected. … We sing the praises of investors who owe their wealth not to creating businesses, but to buying companies in deals that require destroying lives and careers, just so that they could squeeze out more money for themselves … (p. 12-15)*

> The rich and their lobbyists have taken firm control of the levers of power in Washington and the state capitals while remaking the rules in their own interests.
>
> — *David Cay Johnston*

In the growing disparity between the rich and the poor, we see evidence of all four forms of sociocentric thought—groupishness, in which the wealthy pursue more and more money without regard for the rights and needs of those with less; group validation, in which the wealthy collectively validate or justify their greed and its concomitant power; group domination, in which the rich are able to wield power over the mass of people (for instance, by having more political power); and group submission, in which the common people seem to have no choice but to go along with those in power. Of course, many intricacies are entailed in human thought, and it may be possible for people to be wealthy without also being sociocentric in these ways. Every case must be individually examined to determine the extent to which sociocentric forces are at play.

> Not only do the wealthiest Americans have inordinate power over the federal government, but there has, for a number of years, been an alarming relationship between mass media, big business, and military interests.

Not only do the wealthiest Americans have inordinate power over the federal government, but there has, for a number of years, been an alarming relationship between mass media, big business, and military interests. This relationship has given rise to what David McGowan (2000) refers to as the "military-industrial-media complex." In his book *Derailing Democracy*, McGowan details how the military has become increasingly powerful through its associations with capitalists agendas; McGowan also discusses how mass media have come under the power of fewer and fewer corporations— themselves with a capitalist agenda. He notes, for example:

> The number-one purveyor of broadcast news in this country—NBC, with both MSNBC and CNBC under its wing as well as NBC news and a variety of "news magazines"—is now owned and controlled by General Electric, one of the nation's largest defense contractors. Is it not significant that as GE's various media subsidiaries predictably lined up to cheerlead the use of U.S. military force in Kosovo, it was at the same time posting substantial profits from the sale of high tech tools of modern warfare it so shamelessly glorifies? … Following the same course that virtually every other major industry has in the last two decades, a relentless series of mergers and corporate takeovers has consolidated control of the media into the hands of corporate behemoths. The result has been that an increasingly authoritarian agenda has been sold to the American people by a massive, multi-tentacled media machine that has become, for all intents and purposes, a propaganda organ of the state. (pp. 1-2)

This shows how media and military agendas are now dangerously combined with capitalistic forces, enabling the super-wealthy to essentially control how people think. Pathological relationships such as these illuminate the sociocentric forms of *groupishness* (conglomerates accumulating more and more power and money), *group validation* (conglomerates validating war mongering beliefs which enable them to get more money and more power), *group control* (these conglomerates controlling the messages people receive about military campaigns, which in turn serve the vested interests of these companies), and *group conformity* (people naively going along with the war agendas disseminated by biased media outlets, which are largely controlled by these behemoths).

In addition to the obvious problems caused by unrestrained capitalism, there are important hidden problems. In their book *The Winner-Take-All Society*, Robert Frank and Philip Cook (1995) focus on the fact that the American capitalist system encourages economic waste, income inequality, and an impoverished culture. They say:

> Winner-take-all markets have increased the disparity between the rich and poor. They have lured some of our most talented citizens into socially unproductive, sometimes destructive tasks. In an economy that already invests too little for the future, they have fostered wasteful patterns of investment and consumption. They have led indirectly to greater concentration of our most talented college students in a small set of elite institutions. They have made it more difficult for "late bloomers" to find a productive niche in life. And winner-take-all markets have molded our culture and discourse in ways many of us find deeply troubling. (pp. 4–5)

In an article in the *New York Times Review* (March 10, 2013), Graham Hill points out some of the ways in which the pursuit of material possessions can be almost all-consuming, and yet how such pursuit cannot lead us to happiness. He tells how, "flush with cash" from his internet business, he bought things and more things, surrounding himself with all manner of material possessions and gadgetry which ultimately expended his time and exhausted his energy. He says, "somehow this stuff ended up running my life ... the things I consumed ended up consuming me." Studies increasingly show that people in the wealthiest countries are often the least happy.

At some point we may recognize that we cannot find meaning in this endless greed for more things, with the latest bells and whistles. In his book, *Man's Search for Meaning*, Viktor Frankl (1959; 1984) addresses the problem of meaninglessness and boredom that accompanies what he terms "the existential vacuum." He says,

> ... I turn to the detrimental influence of that feeling of which so many patients complain today, namely the feeling of the total and ultimate meaninglessness of their lives. They lack the awareness of a meaning worth living for. They are haunted by the experience of their inner emptiness, a void within themselves ... The existential vacuum is a widespread phenomenon of the twentieth century ... [and] manifests itself mainly in a state of boredom ... ultimately man should not ask what the meaning of his life is, but rather he must recognize that it is he who is asked. In a word, each man is questioned by life; and he can only answer to life by answering for his own life ... (pp. 128, 131)

We can trace much of the meaninglessness of life so often experienced by humans today to our (largely unconscious) capitalistic orientation. This worldview leads to the widespread accouterments in modern cultures that trap us within superficial logics, within trivial and artificial mindsets, but of which we are hardly aware.

> Beginning in infancy and continuing throughout life, the things we see and read profoundly alter the kinds of people we become.
>
> — *Frank & Cook*

In exemplifying ways in which American capitalism affects our culture, Frank and Cook (1995) point to such things as how the book and movie industries tend to foster, in essence, sociocentric thought. They note that publishers tend to publish books by previously successful authors, however ill-written these books might be. They note that books tend to stay on the market to the extent that they are widely read in the culture. The same is true of movies: popular movies are those that stay in the movie theaters longer so more people can see them. Consequently, books and movies that offer dissenting views don't tend to survive, or are never given fair attention. These realities are disturbing because, as Frank and Cook stress, " ... beginning in infancy and continuing throughout life, the things we see and read profoundly alter the kinds of people we become" (p. 19).

Notice how reasonable it seems to make movies and publish books based on what was previously financially successful. If a genre is successful at the box office—violent movies, for example, or as-the-world-turns romance novels—it seems reasonable to make more movies in that genre. But the only reason it seems so reasonable (and natural) is that we've internalized the sociocentrism of a highly advanced capitalist economy. By choosing to produce items on the basis of their profitability, we are choosing to put aside the many more important values we could be emphasizing, such as fostering empathy and concern for the environment, improving the quality of life for humans and other species, and striving to create increasingly fairminded critical societies. The depth of the sociocentrism is apparent by observing that publishing-for-profit often seems, to the common person, less ideological than publishing to further a cause. It seems *almost neutral* compared with other values, such as protecting versus exploiting the environment, or exploring the idea that health care should, or should not, be free to all. But, of course, it's not at all value-neutral. Instead, it is a key part of the ideology of capitalism. This is just one of the many subtle examples of the ill effects of capitalism as we now experience it.

Consider the role advertising plays in the life of the average person today. On a daily basis, if we leave the house at all, or turn on our technological gadgets or TVs, we are heavily influenced by advertising messages designed to continually point out our "flaws"—flaws which a given product promises to "do away with." Again, these messages are often subtle and implicit. Even highly insightful people fall prey to these messages. And as a result of our gullibility, we purchase far more "things" than we need, a phenomenon that contributes to the problem of diminishing resources on the planet.

Perhaps the most serious problem connected with capitalism is that of vested interest—groups exploiting other groups (or individuals) while pursuing their own interests. This problem is documented every day, in every major newspaper in the world. More than 200 years ago, during the early stages of modern capitalism, it was a primary concern of Adam Smith (1776; 1976), who was considered the father of modern economics. Though his name is often invoked by those economic and political theoreticians who advance capitalism, in his book *The Wealth of Nations*, Smith stressed the importance of checks and appropriate controls in capitalist economies. He said, for instance:

> *People of the same trade seldom meet together, even for merriment and diversion, but the conversation ends in a conspiracy against the public, or in some contrivance to raise prices. It is impossible indeed to prevent such meetings, by any law which either could be executed, or would be consistent with liberty or justice. But though the law cannot hinder people of the same trade from sometimes assembling together, it ought to do nothing to facilitate such assemblies; much less to render them necessary.* (p. 152)

> *Civil government, so far as it is instituted for the security of property, is in reality instituted for the defence of the rich against the poor, or of those who*

have some property against those who have none at all. (p. 775)

Our merchants and master-manufacturers complain much of the bad effects of high wages in raising the price, and thereby lessening the sale of their goods both at home and abroad. They say nothing concerning the bad effects of high profits. They are silent with regard to the pernicious effects of their own gains. They complain only of those of other people. (p. 117)

Capitalism is a complex economic system that has fundamentally developed largely over the past two centuries. It is one economic system among a number of possibilities that has been created by human thought and executed by human agents. Unfortunately, as Max Weber said in 1905, uncontrolled capitalism has largely entrapped us in what he called an *iron cage*, replete with its bureaucratic systems that, in effect, imprison us. This *iron cage*—from which, as Weber sees it, no escape seems possible—is a direct consequence of sociocentric human thought. But, again, capitalism is, in the first instance, a human idea; and as with all human ideas, it can be changed. It can be improved. It can be displaced. Insofar as it serves the people and minimizes suffering, it should be applauded. But insofar as it causes suffering and injustice, it should be altered, or, yes, even abandoned.

Critical thinkers want to see things as they are, assess things as they are, and work toward improvement where improvement is needed. They do not blindly accept any system of thought, such as capitalism, even when the majority of people in the world go along with it. Critical thinkers see through terms like "free-market economy," when the use of such terms skews reality (e.g., implying that world economies operate "freely," when in fact they are controlled by any number of variables). Critical thinkers can imagine a world where people emancipate themselves from oppressive economic systems. Critical thinkers work toward egalitarianism; they want to see the world's resources more evenly distributed (as we have seen in movements such as "Occupy Wall Street ... we are the 99%").

Test the Idea

To what extent do you see capitalism, or "free-market economy," causing problems in human societies? Find examples in the news or other literature to support your position. What can be done about these problems?

SCHOOLING IS A PREVAILING SOCIOCENTRIC AGENT

In every country in the world, students are indoctrinated into the ideologies of their culture through schooling. This is, at present, a natural phenomenon stemming from the fact that no human societies now advance or support fairminded critical thinking as a universal ideal. Accordingly, schooling is an agent of the state, of the status quo, and of the mainstream view. Fostering independence of thought in schooling is rare. Teachers who attempt it are often marginalized, removed from the classroom, or otherwise penalized. Consider the *Scopes Monkey Trial* of 1925, a legal case in which John Scopes, a high-school teacher in Tennessee, was indicted and convicted for teaching evolution (in violation of the Butler Act, which made it unlawful to teach evolution). Though the verdict was overturned on a technicality, the trial illuminates the difficulties teachers face in swimming against the main stream of the culture, even when the mainstream view is absurd.

Or consider, again, our example of Socrates, going back to 399 BCE, when he was accused, indicted, and ultimately put to death for two reasons:

1. Introducing and believing in gods other than those sanctioned by the state. (Although some accused Socrates of atheism, all evidence points in the opposite direction, including the fact that Socrates believed in life after death.)
2. Corrupting the young (by fostering their intellectual development and encouraging them to question the status quo).

To understand Socrates' views in connection with education and the problem of sociocentric thought, consider the following passage from *The Encyclopedia of Philosophy* (1967):

> *There was reason for fearing Socrates as a social force. Where arête [excellence, in terms of how to make the best of oneself and live a rational life], education, and state were fused in one image, an educator critical of received assumptions was a revolutionary. Socrates not only publicly raised such fundamental questions as "What is arête?" and "Who are its teachers?" but also by discrediting through their own representatives the accepted educational channels and by creating a climate of questioning and doubt, he was suspected by conservative minds of the dangerous game of discomfiting all authority before a circle of impressionable youths and subtracting from the state the stability of tradition. It was also apparent that the values by which Socrates lived, his indifference to material wealth and prosperity, and his freedom from desire and ambition were themselves a living criticism of all institutions and of politicians who did not seem to know what they were*

doing or who were compromising their principles. (p. 482)

Socrates was perhaps the most original, influential, and controversial figure in the history of Greek thought. ... [H]e was obviously at home in the best society, but he had no respect for social status. ... Tradition holds that by refusing to compromise his principles, he deliberately antagonized the court. (p. 480)

Prominent thinkers throughout history have commented on schooling as an agent of indoctrination. Comenius, a 16th- and 17th-century educator and scholar, said that he was only one of thousands whose youth was wasted in these "slaughterhouses" of the young.

John Henry Newman, a leading 19th-century university president and theologian, who penned one of the most important and well-developed treatises on the educated mind and the educated person, lamented the wretched state of instruction at the university level during his time. Here is just a sampling of his work, taken from *The Idea of a University* (1852; 1996):

I will tell you, Gentlemen, what has been the practical error of the last twenty years—not to load the memory of the student with a mass of undigested knowledge, but to force upon him so much that he has rejected all. It has been the error of distracting and enfeebling the mind by an unmeaning profusion of subjects; of implying that a smattering in a dozen branches of study is not shallowness, which it really is, but enlargement, which it is not; of considering an acquaintance with the learned names of things and persons, and the possession of the clever duodecimos, and attendance on eloquent lecturers, and membership with scientific institutions ... that all this was not dissipation of mind, but progress. All things now are to be learned at once, not first one thing and then the other, not one well, but many badly. Learning is to be without exertion, without attention, without toil; without grounding, without advance, without finishing. There is to be nothing individual in it; and this, forsooth, is the wonder of the age. What the steam engine does with matter, the printing press is to do with the mind; it is to act mechanically, and the population is to be passively, almost unconsciously enlightened. (p. 103)

Emma Goldman (1869-1940) wrote extensively on oppressive governments and the consequences of their unethical behavior. She indicts not just governments, but all of society, for contributing to the problem. She says:

However, it is not only government in the sense of the state which is destructive of every individual value and quality. It is the whole complex of authority and institutional domination which strangles life. It is the superstition, myth, pretense, evasions, and subservience which support authority and institutional domination. It is the reverence for these institutions instilled in the school, the Church, and the home in order that man may believe and obey without protest. Such a process of devitalizing and distorting personalities of the individual and of whole communities may have been a part of historical evolution; but it should be strenuously combated by every honest and independent mind in an age which has any pretense to enlightenment. (Goldman, 1996, pp. 434-435)

C.S. Lewis (1947) points out that authors assume their texts will be accepted uncritically by students, which is itself a form of indoctrination. He says, "The very power of [textbook writers] depends on the fact that they are dealing with a boy: a boy who thinks he is 'doing' his 'English prep' and has no notion that ethics, theology, and politics are all at stake. It is not a theory they put into his mind, but an assumption, which ten years hence, its origin forgotten and its presence unconscious, will condition him to take one side in a controversy which he has never recognized as a controversy at all" (p. 48).

Einstein (Clark, 1979, p. 33) believed that most of his teaching colleagues did little more than encourage "the obedience of a corps." Einstein speaks of the meaninglessness and hypocrisy with which most people plod through life, and of the crushing realization he experienced in seeing through dogmatism by his own self-education (Clark, 1979):

When I was a fairly precocious young man I became thoroughly impressed with the futility of the hopes and strivings that chase most men restlessly through life. Moreover, I soon discovered the cruelty of that chase, which in those years was much more carefully covered up by hypocrisy and glittering words than is the case today. By the mere existence of his stomach everyone was condemned to participate in that chase. The stomach might well be satisfied by such participation, but not man insofar as he is a thinking and feeling being.

As the first way out there was religion, which is implanted into every child by way of the traditional education-machine. Thus I came—though the child of entirely irreligious (Jewish) parents—to a deep religiousness, which, however, reached an abrupt end at the age of twelve.

Through the reading of popular scientific books I soon reached the conviction that much in the stories of the Bible could not be true. The consequence was a positively fanatic orgy of freethinking coupled with the impression that youth is intentionally being deceived by the state through lies; it was a crushing impression. (pp. 3, 5)

In the early twentieth century, Sumner (1906; 1940) was concerned that schools were well on their way to becoming mere extensions of the society—replete with its prejudices and biases. Consider his developed view and ask yourself whether his fears have been realized in schooling today:

The boards of trustees are almost always made up of "practical men," and if their faiths, ideas and prejudices are to make the norm of education, the schools will turn out boys and girls compressed into that pattern. ... We seem likely to have orthodox history (especially of our own country), political science, political economy, and sociology before too long. It will be defined by school boards who are party politicians. As fast as physics, chemistry, geology, biology, bookkeeping, and the rest come into conflict with interests, and put forth results which have a pecuniary effect ... then the popular orthodoxy will extend to them, and it will be enforced as "democratic." ... The reason is because there will be a desire that children shall be taught just that one thing which is "right" in the view and interest of those in control, and nothing else. ... In fact, this is the reason why the orthodox answers of the school boards and trustees are mischievous. They teach that there are absolute and universal facts of knowledge, whereas we ought to teach that all our knowledge is subject to unlimited verification and revision. (p. 632)

In his book *Teachers as Intellectuals*, Henry Giroux (1988) focuses on some of the root problems in schooling that result from, and lead to, sociocentric thought:

The rationality that dominates traditional views of schooling and curriculum is rooted in the narrow concerns for effectiveness, behavioral objectives, and principles of learning that treat knowledge as something to be consumed and schools as merely instructional sites designed to pass onto students a "common" culture and set of skills that will enable them to operate effectively in the wider society. Steeped in the logic of technical rationality, the problematic of traditional curriculum theory and schooling centers on questions about the most thorough or most efficient ways to learn specific kinds of knowledge, to create moral consensus, and to provide modes of schooling that reproduce the existing society. For instance, traditional educators may ask how the school should seek to attain a certain predefined goal, but they rarely ask why such a goal might be beneficial to some socioeconomic groups and not to others, or why schools, as they are presently organized, tend to block the possibility that specific classes will attain a measure of economic and political autonomy. (p. 6)

Richard Paul enriches our understanding of this problem in his classic anthology, *Critical Thinking: What Every Person Needs to Survive in a Rapidly Changing World* (1993; 2012):

No culture sees itself as indoctrinating the young or discouraging intellectual development. Each sees itself as concerned with education worthy of the name. The rhetoric of reason and objective learning is everywhere. Yet classroom instruction around the world, at all levels, is typically didactic, one-dimensional, and indifferent, when not antithetical, to reason. Blank faces are taught barren conclusions in dreary drills. There is nothing sharp, nothing poignant, no exciting twist or turn of mind and thought ... no struggle, no conflict, no rational give and take, no intellectual excitement or discipline, no pulsation in the heart or mind. Students are not expected to ask for reasons to justify what is presented to them for belief. They do not question what they see, hear, or read, nor are they encouraged to do so. They do not demand that subject matter "make sense" to them ... they do not expect to have to think at all. They mechanically repeat back what they were told, or what they think they were told, with little sense of the logicalness of what they are saying. Education for most is drab, empty, passive, and sluggish, a mass of permissions, rules, sanctions, and authorizations. And, if truth be told, educators are not typically disturbed by these facts ... Equally undisturbing [to these educators] is the fact that what teachers teach very often does not even make logical sense to the teachers themselves. (p. xiii)

> **Because teachers themselves are heavily indoctrinated into the ideologies of the culture... they tend to unwittingly pass along their narrow, parochial views to their students.**

Because teachers themselves are heavily indoctrinated into the ideologies of the culture, resulting from the many sociocentric forces that have influenced them, they tend to unwittingly pass along their narrow, parochial views to students. But when genuine education is fostered, schools have the opportunity to emancipate, rather than indoctrinate, the mind.

Schools should be alive with questions, both on the parts of teachers and students. Teachers should encourage students to wonder aloud about truth and meaning. Discussions about controversial issues should be openly encouraged. *No issues should be taboo from discussion in schools.* But where can we find classrooms today in which open dialogue is possible, much less encouraged? What would parents do if students were encouraged to discuss issues considered taboo in the culture? What would happen to teachers if they led such discussions? What would happen to administrators if they encouraged teachers and students to question the status quo—the mainstream views of society? What would happen to teachers and administrators if they encouraged reasoned dissent among students? But perhaps more important, what would happen in the lives of students if they learned the importance of, and the intellectual skill involved in, reasoned dissent? And how would the world be different if they did?

A sense of boredom and lack of zest for learning is clearly marked in this student's demeanor; this is no wonder given the state of schooling today, which for the most part advances neither deep learning nor critical thinking.

In the following passages, Bertrand Russell (1957) emphasizes the significance of open and free inquiry. He stresses the critical need to create education systems that foster fairminded pursuit of knowledge, and warns of the dangers inherent in dogmatic ideologies.

In 1925, John Scopes was tried and found guilty for teaching evolution in school, which was against the law in the state of Tennessee at that time. Was Scopes guilty of encouraging his students to think critically?

The conviction that it is important to believe this or that, even if a free inquiry would not support the belief, is one which … inspires all systems of state education. … A habit of basing convictions upon evidence, and of giving to them only that degree of certainty which the evidence warrants, would, if it became general, cure most of the ills from which the world is suffering. But at present, in most countries, education aims at preventing the growth of such a habit, and men who refuse to profess belief in some system of unfounded dogmas are not considered suitable as teachers of the young. …

The world that I should wish to see would be one freed from the virulence of group hostilities and capable of realizing that happiness for all is to be derived rather from cooperation than from strife. I should wish to see a world in which education aimed at mental freedom rather than at imprisoning the minds of the young in a rigid armor of dogma calculated to protect them through life against the shafts of impartial evidence. The world needs open hearts and open minds, and it is not through rigid systems, whether old or new, that these can be derived. (pp. vi-vii).

Sumner (1906; 1940) implicitly distinguishes between education, which entails developed criticality of mind, and schooling, which is merely what happens in schools—whether reasonable or unreasonable, whether it cultivates the mind or warps it, whether it leads to emancipation or uncritical acceptance of received views. On the relationship between education and developing critical thought, Sumner says:

The critical faculty is a product of education and training. … It is a prime condition of human welfare that men and women should be trained in it. It is our only guarantee against delusion, deception, superstition, and misapprehension of ourselves and our earthly circumstances. … Education teaches us to act by judgment. Our education is good just so far as it produces well-developed critical faculty. … A teacher of any subject who insists on accuracy and a rational control of all processes and methods, and who holds everything open to unlimited verification and revision is cultivating

that method as a habit in the pupils. ... When the schools are not too
rigidly stereotyped they become seats of new thought, of criticism of what is
traditional, and of new ideas which remold the mores. (pp. 632–634)

Sociologist James Loewen (1995; 2007) has extensively studied how students
think of history courses and what high school history textbooks commonly
encompass. He says:

> *High school students hate history. When they list their favorite subjects,*
> *history invariably comes in last. Students consider history "the most*
> *irrelevant" of twenty-one subjects commonly taught in high school ... When*
> *students can, they avoid it ... (p. 1)*

Loewen's work brings to light numerous problems in textbooks commonly
used in U.S. high school history classes, including the
"huge" (and growing) size of the books, the content of
which could not possibly be covered in a semester or
year. Further, he says, "While textbook authors tend
to include most of the trees and all too many twigs,
they neglect to give readers even a glimpse of what they
might find memorable: the forests. Textbooks stifle
meaning by suppressing causation. Students exit history
textbooks without having developed the ability to think
coherently about social life" (pp. 6-7).

> There was reason
> for fearing Socrates
> as a social force
> ... an educator
> critical of received
> assumptions was
> a revolutionary.
>
> — *Encyclopedia of Philosophy*

Since history textbooks have to sell, they tend to be
heavily influenced by social ideologies—by the ways
in which people in the society see their own history. In other words, history
textbooks will sell only to the extent that they validate the views of the society in
which they exist. Those responsible for deciding to purchase (or not purchase)
a given textbook base their decision largely on their own views, i.e., on the way
they see the world and the way they understand history. On the "receiving" end
of these decisions, students come to detest history. They fail to see its importance
to their lives. They fail to see themselves as historical thinkers who naturally
filter and control how they view their own past. They fail to see the power in
understanding the past:

> *As a sociologist, I am reminded constantly of the power of the past. Although*
> *each of us comes into the world de novo, we are not really new creatures.*
> *We arrive into a social slot, born not only to a family but also a religion,*
> *community, and, of course, a nation and culture ... Not understanding their*
> *past renders many Americans incapable of thinking effectively about our*
> *present and future. (Loewen, 1995; 2007, p. 9)*

Loewen points out that history textbooks tend to make people into heroes—
a degenerative process he calls heroification, which often leads to gross
misportrayals. Loewen offers lengthy examples of this problem, including one

focused on Helen Keller. He notes that Keller's life tends to be treated superficially in history textbooks. He stresses that though a section on Helen Keller is often "included" in such books, the story tends to focus on her physical disabilities and how she is taught to read and speak despite these disabilities. What is rarely discussed is the fact that Helen Keller became a radical socialist and helped found the American Civil Liberties Union to fight for freedom of speech. What is frequently excluded from the history of Helen Keller is how her conversion to socialism "caused a storm of publicity—and outrage" (p. 14). Whether or not people agree with her socialistic views is irrelevant to the fact that, importantly, most people have no sense that she held such views. Not only are most students never encouraged to read Keller's essays on social issues, in fact, most never learn that she wrote them. Still, students are highly encouraged to see Keller as a hero.

When we can critique the many ways in which schooling is guided by, and leads to, dysfunctional group thought and action, we can begin to forge a new path—one that effectively deals with these dysfunctionalities and systematically cultivates the educated, emancipated mind.

Test the Idea

Take several quotes from this section. Articulate your understanding of them in your own words, and then interrelate the main ideas of each. If people took these ideas seriously, how might schooling change (both academically and as a social force)?

SPECIESCENTRISM IS A DANGEROUS FORM OF SOCIOCENTRISM

Sociocentrism is based on the notion that human groups intrinsically see themselves as privileged over other groups. Accordingly, humans naturally see their species (their "in-group") as privileged over other species ("out-group"). And it is their speciescentrism that causes humans to be insensitive to the suffering of animals.

Speciescentrism has been exemplified throughout human history.[30] Consider, for instance, the use of primates in research. There is growing concern among reasonable people about whether, and to what extent, primate research is ethically justifiable, given the suffering that it almost always (if not always) causes. Primate research has historically been conducted for, and rationalized by, its potential human benefit. It is based on the (usually unstated) assumption that because human needs and desires take precedence over those of other species, humans are entitled to treat other species as they wish, with little or no regard for the

---

30 It may be that the term "speciescentrism" can be used interchangeably with anthropocentrism and humanocentrism. Keep in mind that my use of the term "speciescentrism" refers to the pathological tendency of humans to see "our" species as privileged over other species, and therefore justified in using other species to serve our vested interests—without regard to the rights and needs of individuals within species.

thoughts or feelings of those species. In his book, *Next of Kin: My Conversations with Chimpanzees*, Roger Fouts (1997) argues, on ethical grounds, against the use of primates for any research purposes. He points out that the chimpanzee (our closest ancestor, alongside the bonobo) has for hundreds of years been viewed as a model research subject because, though virtually "human," chimps are perceived (genetically) to lack human emotions:

Chimpanzees, like all feeling creatures, deserve our empathy.

In 1699, England's best-known anatomist, Edward Tyson, performed the first dissection of a chimpanzee and revealed an anatomy that resembled "Man in many of its Parts, more than any of the Ape-kind, or any other Animal in the World." Tyson was especially troubled by the creature's brain and laryngeal region. They looked almost human, indicating that this animal might be capable of thought and speech. But Tyson was a good Cartesian and he assumed that a thinking, talking animal was simply not possible. So he decided that though this ape-man had all the machinery for thought and speech, it did not have the God-given ability to use them. It was Tyson who invented the paradigm of the mindless ape: the chimpanzee with a human brain but no single thought in it, the chimpanzee with a nervous system but not the slightest emotion, the chimpanzee with the apparatus for language but not a thing to communicate. Tyson dreamed up the view of the chimpanzee that biomedical researchers still cling to today: a beast with the physiology of a human but the psychology of a lifeless machine—a hairy test tube created for the sake of human exploitation. (p. 50)

But Fouts' research, along with that of many ethologists, has shown what is, in fact, obvious to any unbiased observer: that chimpanzees (and indeed all apes) experience feelings just as humans do. Fouts (1997) documents a number of egregious acts perpetrated on chimpanzees for research purposes, which violated their basic rights and caused them tremendous suffering. For instance, he reveals how the Air Force "recruited" infant chimpanzees from Africa in the 1950s and 1960s for its space program:

> Speciescentrism has been exemplified throughout human history, and causes untold suffering to creatures outside the human "in-group."

The military procured the chimps from African hunters who stalked mother chimpanzees carrying a baby. Usually the mother was shot out of her hiding place high up in a tree. If she fell on her stomach, then her infant, clinging to her chest, would die along with her. But many mother chimpanzees shielded their infants by falling on their backs. The screaming infant would then be bound hand and foot to a carrying pole and transported to the coast, a harrowing journey usually lasting several days. If the infants survived this second ordeal, and many did not, then they were sold for four or five dollars to a European animal dealer who kept them in a small box for days until the American buyer arrived—in this case the Air Force. Those still alive when the buyer came were crated up and sent to the United States, a journey that mirrored the slave trade of earlier centuries. Very few babies emerged from the crates. It is estimated that ten chimpanzees died for every one that made it to this country. (pp. 42–43)

Countless research studies conducted each year on innocent creatures center on topics of little practical use, or which merely serve human greed and vanity. In his book *Minding Animals*, Marc Bekoff (2002) offers the following descriptions of two such research projects. The first focuses on learned helplessness, the other on the effects of radiation. Note the conclusions that researchers come to in each case:

When a normal, naïve dog receives escape/avoidance training in a shuttlebox, the following behavior typically occurs: At the onset of electric shock the dog runs frantically about, defecating, urinating, and howling until it scrambles over the barrier and so escapes from the shock. … However, in dramatic contrast … a dog who had received inescapable shock while strapped in a

Jane Goodall has been a powerful advocate for the rights of wild animals for than 50 years.

Pavlovian harness soon stops running and remains silent until shock terminates. … It seems to "give up" and passively "accept the shock."

In one set of tests, [monkeys] had been subjected to lethal doses of radiation and then forced by electric shock to run on a treadmill until they collapsed. Before dying, the unanesthetized monkeys suffered the predictable effects of excessive radiation, including vomiting and diarrhea. After acknowledging all this a DNA [Defense Nuclear Agency] spokesman commented: "To the best of our knowledge, the animals experience no pain." (p. 140)

Jane Goodall, famous for her research on chimpanzees in the wild and for her advocacy of animal rights, illuminates some of the many ways in which humans use animals in research, often causing suffering that, if it were done to humans, would be called torture. In her book *Reason for Hope* (2000), Goodall says:

In the name of science and with the various goals of improving human health, keeping dying people alive, ensuring human safety, testing researchers' hypotheses, and teaching students, animals are subjected to countless invasive, frightening, and sometimes very painful procedures. To test product safety and efficacy, animals such as rats and mice, guinea pigs, cats, dogs, and monkeys are injected with or forced to swallow, or have dripped into their eyes, a whole variety of substances. Surgical techniques are practiced by medical students on animals, and new surgical procedures are tested on animals. To try out experimental techniques for treating burns, vast areas of animals' bodies are subjected to first degree burns.

To discover more about the effect of smoking, taking drugs, eating too much fat, and so forth on human animals, other kinds of animals are forced to inhale huge quantities of smoke, take drugs, and overeat. To learn about biological systems, scientists stick electrodes into animals' brains, deafen, kill and dissect them. To learn about mental functions, researchers subject animals to a vast array of tests; mistakes are punished with electric shocks, food and water deprivation and other cruelties. In short, what is done to animals in the name of science is often, from the animals' point of view, pure torture—and would be regarded as such if perpetrated by anyone who was not a scientist. (pp. 218–219)

> Humans systematically violate the rights of animals.

Bekoff focuses on a number of systematic ways in which humans violate the rights of animals.[31] These violations are easily rationalized by human perpetrators when we assume, quite conveniently, that animals feel no pain. Bekoff details, for instance, the fact that wearing animals as clothing is still a common practice, and that there are no laws in the United States which regulate fur farms or how trapped animals can or cannot be killed. He says:

Wild fur-bearing animals, over 40 million individuals per year, are cruelly captured, injured, and killed for profit. Many are trapped using contraptions that cause psychological and physical suffering. These devices include leg hold traps, wire snares that encircle an animal and pull tight as the animal struggles, and conibears that grip the entire body and break the neck or back. Beavers are often trapped in water and drown after struggling for some time. . . . Animals are also raised on farms only to be slaughtered for clothing. Recently dogs and cats (bred specifically for use as clothing, or strays) have been used to make fur products. These individuals typically are kept in deplorable conditions before being beaten, hanged, suffocated, or bled to death. . . . Animals such as mink are killed by neck-snapping. They show great distress when removed from their cages to be killed—screeching, urinating, defecating, fighting for their lives. (p. 156)

In addition to the many mainstream beliefs that lead to animal suffering, there are many weird beliefs that also cause untold suffering for innocent creatures. In a *National Geographic* article (January 2010), Bryan Christy offers an exposé on the world's most notorious wildlife dealer. In this article, he focuses on Asia's wildlife trade and insatiable demand for traditional medicines, exotic pets, and culinary

---

31 The sociocentric thought on the part of researchers that we see throughout this section on the treatment of non-human research subjects should be apparent when we consider that such treatment often straightforwardly violates our own laws about preventing cruelty to animals.

delicacies. In cataloging these practices, he says:

> *Tigers are all but extinct in the wild. …*
> *There's a valuable black market for tigers.*
> *Tibetans wear tiger-skin robes; wealthy*
> *collectors display their heads; exotic*
> *restaurants sell their meat; their penis is*
> *said to be an aphrodisiac; and Chinese*
> *covet their bones for health cures, including*
> *tiger-bone wine, the "chicken soup" of*
> *Chinese medicine. … In some Asian*
> *countries, tourist attractions called tiger*
> *parks secretly operate as front operations*
> *for tiger farming—butchering captive*
> *tigers for their parts and offering a potential*
> *market for wild-tiger poachers too. (p. 98)*

Tigers have been exploited for human use and "sport" for hundreds of years or more.

The sad fact is that the exploitation of animals throughout human history has been well-documented—from the killing of whales for their blubber to the killing of elephants for their tusks; from the use of wild animals in circuses and animal "parks" to the breeding of animals for display in zoos; from bullfighting in Spain to wild animal "sporting" in all parts of the world; from mass-consumer farming to the use of animals in research. It might be said that every animal that *can* be exploited for human use, *has* been thus exploited.

Peter Singer (2000), a preeminent philosopher who specializes in practical ethics, has had perhaps more influence than any other writer in advancing the rights of animals. In much of his work, he reveals the unnecessary suffering many animals face at the hands of humans. He says:

> It might be said that every animal that *can* be exploited for human use, *has* been thus exploited.

> *… [W]e have no right to discount the interests of*
> *nonhuman animals simply because, for example, we*
> *like the taste of their flesh. Modern industrialized*
> *agriculture treats animals as if they were things, putting*
> *them indoors and confining them whenever it turns*
> *out to be cheaper to do so, with no regard at all paid to*
> *their suffering or distress, as long as it does not mean that they cease to be*
> *productive. But we cannot ethically disregard the interests of other beings*
> *merely because they are not members of our species. Note that this argument*
> *says nothing at all about whether it is wrong to kill nonhuman animals for*
> *food. It is based entirely on the suffering that we inflict on farm animals when*
> *we raise them by the methods that are standard today. (p. xvi)*

Singer (2000) illuminates the powerful role that vested interest plays in people's inability to empathize with animals:

> *More significantly still for the prospects of the animal liberation movement is the fact that almost all of the oppressing group are directly involved in and see themselves benefitting from, the oppression. There are few humans indeed who can view the oppression of animals with the detachment possessed, say, by northern whites debating the institution of slavery in the southern states of the Union. People who eat pieces of slaughtered nonhumans every day find it hard to believe that they are doing wrong; and they also find it hard to imagine what else they could eat. On this issue, anyone who eats meat is an interested party. Meat eaters benefit—or at least they think they benefit—from the present disregard of the interests of nonhuman animals. This makes persuasion more difficult. How many southern slaveholders were persuaded by the arguments used by the northern abolitionists and accepted by nearly all of us today? Some, but not many. (p. 25)*

> Almost all of the oppressing group are directly involved in, and see themselves benefitting from, the oppression.
>
> — *Peter Singer*

Add to the many egregious acts humans inflict upon animals the fact that the sheer number of humans (yes, the human population explosion) has caused increasing encroachments on the natural habitats of other animals, causing their numbers to dwindle, in many cases to the point of extinction. In fact, many scientists believe we are now living through "the sixth great extinction," and that this sad phenomenon is human-caused.

As long as humans see themselves as superior to other species (as a natural part of our sociocentric nature), these problems will continue to plague the unfortunate creatures with whom we share the precious, but dwindling, resources on our planet.

 ## Test the Idea

To what extent do you see speciescentrism as a problem in human societies today? Can you find examples that support the fact that this is a problem, or examples that show awareness of the problem (such as advocacy groups working for the rights of animals)? What can be done to combat it?

Fairminded critical thinkers seek never to exploit other animals to serve their selfish or vested interests. They want to know, and fairly face, the extent to which they and other people use animals to serve their interests (so they can avoid doing so). They try not to hide from these realities or rationalize them. They do not see humans as deserving more advantages than other sentient creatures. They recognize that humans have far more power to harm other creatures than other creatures have to harm humans; consequently, they try to reduce the amount of suffering humans cause other animals. Critical thinkers want to emancipate themselves from slavery to group ideologies—and they want to emancipate other sentient creatures from slavery to human desires.

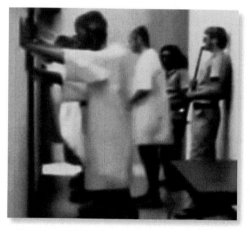

MANY STUDIES ILLUMINATE PROBLEMS IMPLICIT IN SOCIOCENTRIC THINKING

Sociocentric thinking is revealed in a multitude of studies focused on understanding human nature. One of the most famous was conducted by Phillip Zimbardo at Stanford University in 1971, in which students

The Stanford Prison Experiment demonstrated, in just a few days, the potentially toxic combination of group control and group validation.

were randomly assigned to play the role of either guard or prisoner in a two-week prison simulation on the Stanford campus. The study was funded by the U.S. Navy to study human reactions in situations where considerable differences exist in terms of authority and power. In this study, to make the situation seem realistic, "guards" were given wooden batons and wore khaki, military-style uniforms and mirrored sunglasses that minimized eye contact. The "prisoners" were not allowed to wear underwear, and were made to wear loose-fitting smocks and rubber flip-flops on their feet. Each "prisoner" was called by his designated number, rather than by name. The "guards" were not given formal instructions, but were simply told it was their responsibility to run the prison. From the beginning of the experiment, the "guards" misused their power over the "prisoners," who were increasingly subjected to abusive and humiliating treatment—both physical and emotional. "Prisoners" were forced to clean toilets with their bare hands, to sleep on concrete floors, and to endure solitary confinement and hunger. They were subjected to forced nudity and sexual abuse. Because of potential emotional damage to the "prisoners," researchers terminated the Stanford prison experiment after only six days.

This study illuminates how easily people, when placed in positions of high authority and power, will use their power in irrational ways. Further, and what concerns us most here, is how people in such positions will tend to collaborate with one another against the interests of those within their reach of power. In this experiment, both overt and tacit agreement among the "guards" led them to egregiously unethical acts, which seemed to them perfectly justified. They collectively rationalized their behavior toward the "prisoners." This would not have been possible if most, or even many, of the "guards" had objected. In the event, each of the "guards" gained power through the agreement and corroboration of the others. Together, they validated their unethical views and actions. They took control of the "prisoners," who in turn submitted to their control. In his book *The Lucifer Effect*, Philip Zimbardo (2007), head researcher in the Zimbardo experiment, says of the "guards":

> *Some of our volunteers who were randomly assigned to be guards soon came to abuse their newfound power by behaving sadistically—demeaning, degrading, and hurting the "prisoners" day in and night out ... none of [the guards] ever intervened to prevent the "bad guards" from abusing the prisoners; none complained to the staff, left their shift early or came to work late, or refused to work overtime in emergencies. Moreover, none of them even demanded overtime pay for doing tasks they may have found distasteful. They were part of the "Evil of Inaction Syndrome ... (pp. 207–208)*

Another well-known experiment that illuminates the phenomenon and pervasiveness of sociocentric thinking was originally conducted in 1968, and has been described in some detail in the book *A Class Divided: Then and Now* (Peters, 1987). This experiment was not a research study in the traditional sense of the term, but in fact was an experiential learning activity that yielded interesting results from a research perspective. It was conducted in a third-grade classroom by teacher Jane Elliott, for the purpose of helping "Caucasian" students comprehend the problem of racial prejudice. It was devised on the heels of the assassination of Martin Luther King, Jr. to help students empathize with the feelings of blacks, who, at that time, were even more systematically discriminated against than they are today. The experiment was conducted over a two-day period, and students were grouped according to eye color. One group consisted of the blue- and green-eyed students, the other of brown-eyed students. After a brief discussion about the problem of racial discrimination, in which Elliott asked her students whether they wanted to truly understand how it feels to be discriminated against, she told them they would get a taste of it through a class activity she had designed. An excerpt from the book describes what

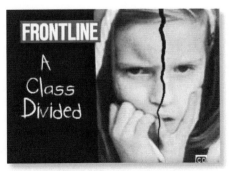

A Class Divided illuminated the problem of group power arbitrarily granted.

happened when the children were placed in the "blue-eyed" or "brown-eyed" groups:

> *"Today," [Elliott] told the class, "the blue-eyed people will be on the bottom, and the brown-eyed people will be on the top." At their puzzled looks, she went on. "What I mean is that the brown-eyed people are better than blue-eyed people. They are cleaner than blue-eyed people. They are more civilized than blue-eyed people. And they are smarter than blue-eyed people." (p. 21)*

What Elliott found was that in a matter of minutes after this introduction, the brown-eyed children were openly discriminating against and gloating over their blue-eyed classmates:

> *One blue-eyed boy slumped way down in his chair. "What color are your eyes?" Jane asked him. "Blue," the boy said, straightening up. "Is that the way we've been taught to sit in class?" "No," the boy said. "Do blue-eyed people remember what they've been taught?" Jane asked the class. There was a chorus of "No's" from the brown-eyed children as they began to see how it would work. The blue-eyed boy now sat bolt upright, his hands folded neatly in the exact center of his desk. A brown-eyed boy near him, one of his close friends in the room, gave him a withering, disdainful look. It all began that quickly." (p. 22)*

Throughout the day, the brown-eyed children had all the advantages. They were treated as smarter, cleaner, more responsible, and so on. The next school day, the tables were turned. The brown-eyed people were no longer privileged. They were dirtier, less intelligent, more slovenly; they were therefore denied the privileges granted their blue-eyed counterparts. Now the blue-eyed children turned on the brown-eyed classmates. They perceived themselves as better, more deserving, brighter than the brown-eyed children.

Naturally, the ethical nature of this experiment has been questioned, but the results seem clear: when people, in this case children, see themselves as superior to others, even without objective data to support their view, they tend to act as if they are in fact superior. When groups of people see themselves as superior to other groups, and when that superiority is validated by those in power, they tend to treat people external to the group as inferior and thus less deserving. In Jane Elliott's words:

> *… even more frightening was the way the brown-eyed children turned on their friends of the day before, the way they accepted almost immediately as true what had originally been described as an exercise. For there was no question, after an hour or so, that they actually believed they were superior. The fact that we were going to change roles on Monday was forgotten. Everything was forgotten in the fact of the undeniable proof that the blue-eyed children were inferior to them. It was as though someone had pointed out to them something they simply hadn't noticed before. Weren't the blue-*

eyed children making more mistakes than they were? Of course. Wasn't the teacher finding fault almost exclusively with the blue-eyed children? Of course. Wasn't it clear that she liked the brown-eyed children better? Of course. What better proof did you need? (p. 25)

In addition to what has already been said, we can see from these passages and the experiment more generally, evidence of at least three important pathological phenomena coming together: 1) that people often hold their views in accordance with what they want to believe, rather than what seems to make the most objective sense ("It's true because I, or we, want to believe it"), 2) people tend to go along with the views of authority figures, and 3) people feed on one another's pathological views within groups (especially views that are self-aggrandizing and self-validating).

Abu Ghraib: U.S. Soldiers in the Iraq War systematically tortured and abused prisoners, behaving in the same egregious ways that were demonstrated in the Stanford Experiment.

This study shows that wanting to believe in one's own superiority, being validated by "authority" in this belief, and being confirmed in this belief by one's peers can easily lead to a sense of arrogance and self-righteousness toward those in the out-group. We see quite keenly in this experiment the sociocentric phenomena of group validation and groupishness. In "the right" circumstances, these combined variables can lead to abuses of the highest magnitude. This has been evidenced in many real-life situations, such as those that led to the Abu Ghraib prison tortures and humiliations in Iraq at the hands of the U.S. military.

Though the military has maintained that the Abu Ghraib tortures resulted from a few bad apples, Zimbardo (2007), among many others, has revealed that the U.S. military was systematically responsible for creating the social conditions that led to these egregious actions in 2003. He quotes from a number of military reports that illuminate the sociocentric nature of the Abu Ghraib events:

General Taguba concludes that these MPs were set up to engage in some of these abuses by higher-ups. He states that "Military Intelligence (MI) interrogators and other U.S. Government agency's interrogators actively requested that MP guards set physical and mental conditions for favorable interrogation of witnesses." ... Major General George Fay's investigative report goes even further ... "Military intelligence personnel allegedly requested, encouraged, condoned or solicited Military Police personnel ... to abuse detainees, and/or participated in detainee abuse, and/or violated established interrogation procedures and applicable law." (p. 158)

According to Zimbardo (2007, p. 357), the long list of abuses at Abu Ghraib included:

1. Breaking chemical lights and pouring the phosphoric liquid on detainees;
2. Threatening detainees with pistols;
3. Pouring cold water on detainees;
4. Beating detainees with a broom and handle;
5. Threatening male detainees with rape;
6. Sodomizing a detainee with a chemical light;
7. Using military dogs to frighten and intimidate detainees with threats of attack;
8. Punching, slapping, and kicking detainees; jumping on their naked feet;
9. Forcibly arranging detainees in various sexually-explicit positions for photographing;
10. Forcing male detainees to wear women's underwear;
11. Forcing groups of male detainees to masturbate themselves while being photographed and videotaped.

> People are far less likely to perpetrate evil actions on others if they have to face the truth in what they are doing. To avoid the truth, they create false beliefs...

In his book *The Lucifer Effect*, Zimbardo (2007) has drawn a number of links between the Stanford Prison Experiment and the Abu Ghraib prison tortures. He comments on the shock he experienced when he learned of the Abu Ghraib abuses, and almost immediately connected them to the behavior of the "normal" students randomly assigned as "guards" in his study almost 30 years earlier. Both the experiment and the Abu Ghraib tortures powerfully exemplify the evil that can be, and is, perpetrated on innocent people when group validation, arrogance, and sense of righteousness are at play. These situations also point to the problem of dehumanization, which occurs when people conceptualize others as subhuman (savage, dirty, barbaric, and so on). This perception leads to all manner of physical and emotional abuses, including humiliation, torture, and murder.

People are far less likely to perpetrate evil actions on others if they have to face the truth in what they are doing. To avoid the truth, they create false beliefs through which they can deal with the situation on their own (dysfunctional) terms.[32] The in-group collectively validates these false beliefs, which enables them to rationalize irrational force (control) used on those who must submit to their power. Again, we see the sociocentric forms of group validation and group control.

Another well-known study, which focuses on the extent to which people will comply with those in positions of authority, is relevant to our discussion here. In this study, Stanley Milgram (1974) demonstrated that the average person will obey those in positions of authority, even if it means causing severe harm to an innocent person. While Milgram's primary study focused on one authority figure

---

32 See the section on egocentricity and self-deception for a better understanding of this phenomenon.

and one "subject," what is less well-known is that Milgram also examined the degree to which group influence might affect subject responses to authority figures. In this study, two confederates of the experimenter posed as teachers (teachers 1 and 2), one confederate posed as "learner," and there was one actual experimental subject—a teacher (teacher 3). Milgram (1974) describes the study as follows:

> Teacher 1 is told to read the list of word pairs, teacher 2 tells the subject [learner] whether his answer is correct or incorrect, and teacher 3 (the naïve subject) administers punishment. As in the basic experiment, the subjects are instructed to raise the shock level one step each time the learner makes an error. ... The confederates comply with the experimenter's orders through the 150-volt shock, which provokes the victim's first vehement protest. At this point teacher 1 informs the experimenter that he does not wish to participate further, because of the learner's complaints. The experimenter insists that teacher 1 continue. However, teacher 1 is not swayed by the experimenter's commands, gets up from his chair in front of the shock generator, and takes a seat in another part of the room ... the experimenter instructs the remaining two subjects [teachers 2 and 3] to continue with the experiment. ... After shock level 14 (210) volts is administered, teacher 2, expressing concern for the learner, refuses to participate further. ... [he says] "I'm willing to answer any of your questions, but I'm not willing to shock that man against his will. I'll have no part of it." ... At this point the naïve subject [teacher 3] is seated alone in front of the shock generator. He has witnessed the defiant actions of two peers. The experimenter orders him to continue, stating that it is essential that the experiment be completed. (pp. 116–118)

The Milgram Experiment illuminated the power people grant to those in positions of perceived authority; follow-up studies showed the influence of peer pressure during this process.

Unlike the initial Milgram experiment in which the vast majority of subjects went along with the experimenter to the point of believing themselves to be causing severe pain to the learner, "in this group setting, 36 of the 40 subjects defy the experimenter" (p. 118). The question, for our purposes here, is why? Milgram answers for us. "The effects of peer rebellion are very impressive in undercutting the experimenter's authority." Consider some of the reasons subjects gave for refusing to proceed with the experiment:

> [One] subject [said], "Well, I was already thinking about quitting when the

guy broke off." Most defiant subjects praised the confederates with such statements as, "I thought they were men of good character, yes I do. When the victim said 'stop,' they stopped ... I think they were very sympathetic people." ... A subject who defied the experimenter at level 21 qualified his approval: "Well, I think they should continue a little further, but I don't blame them for backing out when they did." ... Four defiant subjects definitely acknowledged the importance of the confederates' actions to their own defiance: "The thought of stopping didn't enter my mind until it was put there by the other two." ... The reason I quit was that I did not wish to seem callous and cruel in the eyes of the other two men who had already refused to go on with the experiment." ... A majority of defiant subjects, however, denied that the confederates' action was the critical factor in their own defiance. (p. 118–120)

This part of Milgram's study, focused on the power of peer influence, shows that, though most subjects were strongly influenced by their peers, these same subjects mostly denied the role of this influence in their decisions to stop punishing the "learner." This disconnect between what is actually happening (subjects are being influenced by the group) and what the subjects think is happening (they are acting in accordance with an autonomous decision) illuminates one of the primary pathological forces in the mind: that people often see themselves as independent thinkers, while in fact they are heavily influenced by the actions of others.[33] In analyzing the results of the experiment, Milgram (1974) offers these helpful suggestions:

There are at least three forces that compete for power in the human mind when it is faced with ethical dilemmas: one's own sense of what is right, what authority figures expect from us, and what the group expects of us.

The peers instill in the subject the idea of defying the experimenter. It may not have occurred to some subjects as a possibility ... The reactions of the defiant confederates define the act of shocking the victim as improper. They provide the social confirmation for the subject's suspicion that it is wrong to punish a man against his will ... The defiant confederates remain in the laboratory even after withdrawing from the experiment. ... Each additional shock administered by the naïve subject then carries with it a measure of social disapproval from the two confederates. (p. 120)

The fact that groups so effectively undermine the experimenter's power reminds us that individuals act as they do for the principal reasons: they carry certain internalized standards of behavior; they are acutely responsive to the sanctions that may be applied to them by authority; and finally, they are responsive to the

33 This paradox is well-documented in the studies conducted with children by Jean Piaget, and has been explained in the section titled "The Logic of Group Validation."

sanctions potentially applicable to them by the group. (p. 120)

Milgram's summary captures at least three forces that compete for power in the human mind when it is faced with ethical dilemmas: one's own sense of what is right, what authority figures expect from us, and what the group expects of us.

What we see in this experiment, among other things, is that, when under social pressure to do so, people might well behave in ways that are ethical, but—and here is the material point—they will often do this *not because it is the right thing to do, but because they want to be perceived as "good" persons by their peers.* In other words, they get something for doing the right thing, namely validation and acceptance. But as our other studies show, people also tend to behave unethically for the same reasons.

Fairminded critical thinkers try to avoid doing the right thing for the wrong reasons. They want to *know* that what they are doing is ethically commendable or "correct." If they go along with others in an acting on a question of ethics, they attempt to analyze the situation for themselves, using the standards of critical thought.

We have dealt with a few powerful studies that have implications for our understanding of sociocentric thought. Again, there are many others. Taken together, these studies illuminate the problems of group control, influence, vested interest, validation, and conformity—all of which lie at the heart of sociocentrism. Critical thinkers look for these four forms of sociocentric thought in studies they read about in the news, and in studies they examine in their professions. They look for implications of sociocentricity being illuminated by researchers; they also look for the problem of sociocentric thought influencing the work of researchers.

Test the Idea

Be on the lookout for research into social behavior that illuminates the problem of sociocentric thought. Identify which of the four forms of sociocentric thought are being illuminated. Also look out for sociocentric thought on the parts of researchers.

SOCIOCENTRIC THOUGHT IN ACADEMIC DISCIPLINES AND IN THE PROFESSIONS

Sociocentric tendencies, perhaps surprisingly, are often found in academic professions. It is thus common to find any and all of the problems implicit in sociocentric thought within the professions, as well as within academic departments, subjects, and disciplines. Where people think *collectively*, we are likely to find people vying for power, using power over others in unethical ways, pursuing vested interests without regard to the rights of others, behaving in subservient ways to those in positions of power, and so on.

The implications of sociocentric thought in the professions can be far-reaching and highly significant. In his book, *How Doctors Think*, Jerome Groopman (2007) details the following problems in medicine, all of which are caused by or connected with sociocentric thought:

1. Physicians tend to overly rely on classification schemes and algorithms when treating patients. Such an approach often fails to take into account the course of a specific person's disease, and the individual characteristics of the patient, sometimes leading to dire consequences. Groopman says, "scoring schemes are proliferating in all branches of medicine" (p. 238) and these schemes suit the "hectic pace of today's clinical care" (p. 239). (Physicians thus sociocentrically validate one another in using this oversimplified approach to complex medical problems.)

2. Physicians often stick with traditional approaches to medical problems, even when such approaches are ineffective. These doctors rationalize their behavior through the mantra, "it's a bad disease" (p. 240) rather than risking failure by trying a different approach. (Traditional ways of doing things, despite evidence which suggests need for change, continue because group members validate one another in maintaining the established views.)

> Where people think *collectively*, we are likely to find people vying for power, using power over others in unethical ways, and behaving in subservient ways to those in positions of power.

3. Doctors do not generally tend to focus on their mistakes. They do not tend to analyze their mistakes, document them, or use knowledge of these mistakes to improve. Groopman says, "During my training, I met a cardiologist who had a deserved reputation as one of the best in his field. Not only a storehouse of knowledge but also a clinician with excellent judgment. He kept a log of all the mistakes he knew he had made over the decades, and at times revisited this compendium when trying to figure out a particularly difficult case. He was characterized by many of his colleagues as eccentric, an obsessive oddball" (p. 21). (These colleagues were engaging in sociocentric validation: "Doctors who meticulously document and analyze their mistakes are kooky eccentrics, while we are the real professionals.")

4. Doctors often ignore information that contradicts a fixed way of diagnosing or treating patients. (This is an example of doctors being trapped within a sociocentric paradigm of diagnosis and treatment—providing sociocentric validation—i.e., "this is the way we do things. Our way is the correct way.")

5. Doctors almost always use heuristics, or shortcuts, in diagnosing and treating patients. Groopman says, "the problem is that medical schools do not teach shortcuts. In fact, you are discouraged from using them, since they deviate sharply from the didactic exercises in classrooms or on bedside rounds

conducted by the attending physicians" (p. 36). Groopman believes that because doctors naturally use shortcuts in their thinking, they need to know how and when they are taking shortcuts; they need to know the advantages of doing this and the disadvantages of doing it. Groopman thinks that medical schools need to teach students how to take command of this process of using shortcuts in thinking. (By ignoring how doctors actually think and work, medical schools are stuck in a sociocentric paradigm of group validation—"this is the way we have always done things. This is the way we will continue to do things.")

To appreciate the problem of sociocentric validation in the medical profession, consider the case of Barry Marshall, an Australian doctor who in 1981 traced both ulcers and stomach cancer to a gut infection. This suggested that both might be treatable by antibiotics. For many years, mainstream gastroenterologists dismissed his theory, holding fast to the established view that ulcers were caused by stress. Marshall, who presented his views to the annual meeting of the Royal Australasian College of Physicians, said, "To gastroenterologists, the concept of a germ causing ulcers was like saying that the Earth is flat."[34] Marshall tried to get funding for his work from pharmaceutical companies, all of which initially refused him. This is not surprising, given that these companies were making billions of dollars a year selling Zantac and Tagamet to treat ulcers as consequences of stress. Though the view that ulcers are caused by bacterial infection is now widely accepted, it required a decade for this view to take root, and then only after Marshall, in desperation, resorted to the surreal to prove his theory. He infected himself with the ulcer-causing bacteria he obtained from one of his patients (to prove the cause of ulcers) and then treated himself with antibiotics (to prove the cure). This example highlights the fact that even highly-skilled professionals can fall prey to the phenomenon of groupthink, and that when they do so, the consequences can be quite harmful.

> Even highly skilled professionals can fall prey to the phenomenon of groupthink.

In an attempt to explain why a doctor at Johnson & Johnson failed to warn his peers about the artificial hip sold by the company, which was so poorly designed it was causing patients to suffer unnecessarily, Dr. Harlan Krumholz, a professor at Yale School of Medicine, said, "Questioning the status quo in medicine is not easy." Dr. Robert Hauser, a cardiologist who warned other doctors about a defective heart implant in 2005, said, "the standard in the medical community is not to report"—not to report, in other words, medical mistakes. When, in 2008, Dr. Lawrence D. Dorr, an orthopedic specialist, warned his peers in an open letter that a hip implant made by Zimmer Holdings was flawed, he "became the subject of a whisper campaign that questioned his skills as a surgeon."[35] Such campaigns,

---

34 See interview with Barry Marshall, *Discover Magazine*. March 2010, pp. 66-74.

35 These quotes are taken from Barry Meier's article "Doctors Who Don't Speak Out," found in the *New York Times*, February 6, 2013.

according to Dorr, are put out by the companies at the germ of the critique. Doctors may remain silent, or participate in these campaigns, for reasons of vested interest. Going along with the campaign may better line their pockets than being honest with patients and acting in the public interest.

To what extent is freedom of speech valued in the professional disciplines? Will professionals stand up for it, or cave in to sociocentric pressure from vested interest groups? Richard Bove, a bank analyst who writes reports about the banking industry, predicts potential problems arising from banking practices and ranks banking companies from the riskiest to the least risky. Though he is among the best-known analysts on Wall Street, most of his colleagues deserted him after Bank Atlantic filed a law suit against him for his writings. The *New York Times* (September 12, 2010) reported, "None of the professional associations that represent analysts or the securities industry rallied to his side, and his employer ultimately abandoned him. ... As it turns out ... Mr. Bove's rankings have proved to be largely correct."

The very way that academicians think about their instruction is often sociocentric at its foundation. For instance, a study I conducted with my colleagues some years ago (Paul, et al. 1997) showed that though most college faculty believe critical thinking to be of primary importance to instruction, and believe they are fostering critical thinking in student thought, few can clearly articulate a reasonable conception of it or demonstrate how they teach for it. A recent study by sociologists Richard Arum and Josipa Roska (2010) supports our findings, demonstrating that most college instruction has "a barely noticeable impact on students' skills" in critical thinking and complex reasoning, and that "there are no universal standards for learning in higher education." This study adds to the growing body of literature which suggests that, for the most part, critical thinking is not fostered in higher-education instruction. Though most faculty would say that fostering students' abilities to think critically is essential to instruction, as Arum and Roska point out, this belief seems to be more in "principle" than in action. Faculty are often highly resistant to changing their instruction. Most still primarily use didactic, lecture-based instruction, while at the same time deceiving themselves into believing they are fostering critical thinking. Working collectively, they validate these views and scorn those who critique their instruction.

Test the Idea

Come up with examples from your own profession or discipline that illuminate the problem of sociocentric thought within it. If you can't think of any, think again.

Again, examples of sociocentric thought can be found in all disciplines and professions. Let us now consider a few such examples from the "mental health" professions.

Case Notes: Psychology and Psychiatry Often Foster Socientric Thought

The social disciplines, such as social work, psychology, and psychiatry, often directly foster sociocentric thought. Consider, for example, the history of psychology in relation to social convention and ideology. For many years, the dominant social belief about homosexuality was that it was morally perverted, mentally pathological, and disgusting. Psychologists and psychiatrists often reinforced this conception. They classified homosexuality as a mental illness and treated it as such. They cooperated in its criminalization. This was true despite historical evidence indicating that many societies have considered homosexuality to be normal and healthy. Much of the misunderstanding of homosexuality resulted from mental health professionals mislabeling it as a mental disease in the nineteenth century. Only after social attitudes toward homosexuality began to be liberalized did psychologists and psychiatrists reconsider their "professional" views.

The manner in which this reconsideration took place is instructive. In 1974, the American Psychiatric Association removed homosexuality from its official list of mental disorders. This reclassification came about as a result of a poll taken of the association's general membership. The views of each association member were given equal weight, even though most members had done no research on the subject. Imagine a science that determines what is true and what is false by taking polls of its members! This vote was taken some 17 years after a 1957 landmark study was conducted at the University of California, Los Angeles, which concluded that no pathological differences exist between homosexuals and heterosexuals. Despite evidence that homosexuality was not pathological, many psychiatrists still opposed removing it from the official list of mental disorders. Psychiatrist Lee Coleman (1984) describes the manner in which the official list changed:

> What particularly struck many observers was the obviously political rather than scientific basis for the change. Under growing pressure from the homosexual community, the trustees of the American Psychiatric Association (APA) declared, by a majority vote in December 1973, homosexuality to be no longer a mental disorder. So much controversy resulted from this [that] a referendum was called to enable the entire APA membership to vote. Of the total votes cast, 5,854 called for elimination, 3,810 for retention, and 367 abstained. (p. 18)

Classification of a sexual practice as pathological is much more than a mere academic distinction. It has far-reaching implications for the well-being of millions of people. For example, as late as the 1940s, homosexual acts were classified as felonies in all the states, with punishments of up to life in prison. Homosexuals were fired, persecuted, scorned, physically attacked, and in some cases killed.

Historically speaking, mental health professionals have frequently supported the criminalization of social behavior merely because it was considered abnormal in a given society. They have more often reflected public opinion than led it.

The publication of Alfred Kinsey's now classic study, *Sexual Behavior in the Human Male* (1948), received both positive and negative reviews. One of the most vocal negative reviewers came from Lewis M. Terman, retired psychologist from Stanford University, past president of the American Psychological Association, father of intelligence testing, and sex researcher. But as James Jones (1997) points out, Terman "had a personal score to settle with Kinsey," because in his study, Kinsey criticized Terman's research methodology in his studies on marital happiness. Terman's scathing review was seen by the foundation that supported Kinsey's work as based in jealousy and spite. But as Jones says,

> "Terman was not through ... After his review was published, he pursued a personal vendetta against Kinsey ... Terman busied himself with academic intrigue ... Terman directed a growing chorus of Kinsey's detractors in the social sciences—cheering on his fellow critics, critiquing drafts of their reviews, and recommending journals that might welcome negative assessments. And because he was perceived as a Kinsey foe, Terman became a clearinghouse for tales, criticisms, and gossip that his fellow academics were not willing to air in print."

> Mental health professionals have frequently supported the criminalization of social behavior merely because it was considered abnormal in a given society. They have more often reflected public opinion than led it.

Jones reveals that Kate Mueller, a longtime enemy of Kinsey at Indiana University, wrote to Terman, "happy to share local gossip about Kinsey." After describing, in a mildly shocked tone, the erotic art object Kinsey was collecting, she confided, "There has been a good deal of discussion as to whether or not Mr. Kinsey's interest in his collection is scientific and objective or emotional, and pretty general agreement that it is the latter." Jones points out that members of the art department who had consulted with Kinsey, she revealed, thought that he was weird (Jones, 591). Thankfully for Kinsey and his institute, Herman B. Wells, the president of his university "had correctly foreseen that Kinsey's research would provide the most severe test to academic freedom in the university's history ... Wells declared 'I am proud to record the fact that, although the individual members of the board and the board as a whole were harassed and subjected to all manner of pressure, they never once wavered in their support of our policy toward the Kinsey Institute' " (Jones, 1997, pp. 592-593). This seems a clear-cut case of sociocentric thought on the part of Kinsey's detractors, with a ringleader to lead the charge, inflate the group's sense of power, and recruit as many people as possible to the "cause." Their purpose was not to illuminate serious weaknesses in Kinsey's work, but to advance personal vendettas.

In her book, *Manufacturing Victims*, psychologist Tana Dineen (1996) writes a devastating critique of what she terms the "psychology industry." Her basic thesis, in her own words, is this:

> *Psychology presents itself as a concerned and caring profession working for the good of its clients. But in its wake lie damaged people, divided families, distorted justice, destroyed companies, and a weakened nation. Behind the benevolent facade is a voracious self-serving industry that proffers "facts" which are often unfounded, provides "therapy" which can be damaging to its recipients, and exerts influence which is having devastating effects on the social fabric. The foundation of modern psychology, its questioning and critical thinking, if not an illusion from its inception, has at the very least been largely abandoned in favor of power and profit, leaving only the guise of integrity, a show of arrogance, and a well-tuned attention to the bottom line. What seemed once a responsible profession is now a big business whose success is directly related to how many people become "users" ... No matter where we turn, one finds the effects of the psychology industry. Its influence extends across all aspects of life, telling us how to work, how to live, how to love, and, even, how to play ... While people have become used to hearing about all sorts of victims, from those of sexual harassment and verbal abuse, to those of "dysfunctional families," divorce, academic discrimination, even vacation cancellation and home renovation, they have not yet paid attention to the psychological techniques which are being used to create and cater to these "victims" ... There are many incentives for acquiring, and even seeking, victim status and, in the sort term, there are some pay-offs. The tragedies, the failures, the hardships, the health problems, and the disappointments of life become explained, relieving people of at least three of life's natural burdens: dealing with complexity, facing things beyond their control, and accepting personal responsibility for decisions and actions. (pp. 17-21)*

Dineen says that psychology is not the profession it claims to be. Rather, it is a powerful and dangerous business, replete with advertising slogans, sales and

"Rebirthing" is a controversial psychological technique designed to help people get past negative emotions and destructive behaviors "caused" by the birthing process. Through the "rebirthing" process, people presumably become more rational. In 2001, Candace Newmaker, a 10-year-old child, was suffocated by "mental health professionals" during a "rebirthing process." The two therapists each received 16 year prison sentences for their work in this case.

marketing programs, and research and development. She says that once people accept a "victim" label, they open themselves up to a wide variety of psychological services, and their lives begin revolving around them. "As well, the entrepreneur, the workshop or seminar leader, the psychological expert, can use victim terminology to promote the industry's view that everyone needs help whether they know it or not" (p. 25).

To the extent that Dineen's thesis is true, and she presents powerful evidence to support her view, the forces of sociocentric groupishness, validation, control, and conformity are all at play. The psychology industry has a powerful motive to manufacture victims—money and more money for psychologists feeding on the industry. Psychologists who prey on their "victims" validate one another in their views. They use various manipulative methods to recruit potential "victims." The people largely go along with these views, sheepishly accepting their roles as victims in need of help (from, of course, the psychologists).

Interestingly, and not surprisingly, in the preface to her second edition of *Manufacturing Victims*, Dineen says that the first edition "drew volatile reactions from within The Psychology Industry." Naturally, they will defend their turf; collectively, they wield considerable power, which they will muster up to "advance" their (sociocentric) cause.

Focusing on one important manifestation of this problem, Margaret Hagen (1997) targets how psychologists present themselves as experts for court cases when, in fact, they have no reasonable tools for their so-called expertise. In her book, *Whores of the Court*, Hagen says:

> Defining healthy behavior by how most people behave is problematic. . . . It would treat racist and chauvinistic practices as healthy wherever they were socially dominant.

> It is assumed that children who experience terrible trauma like witnessing murder or experiencing sex abuse, often suffer, like some Vietnam vets, from post traumatic stress syndrome. It is also said that one of the most common features of this stress disorder is the loss of the memory of the precipitating traumatic event—what psychiatrists call "repression" of the traumatic memories—because the mind seeks unconsciously to protect the person from having to re-experience the trauma in memory. Lastly, it is assumed that repressed memories can be recovered in the proper conditions, usually in the context of therapy, but perhaps through an accidental triggering … These psychological assumptions and countless others like them—lacking any scientific basis but embraced unquestionably by their adherents—over the last twenty-five years have crept insidiously into our legal system, into legislative bodies and courtrooms all over the country … Psychology's takeover of our legal system represents not an advance into new

but clearly charted areas of science, but a terrifying retreat into mysticism and romanticism, a massive suspension of disbelief propelled by powerful propaganda … The demand is great, the supply is huge, and the science behind it all is nonexistent."

In cases such as those with which Hagen is concerned, psychologists have a vested interest in presenting their views as scientific; collectively, they validate these erroneous views which serve their selfish and groupish interests; they manipulate judges, juries, prosecutors, and the public into seeing them as experts on matters where they can't be experts. The people are then effectively recruited to the psychologists' views.

Awareness of questionable practices in the mental health professions should make us cautious in accepting, without question, the present dominant views in these fields. We should understand that the views of mental health professionals are transitory, and will change as political and social attitudes change. Until mental health professionals are taught to see through the social ideologies that influence their practices, they will continue to make decisions based on pseudoscientific (and sociocentric) conformity.

Test the Idea

See if you can think of additional examples within the social disciplines (psychology, sociology, social work, psychiatry, counseling, and so on) that illuminate how these disciplines sometimes encourage, or engage in, sociocentric thought. What are some important implications of these "professionals'" sociocentric beliefs?

Social ideology is often confused with objective fact. This is reflected in the failure of the mental-health field to ensure that its fundamental evaluative concepts (such as "healthy" and "pathological") are established by truly independent research, and not from the influence of social beliefs. For example, behavior falling outside the "normal distribution" is often viewed by the mental health professions as "pathological."

Consider the very definition of "abnormal" as defined by J. P. Chaplin in the *Dictionary of Psychology* (1985). Note that this definition is debatable among clinical practitioners:

… diverging widely from the normal; descriptive of what is considered normative, healthy or psychological from an adjustmental point of view. … Some authorities have suggested that abnormality be defined in statistical terms—that individuals who fall outside certain limits along the normal probability curve be considered abnormal. … Others have suggested that normalcy and abnormalcy be defined in terms of cultural standards, thus

allowing considerable latitude for cultural relativity. ... In applying such a
definition, considerable latitude must be allowed for clinical judgment. (pp. 3–4)

Clearly, defining healthy behavior by how most people behave is problematic. Such a position would make mental health vary, not only from culture to culture but from social group to social group as well. It would treat racist and chauvinistic practices as healthy wherever they were socially dominant. There appears no good reason to think either that all "normal" behavior is "healthy," or that all "abnormal" behavior is "unhealthy."

The problems we find in the mental health professions that are caused by sociocentric thought do not make these professions unique. Again, sociocentricity can cause problems in any field of study. Some of these problems have greater significance and are more far-reaching than others. Critical thinkers look for these tendencies in their own work with others and in their professions more generally. Critical thinkers work to move their professions away from sociocentric thought, even if it means being ostracized by others in the profession.

Some critical questions that can help you determine the extent to which sociocentric thought is actively fostered or discouraged within a discipline or profession:

- To what extent is sociocentric thought implicit in this subject or tradition? What concrete examples illuminate sociocentric thinking within the field?
- To what extent are professionals within this field sensitive to social ideologies, and to the role these ideologies play within the field?
- To what extent does this discipline foster the critique of norms in culture and society?
- How does the field treat critics of social norms?
- How tolerant is the profession of socially diverse, but not ethically harmful, practices?
- What degree of freedom of speech or belief is tolerated in the field?

Test the Idea

Answer the questions above for your own professional field or academic subject.

CHAPTER THREE
SOCIOCENTRIC AND OTHER IRRATIONAL
USES OF LANGUAGE

Groups often use language in sociocentric ways. In doing so, they rationalize unjust acts and irrational thought by misusing language and conceptualizing the world in largely groupish terms. Consider: sociocentrism can be exemplified by the very names groups choose for themselves, and the ways in which they differentiate themselves from groups they consider inferior. More than 100 years ago, Sumner (1906; 1940) catalogued numerous examples of this phenomenon among many peoples:

> *When Caribs were asked whence they came, they answered, "We alone are people." The meaning of the name* Kiowa *is "real or principal people." The Lapps call themselves "men." Or "human beings." The Greenland Eskimo think that Europeans have been sent to Greenland to learn virtue and good manners from the Greenlanders. (p. 14)*

In the everyday life of human thought, we can find many group-serving uses of language that obscure unethical behavior. When Europeans first inhabited the Americas, they forced native peoples into slavery, tortured them, and murdered them, all in the name of "progress and civilization." By thinking of natives as "savages," they could readily justify their inhumane actions. At the same time, by thinking of themselves as "civilized," they

Depicting the Spaniard's treatment of native people upon the "discovery" of America; this treatment was justified under the label "progress," and allegedly sanctioned by God.

could deceive themselves into believing they were bringing something valuable to the "savages," namely "civilization." The terms "progress," "savagery," "civilization," and "the true religion" were developed and used collectively as vehicles to gain material wealth and property. Gross exploitation of native peoples resulted.

Sumner notes that social groups often construct language to maintain a special, superior place for themselves:

> The Jews divided all mankind into themselves and the Gentiles. They were "chosen people." The Greeks called outsiders "barbarians." ... The Arabs regarded themselves as the noblest nation and all others as more or less barbarous. ... In 1896, the Chinese minister of education and his counselors edited a manual in which this statement occurs: "How grand and glorious is the Empire of China, the middle Kingdom! ... The grandest men in the world have come from the middle empire." ... In all the literature of all the states equivalent statements occur. ... In Russian books and newspapers the civilizing mission of Russia is talked about, just as, in the books and journals of France, Germany, and the United States, the civilizing mission of those countries is assumed and referred to as well understood. Each state now regards itself as the leader of civilization, the best, the freest and the wisest, and all others as their inferior. (p. 14)

In her book *The Second Sex*, Simone de Beauvoir (1949; 1974) illuminates the same problem. She offers a number of powerful examples, focusing on how people use terms to stereotype and, hence, to dismiss groups considered inferior:

> Thus it is that no group ever sets itself up as the One without at once setting up the Other over against itself. If three travelers chance to occupy the same compartment, that is enough to make vaguely hostile "others" out of all the rest of the passengers on the train. In small-town eyes all persons not belonging to the village are "strangers" and suspect; to the native of a country all who inhabit other countries are "foreigners"; Jews are "different" for the anti-Semite, Negroes are "inferior" for American racists, aborigines are "natives" for colonists, proletarians are the "lower class" for the privileged. (p. xix)

> Each state now regards itself as the leader of civilization, the best, the freest and the wisest, and all others as their inferior.
>
> — *Sumner*

A popular book written in the 1970s, *Psychobabble: Fast Talk and Quick Cure in the Era of Feeling* (Rosen, 1977), targeted the problem of people in the counterculture (at that time) embracing uses of language which, though appearing to liberate the mind, had in fact the opposite effect. In portraying "psychobabblers," Richard Dean Rosen says:

> Their jargon seems ... to free-float in an all purpose linguistic atmosphere, a set of repetitive verbal formalities that kills off the

*very spontaneity, candor, and understanding it pretends to promote. It's
an idiom that reduces psychological insight to a collection of standardized
observations, that provides a frozen lexicon to deal with an infinite variety
of problems. Uptight, for instance, is a word used to describe an individual
experiencing anything from mild uneasiness to a clinical depression. To
ask someone why he or she refers to another as being* hung-up *elicits a reply
that reveals neither understanding nor curiosity: 'Well, you know, he's just,
well,* hung-up *... Increasingly people describe their moody acquaintances as*
manic-depressives, *and almost anyone you don't like is psychotic or at the
very least* schizzed-out." *(p. 11)*

Those in the counter culture today have their own special uses of language that
parallel Rosen's examples. But as Rosen aptly points out:

*If psychobabble were a question of language alone, the worst one could say
about it is that it is just another example of the corrosion of the English
language. But the prevalence of psychobabble signifies more than a mere
"loss for words." One never loses just words, of course, and so psychobabble
represents a loss of understanding and the freedoms that accompany
understanding as well. (p. 12)*

Wittgenstein said, "a picture held us captive," meaning that the definition
we give of some set of events or circumstances can not only distort reality, but
hold us hostage within that distorted definition. This definition, and hence this
picture, is infused with meanings from the language that underpins it. Rosen's
"psychobabblers" created and used words that then held them captive—words that
concealed what was really going on. A great many things in the 60s and 70s were
"groovy" and "cool." But, what about the reality underneath the words? Rosen
quotes an Esalen group leader named Shirley, in a conversation reported in the
Village Voice:

*"Leo," said Miriam, "you have to realize the important thing is living in the
present moment, You have to be fully aware in the now, that's the trick."*

*"Beautiful," said Leo, "you've got to stop that Aquarian Age stuff. If this is
the Aquarian Age, we're in trouble, we've been screwed by Nixon, we've been
screwed by Ford, and we're letting Kissinger screw everyone he wants."*

*"I don't understand politics," said Shirley. "I don't know anything about
politics, so I don't feel as if I'd been screwed. It's not part of my reality, so it's not
true for me." (p. 14)*

In the United States, throughout the past century, the use of expressions like
"advancing the cause of freedom," "spreading democracy across the world,"
"standing up for the American flag," and "bringing civilization to developing
countries" all exemplify the manipulative use of language when these words
are intended to mask what is really happening—taking over another country,
seizing precious resources to serve U.S. interests, supporting oppressive and

secret military forces, sending in the CIA to foil free elections, declaring war on innocent peoples, or growing the military-industrial complex.

Consider, again, the Vietnam War. Prior to the war, the U.S. government supported the occupation of Vietnam by the French and, in fact, was financing 80 percent of the French war effort against the Vietnamese. To the public (Zinn, 1980; 2006), U.S. officials said we were helping to stop the spread of communism in Asia. A secret memo of the National Security Council from June of 1952 shows that the main concern of U.S. officials was advancing the United States' financial interests in Asia (specifically so we could get our hands on petroleum, rubber, tin, and other commodities). In 1963, President Kennedy's undersecretary of State, in speaking before the Economic Club of Detroit, said:

What is the attraction that Southeast Asia has exerted for centuries on the great powers flanking it on all sides? Why is it desirable, and why is it important? First, it provides a lush climate, fertile soil, rich natural resources … The countries of Southeast Asia produce rich exportable surpluses such as rice, rubber, teak, corn, tin, spices, oil, and many others. (Zinn, 1980; 2006, p. 475)

But President Kennedy used very different language in explaining to the American people why we needed war in Vietnam. President Kennedy "talked of Communism and freedom." In a news conference February 14, 1962, he said "the U.S. for more than a decade has been assisting the government, the people of Vietnam, to maintain their independence" (Zinn, 1980; 2006, p. 475). This, of course, could not have been true when the U.S. had been largely funding the French war against the Vietnamese people.

To create our needed war in Vietnam, the U.S. government fabricated an unprovoked attack against the U.S. off the Vietnamese coast, then lied to the American people. To accomplish this, according to Zinn (1980; 2006), President Johnson (in 1964):

… used a murky set of events in the Gulf of Tonkin, off the coast of North Vietnam, to launch a full-scale war on Vietnam. Johnson and Secretary of Defense Robert McNamara told the American public there was an attack by North Vietnamese torpedo boats on American destroyers. "While on routine patrol in international waters," McNamara said, "the U.S. destroyer Maddox underwent an unprovoked attack." It later turned out that the Gulf of

Bodies of some of the hundreds of Vietnamese villagers killed by US soldiers during the My Lai Massacre in the Vietnam War.

Tonkin episode was a fake, that the highest American officials had lied to the public—just as they had in the invasion of Cuba under Kennedy. (pp. 475–476)

According to available data, a little more than 58,000 U.S. soldiers died in the Vietnam War. No one knows how many Vietnamese died, but estimates are as high as 3,000,000 or more, most of them civilians. According to Bertrand Russell in *War Crimes in Vietnam* (1967, p. 50), in November 23, 1962, the *New York Herald Tribune* stated:

The United States is deeply involved in the biggest secret war in its history. Never have so many U.S. military men been involved in a combat area without any formal program to inform the public about what is happening. It is a war fought without official public reports or with reports on the number of troops involved or the amount of money and equipment poured in.

For further support of the fact that the U.S. government has, throughout its history, often manipulated the American people through misuse of language, consider U.S. support of the brutal Pinochet administration in Chile, the U.S.-supported overthrow of the Nicaraguan government in 1979 (facilitated by the CIA), and the U.S. war in Iraq, among many other examples.[36]

Test the Idea

Identify one story from the news each day (or week) that exemplifies misuse of language by a politician for the purpose of hiding or obscuring the truth. What precisely is this politician hiding, and why is he or she hiding it? What is gained by this purpose through fabrication?

Critical thinkers are keenly aware of the many ways in which the human mind routinely distorts, and is taken in by, ideas. They are on the lookout for sociocentric uses of language; they strip off the words being used and look at the reality underneath them. They try to avoid being manipulated by others' use of language; they try never to manipulate others through their words.

THE MIND NATURALLY GENERATES CONCEPTS AND PERSPECTIVES THAT SERVE ITS INTERESTS

To deeply understand the role sociocentrism plays in our conceptualizations, we must first understand the role of concepts in human thought. This isn't an easy task, but we can begin with this: humans primarily live in their ideas, in their

---

36 To learn more about the secret work of the U.S. government, see the following books by Phillip Agee: *Inside the Company: CIA Diary; Dirty Work: The CIA in Western Europe; Dirty Work 2: The CIA in Africa;* and *On the Run.* Also see the political writings of Noam Chomsky and back copies of *Covert Action Quarterly* (if you can find them), as well as "allegations of state terrorism" in Wikipedia: http://en.wikipedia.org/wiki/Allegations_of_state_terrorism_committed_by_the_United_States.

conceptualizations of things. We naturally place things in categories to understand them; we have no choice. This process of categorization is intrinsic to the human mind. We categorize the material things we use or refer to on a daily basis—things like chairs, tables, ink pens, and windows. This natural process of classifying things in our world is essential to our ability to communicate with one another. Through codification of language, (and hence ideas), humans learned increasingly, over evolutionary time, to read as well as understand words and what they are referring to. We can give and receive directions, we can order food at a restaurant, and so on.

We have the intrinsic "need" to be validated by others. Without this validation, we tend to believe that something is inherently wrong with us.

But things become more complex when we conceptualize more abstract—rather than, let us say, concrete—realities. To discuss the concept of a chair, for instance, is very different from discussing the concepts of democracy, love, sexuality, freedom, or justice.

Further, as mentioned, humans tend to *create* ideas to fit their agendas. We often distort ideas in accordance with what serves our interests, what gets us what we want, what keeps us from having to change, and what leads to getting more for ourselves or the groups with which we identify. In short, we often conceptualize things to advance our egocentric or sociocentric interests.

In fact, this distorted way of conceptualizing reality seems the natural state of the human mind. We often define love, for instance, in egocentric ways, focusing on what we will get from other persons who "love" us—on whether and to what extent they will make us feel good, do things for us, give us things, stroke our ego, etc. In short, we humans frequently think more about *what others will do for us* in a "loving" relationship than what we can, or will, do for them. This concept of love, of course, is largely unconscious in the mind. Otherwise we would notice it, and in some way have to face it. This way of thinking about love *keeps people trapped in a definition of love* that they replay whenever things are not working in their "love" relationship. It defines how they interpret their partner's behavior. For example, when this is the way you think of love—when this is your *concept* of love—then whenever your partner doesn't agree with you, you might decide the relationship isn't working. When your partner doesn't make you feel good or give you what you want, you feel the relationship is failing. These are natural implications of a distorted or false conception of "love." This conception of love, alas, is too common.[37]

This represents only one example of the potentially limitless number of concepts—and, accordingly, the multitude of belief systems—the human mind creates that cause problems for ourselves and others. Because we are born with powerful egocentric and sociocentric predispositions, the ideas, concepts, and theories generated by our minds are often driven by these innate tendencies. For example, humans tend to gravitate toward that which is easy and undemanding,

---

37 For a substantive conceptual analysis of love, see Eric Fromm's *The Art of Loving*.

and to avoid that which is difficult and demanding. We want life to be easy and free from complications and complexities. In other words, this is how we tend to *conceptualize* life. Consequently, we often seek that which is effortless and pain-free. We avoid that which is confusing. Likewise, as has already been dealt with in some detail, we tend to conceptualize ourselves as needing validation from others. Without this validation, people often see themselves as inferior in some way. Their self-esteem suffers. Concepts such as these, and many others created by our minds, keep us trapped in neurotic ways of thinking.

Critical thinkers take command of their ideas. They study their minds to understand how they form their ideas. They avoid blindly conforming to group ideas. They work to see through ideas that others try to thrust upon them. They seek to weed out the dysfunctional ideas they have uncritically accepted throughout their lives.

Test the Idea

Think of a concept you use in your thinking to get something you want for yourself. Use my example of "love" as a model for your thinking.

Look for an idea that you distort in order to get something you couldn't otherwise justify in your own mind. Another example might be "reasonable use of power." If you think of this as justifying asking people to do things (or making them do things) that are contrary to their interests, this would not be a "reasonable use of power." This form of rationalization is commonly seen in cultures where some people have inordinate power over others and, when group-sanctioned, exemplifies sociocentric control.

To further understand how concepts are used and created in human thought, think of the mind as creating lenses through which we see the world. These lenses develop over a lifetime in each of us. They entail, in essence, all the ideas, beliefs, and assumptions we have created in our minds that cause us to experience the world in certain ways. If we could examine these lenses, we would find in them a mixture of ideas that are sound and unsound, logical and illogical, just and unjust. *But all appear to the mind as perfectly reasonable.* It is through these conceptual lenses that we give meaning to our world, that we define things, that we determine whether to accept or reject new ideas, practices, values, viewpoints, and so on. The way one sees parenting might result from a combination of the way one's parents parented, the way one's spouse parents, the way some particular "authorities" on parenting suggest that one should parent, the ways most encouraged in the culture, and so forth. Each of these represents a set of "lenses" through which we see parenting. It should be quite clear that none of them ensures, in and of themselves, high-quality parenting.

Many of these lenses come from the groups in which we are or have been members. A large number of them are *sociocentric* in orientation. They are

Humans Often Distort Reality Through Irrational Lenses

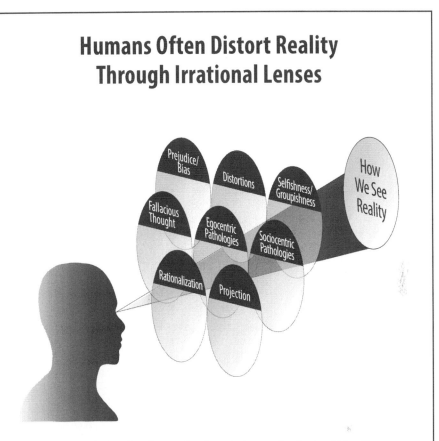

When engaging in irrational pursuits, the mind must deceive itself; it relies on pathologies of thought to do it. The pathologies of thought can be pictured as a set of filters or lenses that:

- cause or "enable" us to see the world according to our perceived interests, without regard to others,
- distort reality so we can get what we want,
- lead us to ignore relevant information to paint a favored picture of the world, based on our vested interests.

These pathologies allow us to deceive ourselves into believing what we want to believe (in order to get what we want or maintain our viewpoint). Pathologies of thought, hence, serve their master—self-deception. They are manifest in both egocentric and sociocentric thought.

> There may be
> layer upon layer of
> social ideologies in
> any given human
> mind that affect
> one's perspectives,
> layer upon layer
> of lenses through
> which one looks
> at the world.

unconscious internalizations of false beliefs and values, resulting from group membership, that unconsciously prejudice how we think. Layer upon layer of social ideologies usually affect one's perspectives in different settings, representing layer upon layer of lenses through which one looks at the world. Many of these lenses or filters have been handed down through human societies for hundreds of years or more. Until we make them explicit in the mind, we can't examine them. We can't see them as they are. Though we largely experience the world through them, we don't have command of them. See on p. 103 a diagram that attempts to visually capture what we might term, "the toxic lenses of the human mind." In *Critical Reasoning in Contemporary Culture* (1992), Richard Talaska illuminates this problem. He says:

> *The foundational values of a culture or society are not determined by reasoning but are merely handed down from some time in the distant past and assumed to be the correct ones. The origins of such values, and the values themselves, remain unquestioned. The nomoi (Greek term for cultural norms) operate at the most basic, nonreflective, emotional level … [They] are not themselves scrutinized for their validity but all else is scrutinized through them. So basic are the nomoi that it is rare, even in a society of many highly educated individuals, for such opinions to be questioned. … Such ruling opinions … are so basic that they are, as it were, no longer seen themselves, but that through which everything else is seen. (pp. 251–252)*

Again, consider mainstream views on sexuality in many cultures today. Such views tend to be highly Puritanical. People tend to apply any number of arbitrary rules to sexuality—rules originally connected with religious beliefs, but which have become part of mainstream culture. For instance, girls who enjoy sex with different men are often referred to as "whores" in a Puritanical society; people who like to be nude outdoors are considered perverted, since such behavior is said to cause sexual arousal in those who see them nude (which is, by implication, considered "bad"); certain sexual acts are considered nasty and dirty, such as anal sex; certain sexual orientations or forms of self-identification are considered dysfunctional, such as homosexuality, bisexuality, transexuality, and so on.

Puritanical roots are so deeply embedded in cultural rules and taboos that even the most liberal-minded, highly-educated, and otherwise insightful people often think puritanically when it comes to sex (though they themselves are not aware of this). Accordingly, they are not sexually free persons. They are born into cultures that impose parochial sexual ideologies on them; they uncritically accept these ideologies with little or no realization that they have done so.

If people want to think reasonably about sexuality, they must first strip away their old ideas on sexuality and begin again with bedrock. This is difficult, if not impossible, to do; people don't easily give up ingrained beliefs and take on new ones. Instead, they have to actively and deliberately discard old ideas, a process to which the mind is intrinsically averse. We would "rather" see new ideas through the lenses of our already-established ones, even if these old ideas keep us imprisoned in our own minds and lead us away from the emancipation of the species.

Puritanical roots are so deeply embedded in cultural rules and taboos that even the most liberal-minded, highly-educated, and otherwise insightful people often think puritanically when it comes to sex.

If I have been raised in a Puritanical culture and have uncritically absorbed puritanical beliefs, and want now to think openmindedly about sexuality, this may be very difficult, since the Puritanical lenses may always be there to some degree, deeply rooted in my thinking and distorting the way I see things. For instance, Americans tend to view open marriage puritanically. People are often appalled at the very idea of it, not because there is anything inherently unethical in a reasonable conception of it (because there isn't), but because they have been raised in a culture that defines marriage in terms of monogamy. They have uncritically accepted a narrow definition of marriage. As far as they are concerned, it simply isn't something you question.[38] If pressed, most people would have to admit they have never thought deeply about it. They just "know" it is wrong. If called upon to fairmindedly consider the pros and cons of open marriage, they probably couldn't do it. They most likely could view it only through distorted lenses, received conventions, and preconceived notions. Accordingly, in terms of marriage and sexuality, they are not free-thinking persons. Instead, they are trapped in sexual rules, conventions, and taboos.

---

38 Though a large percentage of people engage in sex outside of marriage, they tend to do so surreptitiously. This isn't compatible with a concept of open marriage in which the parties agree to explore, in agreed-upon terms, sexual relations that go beyond marital sex. An excellent book that deals with the issue of human sexuality from a biological standpoint is *The Myth of Monogamy* by David Barash and Judith Lipton (2002). In their culminating chapters, the authors briefly discuss the tension between the human desire for, at one and the same time, monogamy and sexual exploration beyond marriage (due to biological roots). How marital partners work through this tension is a private matter. But we know, for instance, that prior to the most current times, polygamy was not uncommon. For our purposes here, the main point is that, again, a reasonable conception of open marriage would be, in-and-of-itself, ethical. If marital partners agree on the terms of such a marriage, and live up to that agreement, then they are acting in good faith. Of course, since human sexuality is complex, finding a workable plan may not be easy.

Test the Idea

To what extent is your view of sexuality taken from the groups in which you have been a member? List all the groups that you realize have influenced your view of sexuality. How has your view been shaped by these different groups? If a parent heavily influenced your view of sexuality, what groups might have influenced her or him? How do you think of marriage in terms of sexuality? How might a healthy open marriage work, or could it work? To what extent has your culture's view of sexuality changed over time? Is it more healthy than it was 100 years ago, less healthy, or a mix? How are you defining "healthy sexuality," and where are you getting your conception of it?

To transcend Puritanical views of sexuality, it should be clear that we cannot trust our culture for guidance, for it will likely advance a narrow, parochial view of sexuality. Accordingly, we can't trust our friends for guidance, as they have likely been indoctrinated into the same puritanical belief systems as have we. And it won't do to blindly trust the professions (like social work, psychology, psychiatry, medicine, and the like) for guidance, for they are as likely to be entrenched in tacit social ideologies as those outside the professions. Instead, we should take a historical view of sexuality. We should look at it in the broadest possible light. It would be best to see it as a healthy part of our biological makeup. We should be open to healthy sexual possibilities.

In sum, we tend to see things through our society's implicit, unconscious, given view, which is quite often warped. (The fact that people have difficulty seeing this, and exemplifying it themselves, rather supports the point.) We naturally see our group's views as the "correct" ones, though we haven't examined them. And these views function as distorting lenses through which much of our world is interpreted and understood.

Critical thinkers are not afraid of ideas. They don't feel the need to go along with the ideas of their culture or group, even if those ideas are comfortable. They can enter and think within any idea, however unusual or "socially unacceptable." They are moved to change their ideas when presented with reasons superior to those they previously held.

PEOPLE OFTEN HAVE TROUBLE SEEING THROUGH IDEOLOGICAL USES OF WORDS

Most people are unaware of the fact that their concepts guide their interpretations of reality; hence, they tend to have little command of the words they use, and they tend to be unaware of how these words influence their thinking. Consequently, they often have trouble differentiating between ideological and nonideological uses of words, and thus are unable to use words like these in a nonloaded way: capitalism, socialism, communism, democracy, oligarchy, plutocracy, patriotism, freedom, liberty, terrorism, nationalism. When these words are used ideologically, their root meanings are often lost or distorted. The words are used to put a positive or negative gloss on events, obscuring what is really going on. Hence, in countries where the reigning ideology extols capitalism, diverging economic systems like socialism and communism are demonized; democracy is equated with capitalism, and plutocratic realities are ignored or hidden. In countries where the reigning ideology is communism, the ideology of capitalism is demonized. Democracy is equated with capitalism, and oligarchic realities are ignored or hidden. Those called "terrorists" or "insurgents" by one group are called "patriots" and "freedom-fighters" by another.

> Most people are unaware of the fact that their concepts guide their interpretations of reality; hence, they tend to have little command of the words they use, and they tend to be unaware of how those words influence their thinking.

If we examine these words and use them in keeping with the core meanings they have in the English language, we may more easily recognize contradictions and inconsistencies in their common use. We may more easily notice when any group misuses them to advance its agenda. Let us review the core meanings of these terms as defined by *Webster's New World Dictionary*:

- *capitalism:* an economic system in which all or most of the means of production and distribution, such as land, factories, railroads, etc., are privately owned and operated for profit, originally under fully competitive conditions; it has generally been characterized by a tendency toward concentration of wealth
- *socialism:* any of the various theories or systems in which society or the community, rather than private individuals, own and operate the means of production and distribution, with all members sharing in the work and products
- *communism:* any economic theory or system based on the ownership of all property by the community as a whole
- *democracy:* government in which the people hold the ruling power, either directly or through elected representatives; rule by the ruled
- *oligarchy:* a form of government in which the ruling power belongs to a few persons
- *plutocracy:* (1) government by the wealthy, (2) a group of wealthy people who control or influence a government
- *patriotism:* love, and loyal or zealous support, of one's own country
- *terrorism:* use of force or threats to demoralize, intimidate, and subjugate—especially such use as a political weapon or policy

To this day, countries in which the reigning ideology is capitalism tend to use the words *socialism* and *communism* as if they meant "a system that discourages individual incentive and denies freedom to the majority of people." Countries in which the reigning ideology is socialism or communism, in their turn, tend to use the word *capitalism* to imply exploitation of the majority by the wealthy few. Both see the use of force by the other as *aggressive* in intent. Both tend to ignore their own inconsistencies and hypocrisy. Neither see the sociocentric belief structure— "our group is better than your group"—guiding their distortions of these terms.

We begin to gain significant command of our minds when we begin seeing our egocentric and sociocentric tendencies at work in the creation of our concepts—when we begin to see these forces guiding the way we see things, and the way we behave, in everyday life situations.

Test the Idea

Be on the lookout for groups using words in ways that serve their interests, but which violate or negate educated uses of those words. A good place to look is in news articles. Identify the words being used and the reasons such words are used. What might the group gain through this use of language? What do their words really mean (as compared with what they want the reader to think they mean)?

PEOPLE FREQUENTLY USE INAPPROPRIATE ANALOGIES TO SERVE SOCIOCENTRIC INTERESTS

Analogies can be used to make sense of things. "This thing I am trying to explain to you (which you don't understand) is like this other thing that you should find intuitive." For instance: critical thinking is like an onion. There are many layers to the onion. As you work your way through one layer, and you begin to think you understand critical thinking, you are faced with another layer, and then eventually another, and so on until you see that there is great depth to a substantive conception of critical thinking. The thing I am trying to explain is critical thinking. The thing I am relating it to is an onion with many layers (which I hope you find intuitive). Perhaps this analogy helps you see that there are multiple complexities in critical thinking that must be, over the long run, understood and internalized.

Analogies can be very useful in understanding ideas and issues. However, analogies can also be used to manipulate people—to encourage them to think in ways contrary to their interests, and in ways that violate proper uses of words. Groups often use analogies inappropriately to get what they want or hide something. Such metaphors and similes are so commonly used, and can so obscure what is really happening, that they frequently go unnoticed.

Looking at a given news source on a given day, we can find many examples of the misuse of analogies to serve sociocentric purposes. On March 16, 2012, I identified the following examples in just one article from the *New York Times*: "G.I. 'Snapped' Under Strain, Official Says" (p. 1). Note the analogy terms italicized.

This article focuses on the American staff sergeant suspected of killing 16 Afghan villagers. The sergeant was moved to a *detention* site in Kuwait. The article states that this move caused an *uproar* in Kuwait. A senior American official said "when they learned about it, the Kuwaitis *blew a gasket*" ... It was said of the sergeant accused that "he felt it was his duty to *stand up* for the ... [U.S.]." His attorney said the man had "been *decorated* many many times ..." and that he did *"blue collar"* work.

Consider a brief analysis of the analogies found in this article. First, using the term "uproar" in reference to the Kuwaitis' reaction might imply that the Kuwaitis had no right to be upset by the sergeant being imprisoned in their country. The words used by the senior American official, that the Kuwaitis' "blew a gasket," seems clearly to imply that the Kuwaitis overreacted and behaved inappropriately, and indeed irrationally, in the situation. The sergeant was said to believe it was his duty to "stand up for" the U.S. This implies that people who go to war when asked to do so by their government are "standing up for" their country. It might imply the opposite as well, that those who are unwilling to go to war are unwilling to "stand up for" their country (and, therefore, their behavior should be considered ethically reprehensible). It was said that the sergeant had been "decorated many many times." The use of the term "decorated" implies that the sergeant had been given many medals (which are called decorations by the military), and therefore that he had done many good things for "our country" which should be considered in dealing with the fact that he murdered 16 innocent people. All of these terms—*uproar, blew a gasket, stand up for* [their country], *decorated*—come out of sociocentric ideologies and are used to manipulate the reader into believing that the "American way" is best, that the military should be glorified, and that those willing to go to war for their country should be applauded—all of which obscures the heinous truth that 16 innocent people were killed by this sergeant, whom our government has exalted.

CHAPTER FOUR
SOCIOCENTRIC COUNTERFEITS OF
ETHICAL REASONING[39]

We have touched on ethics in numerous places thus far. But let us now deal with the concept more directly. The proper role of ethical reasoning is to highlight acts of two kinds: those that enhance the well-being of others—acts that warrant our praise—and those that harm or diminish the well-being of others, and thus warrant our criticism. The ultimate basis for ethics is clear: Human behavior has consequences for the welfare of others. We are capable of acting toward others in such a way as to increase or decrease the quality of their lives. We are capable of helping or harming. What is more, we are theoretically capable of recognizing when we are doing one or the other. This is so because we have the capacity to put ourselves imaginatively in the place of others, and to recognize how we would be affected if someone acted toward us as we do toward others.

> Fairminded thinkers routinely distinguish ethics from other domains of thinking with which it is often confused— domains such as social conventions, religion, theology, politics, and the law.

It is essential to understand the importance of ethical reasoning in human life and the importance of ethics in countering the problem of sociocentric thought. Fairminded thinkers routinely distinguish ethics from other domains of thinking with which it is often confused—domains such as social conventions, religion, theology, politics, and the law. It is not uncommon, for example, for variant, conflicting social values and taboos to be treated as if they were universal ethical principles.

Thus, religious ideologies, social "rules," and laws, which are often sociocentric in nature, are frequently mistaken to be ethical in nature. If we accepted this amalgamation of domains, by implication, every practice within any religious system, every social rule, and every law would be considered ethically justified.

If religion were to define ethics, we could not judge any religious practices (e.g., torturing unbelievers or burning them alive) to be unethical. In the same way, if ethical and conventional thinking were one and the same, every social practice within any culture would necessarily be ethically obligatory—including social conventions in Nazi Germany. We could not, then, condemn any social traditions,

---

39 For a deeper understanding of ethics, see Richard Paul and Linda Elder (2006), *The Thinker's Guide to Ethical Reasoning*. Dillon Beach: Foundation for Critical Thinking Press.

norms, and taboos from an ethical standpoint—however ethically bankrupt they were. What's more, if the law were to define ethics, then, by implication, politicians and lawyers would be considered experts in ethics. Every law they finagled to get on the books would take on the status of an ethical truth.

We must remain free to critique commonly accepted social conventions, religious practices, political ideas, and laws (using ethical concepts not defined by them). No one lacking this ability can become proficient in ethical reasoning. Let us consider each of these domains from this perspective.

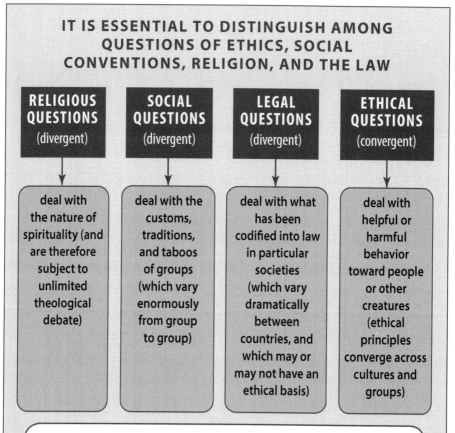

IT IS ESSENTIAL TO DISTINGUISH AMONG QUESTIONS OF ETHICS, SOCIAL CONVENTIONS, RELIGION, AND THE LAW

RELIGIOUS QUESTIONS (divergent)	SOCIAL QUESTIONS (divergent)	LEGAL QUESTIONS (divergent)	ETHICAL QUESTIONS (convergent)
deal with the nature of spirituality (and are therefore subject to unlimited theological debate)	deal with the customs, traditions, and taboos of groups (which vary enormously from group to group)	deal with what has been codified into law in particular societies (which vary dramatically between countries, and which may or may not have an ethical basis)	deal with helpful or harmful behavior toward people or other creatures (ethical principles converge across cultures and groups)

Any given religious, social, or legal edict or practice may, or may not, be ethical in orientation. If we are ever to reach a point in human development where skilled ethical reasoning is the norm, each of us must cultivate in ourselves the ability to determine whether any belief system, practice, rule, or law is ethical. To be skilled in ethical reasoning means to develop a conscience not subservient to fluctuating social conventions, theological systems, or unethical laws.

As we face problems in our lives, we must distinguish the ethical from the unethical (or the pseudo-ethical), and we must routinely apply ethical principles to those problems that are genuinely ethical in nature. The more often we do so, the better we become at ethical reasoning.

ETHICS VERSUS RELIGION

Religious variability derives from the fact that theological beliefs are intrinsically subject to debate. There are an unlimited number of alternative ways for people to conceive and account for the nature of the "spiritual." The *Encyclopedia Americana*, for example, lists more than 300 different religious belief systems. These traditional ways of believing, which are adopted by social groups or cultures, typically take on the force of habit and custom. They are then handed down from one generation to another. To the individuals in any given group, their particular beliefs seem to them the only way, or the only reasonable way, to conceive of the "divine." They cannot see that their religious beliefs are just one set among many tendentious religious belief systems.

Theological reasoning answers metaphysical questions such as:

- What is the origin of all things?
- Is there a God?
- Is there more than one God?
- If there is a God, what is his/her nature?
- Are there ordained divine laws expressed by God to guide our life and behavior?
- If so, what are these laws?
- How are they communicated to us?
- What must we do to live in keeping with the will of the divine?

Consider these categorical examples of how religious beliefs become confused with ethical principles:

- Members of majority religious groups often enforce their beliefs on minorities.
- Members of religious groups often act as if their theological views are self-evidently true, scorning those who hold other views.
- Members of religious groups often fail to recognize that "sin" is a theological concept, not an ethical one. ("Sin" is theologically defined.)
- Divergent religions define sin in different ways (but often expect their views to be enforced on all others as if a matter of universal ethics).

Religious beliefs, when dominant in a human group, tend to shape many, if not all, aspects of a person's life—with rules, requirements, taboos, and rituals. Religious groups often exemplify the problems of group validation and group control through the imposition of religious beliefs. Everyone in the group is expected to accept and validate the beliefs. The members are largely controlled (or recruited) through indoctrination. Many religious regulations are neither right nor wrong, ethically speaking, but simply represent social preferences and culturally subjective choices.

It is every person's human right to choose his or her own religious orientation, including that of agnosticism or atheism. There is a provision in the United Nations Declaration of Human Rights concerning this right:

> *Everyone has the right to freedom of thought, conscience, and religion; this right includes freedom to change his religion or belief ... (Article 18)*

Beliefs about divinity and spirituality are notoriously divergent, and should therefore be noncompulsory. There is no definitive way to prove any given set of religious beliefs to the exclusion of all others. For this reason, religious freedom is a human right. One can objectively prove that murder and assault are harmful to persons, but not that nonbelief in God harms anyone.

Beliefs about divinity and spirituality are notoriously divergent, and should therefore be noncompulsory.

That ethical judgment must trump religious belief is shown by the undeniable fact that many persons have been tortured and/or murdered by people motivated by religious zeal or conviction. Indeed, religious persecution is commonplace in human history. Humans need recourse to ethics in defending themselves against religious intolerance and persecution.

Consider this example: if a religious group were to believe that the firstborn male of every family must be sacrificed, and if this group confused religion with ethics, everyone in that group would think themselves ethically obligated to kill their firstborn male. Their religious beliefs would lead them to unethical behavior and lessen their capacity to understand the cruel nature of their acts.

Or consider this: according to the *Press Democrat* (January 1, 2011), "a senior Iranian cleric says women who wear immodest clothing and behave promiscuously are to blame for earthquakes." Hojatoleslam Kazem Sedighi, Tehran's acting Friday prayer leader, said, "Many women who do not dress modestly ... lead young men astray, corrupt their chastity and spread adultery in society, which (consequently) increases earthquakes." Those who accepted this view as based in ethics would require women to dress in accordance with a particular religious code and would blame women who refused to dress in this way, as this cleric has done, for causing earthquakes. This example illustrates how far, indeed, the human imagination may be stretched.

No religious belief, as such, can justify overriding basic human rights.

A society must be deemed unethical if it accepts among its religious practices any form of slavery, torture, sexism, racism, persecution, murder, assault, fraud, deceit, or intimidation. Remember, atrocities have often been committed in the name of God. Even to this day, religious persecution and religiously-motivated atrocities are commonplace. *No religious belief, as such, can justify overriding basic human rights.*

In short, theological beliefs cannot override ethical principles. We must turn to ethical principles to protect ourselves from intolerant and oppressive religious practices.

Test the Idea

On page 113, look at the list of categorical examples of religious beliefs being confused with ethical principles. See if you can give actual examples of beliefs for each category.

ETHICS VERSUS POLITICAL IDEOLOGY

A political ideology advances a given perspective on the present distribution of wealth and power, and devises strategies in keeping with that perspective. This point of view offers either a "justification" of the present structure of power or a "critique." It seeks either to protect and maintain the way things are or to change them. It seeks to change things in small ways or in big ways. It compares the present to the past, and both to a future it projects.

> Virtually all political ideologies speak in the name of "the people." Yet most politicians are committed not to the people, but to powerful vested interest groups who fund their election campaigns.

Conservative ideologies, at least in many twenty-first-century societies, "justify" the status quo or seek a return to a previous, "ideal" time. Liberal ideologies critique the status quo and seek to justify "new" forms of political arrangements designed to rectify present problems. Reactionary ideologies plead for a "radical" return to the past; revolutionary ideologies plead for a "radical" overturning of the fundamental ("corrupt") structures. Conservative ideologies tend to consider the highest values to be private property, family, God, country, individual advancement, and responsibility for self. Liberal ideologies consider the highest values to be liberty, equality, social justice, public interest, and responsibility for the disadvantaged. Of course, conservative and liberal ideologies occur on a continuum, and thus we often see a blending of these viewpoints in those who lean toward the middle of the continuum.

Ideological analyses have highly significant ethical implications. Put into action, they often have profound effects on the well-being of people. What is more, the ideologies officially espoused by politicians are often widely different from the personal ends they pursue. Virtually all political ideologies speak in the name of "the people." Yet most politicians are committed not to the people, but to powerful vested interest groups who fund their election campaigns. The same people often end up ruling, independent of the "official" ideology. Thus, in the post-Soviet power structure, many of those who were formerly powerful in the communist party are now among the most prominent and acquisitive neo-capitalists.

In short, it appears that politicians rarely act for ethical reasons. Struggling against each other for power and control, people in political movements and with differing interests often sacrifice ethical ideals for practical advantage. They often rationalize unethical acts as unavoidable necessities ("forced on them" by their opponents). They frequently use propaganda to further vested-interest agendas (or groupishness). They routinely engage in group validation. They often "control" the people through manipulation. The people usually submit to those in power (while perceiving themselves to be autonomous, independent thinkers).

In conceptualizing a "new ethic" for future societies, Erich Neumann (1969; 1973) says of politicians:

> *The incompetence of the politicians, which has become so cruelly and sanguinely obvious to modern man, is essentially due to their human inadequacy—that is, to a morally undermining of their psychic structure which culminates in their total breakdown when faced with any real decision. To future ages, the fact that the leading politicians of our period were not required to pass a test of any kind to determine their human and moral qualifications will appear exactly as grotesque as it would seem to us today if a diphtheria-carrier were to be placed in charge of the children's ward in a hospital.*

One might question whether such a test could be developed, but Neumann's comments remind us that in human societies today, politicians are usually chosen not for their ethical reasoning abilities, but instead for their charismatic style and in accord with the amount of money they can rake in to support their candidacies. Politicians in most societies today are held only to minimal ethical standards (if any at all). Indeed, given the usually unethical nature of the election process itself, truly ethical, honest persons can rarely gain entrance into today's political arenas, much less survive in them. Since voters tend to confuse ethics with social rules and conventions, and since most are indoctrinated into mainstream views, they usually elect politicians who reflect (their) mainstream views and who will therefore maintain the status quo (within some minimal range). Mainstream voters tend to view social rules as inherently illuminating "the right way to live." They want these rules to be maintained in the society, and hence supported, rather than questioned, by politicians. They are easily swayed by political manipulation through media bias and propaganda.

Critical thinkers, however, are not manipulated by unethical politicians. They look beneath the surface of the words politicians use to their actions. Critical thinkers are keenly aware of the problem of vested interest in politics. Though critical thinkers do not assume that every politician is corrupt, they recognize that systems of power are frequently dysfunctional and, hence, lead to corruption. Those who think critically work toward the cultivation of political systems that serve the people rather than special interest groups.

Test the Idea

Identify examples of politicians speaking and acting as if they are concerned with the welfare of the people, when in fact there is strong evidence to suggest that they are primarily concerned with advancing the agendas of special-interest groups with which they are connected.

ETHICS VERSUS THE LAW

Anyone interested in developing their rational capacities should be able to differentiate ethics from the law. What is illegal may or may not be a matter of ethics. What is ethically obligatory may be illegal. What is unethical may be legal. Hence, there is no essential connection between ethics and the law.

Laws often emerge out of social conventions and taboos. And because we cannot assume that social conventions are ethical, we cannot assume that human laws are ethical. What is more, most laws are ultimately made by politicians, who routinely confuse social values with ethical principles. Again, their primary motivation is (except in special cases) power, vested interest, or expediency. For example, from 1900 through 1930, American politicians, in response to an electorate dominated by fundamentalist religious believers, passed laws which made it illegal for anyone, including doctors, to disseminate information about birth control. The consequence was predictable: hundreds of thousands of poor and working-class women suffered severe injuries or death from the effects of illegal drugs and unsanitary abortions. To "criminalize" violations of social conventions is one of the time-honored ways for politicians to get re-elected.

> Laws often emerge out of social conventions and taboos. And because we cannot assume that social conventions are ethical, we cannot assume that human laws are ethical.

Examples of Laws Being Confused with Ethics:

- Many sexual practices (such as homosexuality) have been unjustly punished with life imprisonment or death (under the laws of one society or another).
- Many societies have enforced unjust laws based on racist views.
- Many societies have enforced laws that discriminated against women.
- Many societies have enforced laws that are oppressive to children.
- Many societies have made torture and/or slavery legal.
- Many societies have enforced laws that arbitrarily punish people for using and selling some drugs, but not others.

Test the Idea

Look at the categories (on page 117) of examples of laws being confused with ethics. For each category, articulate/write out two actual examples in a given society (for example, enslaving Africans in the U.S. was legal until the mid-nineteenth century, but it was never ethical).

When people confuse the law with ethics, the laws in society are seen as inherently ethical. The laws are validated by the group as right and good. People in the society conform to the laws rather than critically analyzing them. Those in power positions often manipulate the people into seeing the laws as ethical, in order somehow to gain from this manipulation. These realities emerge from, and are guided by, sociocentric thought.

Overturning Unethical Laws Is Often Difficult Due to Groupthink

In considering the ethical or unethical nature of laws, let's look at what is termed "child pornography." For many people, this is a very threatening issue. These people experience a strong gut-reaction to the idea of people viewing children in the nude, seeing such viewing as a horrific crime and one that should be severely punished.

And yet, ethically considered, the viewing of such images is not wrong in itself; yet, people frequently serve long prison sentences for such "crimes." Few attorneys or judges advocate against these harsh sentences. Jack Weinstein, a federal judge who has come "to be identified by his efforts to combat what he calls 'the unnecessary cruelty of the law' " (*New York Times*, May 22, 2010), has gone to extraordinary lengths to challenge the strict punishments connected with possession of child pornography. The *New York Times* article states, "Last week, the United States Court of Appeals for the Second Circuit vacated a 20-year child pornography sentence by ruling that the sentencing guidelines for such cases, 'unless applied with great care, can lead to unreasonable sentences.'" Judge Weinstein was quoted as saying he does not believe that those who view the images of children, as opposed to those who produce or sell them, present a threat to children. "We're destroying lives unnecessarily," he said. Douglas Berman, a professor at Moritz College of Law, Ohio State University, who studies sentencing issues, agrees. He says, "What has caused concern in courts across the nation is that we have a lot of relatively law-abiding individuals sitting in the basement downloading the wrong kind of dirty pictures facing not just prison sentences but incredibly long prison sentences." According to the *Times* article, supporters of Judge Weinstein, who is 88 years old and has served on the federal bench for 43 years, "praise his taking unusual actions in pursuit of his notions of justice, like for a time refusing to handle drug cases out of opposition to mandatory minimums."

Some other few professionals question the extraordinarily lengthy sentences being given for the possession of child pornography, as is pointed out in an article in the *New York Times* (November 5, 2011) entitled, Life Sentence for Possession of Child Pornography Spurs Debate Over Severity. This article focuses on the fact that a 26-year-old stockroom worker whose computer contained hundreds of "pornographic" images of children was sentenced to life in prison without the possibility of parole. Some law professors and attorneys interviewed for the article point out that this sentence violates the rights of the accused. The same sentence is given for first-degree murder.

Kids bathing in a small metal tub, 1939. This picture might be considered "pornographic" today, and "exploitative" of children's rights.

Taken from: http://en.wikipedia.org/wiki/File:
KidsBathingInASmallMetalTub.jpg

The judge who handed down this life sentence is reminiscent of the judge in the trial of Oscar Wilde in 1895 (Ellmann, 1987). Wilde was accused, tried, and convicted of sodomy with Lord Alfred Douglas. In speaking to Wilde, and fellow accused, Alfred Taylor, during sentencing, Justice Charles said of the case:

> *"Oscar Wilde and Alfred Taylor, the crime of which you have been convicted is so bad that one has to put a stern restraint upon one's self to prevent one's self from describing, in language which I would rather not use, the sentiments which must rise to the breast of every man of honour who has heard the details of these two terrible trials ... People who can do these things must be dead to all sense of shame, and one cannot hope to produce such effect upon them. It is the worst case I have ever tried ... I shall, under such circumstances, be expected to pass the severest sentence that the law allows. In my judgment it is totally inadequate for such a case as this." (pp. 448-449)*

The Bathers by British painter Henry Scott Tuke (1858-1929).

When it comes to hot-button issues such as viewing nude images of children (or, in the past, witch hunts or homosexuality), people are often swept along by mass hysteria, which emerges from a powerful interrelationship between and among group validation, indoctrination, and group righteousness. An interesting summary of a report in *Time* magazine (December 13, 2010) suggests that "making pornography more accessible could lead to a drop in child sex abuse." The report from the Czech Republic points out that "rates of abuse in that country declined after a ban on sexually explicit material was lifted." This included child pornography.[40]

Because many people assume that viewing photos of nude children and taking illegal drugs lead to criminal behavior (or should be criminal in themselves), legalizing behaviors such as these is an uphill battle. Thus, to stand against the majority on these issues takes a degree of intellectual courage and autonomy uncommon in today's societies.

Test the Idea

Make a list of the laws in your country that you believe are unethical, or for which you think the prison sentences are too harsh. How do these laws emerge from socientric thought? How many are based in hysteria resulting from groupthink? Take a look at this and related books: *Ain't Nobody's Business If You Do: The Absurdity of Consensual Crimes in Our Free Country* by Peter McWilliams. See if it adds to your understanding of this problem.

ETHICS VERSUS SOCIAL CONVENTIONS

It should be clear by now that humans are, in the first instance, socially conditioned. Consequently, we do not begin with the ability to critique social norms and taboos. Unless we learn to critique the social mores and taboos imposed upon us from birth, we will most likely accept those traditions as "right."

Consider the history of the United States. Until the mid-19th century, most Americans considered slavery to be justified and desirable. It was part of this country's social customs. Moreover, throughout history, many groups of people, including people of various nationalities and skin colors, as well as females, children, and individuals with disabilities, have been victims of discrimination as the result of social conventions treated as ethical obligations. Yet all social practices that violate human rights should be rejected—and have been rejected by

---

40 Many will argue that the rights of children are violated when nude pictures are taken of them. This is a debatable question and directly depends on the context in which the images are produced, on whether children are coerced during the process—i.e., on whether the children are *in fact* abused. Some will argue that taking pictures of children in the nude is inherently psychologically abusive, without regard to context. This is *ipso facto* illogical, given that there are any number of contexts in which nudity of children is properly justified, including images of nude children in medical books that are essential to the training of medical practitioners. Thus, creating images of children in the nude is not in itself harmful, and has been freely done at many times and in many cultures in human history. For instance, many parents have taken, and do take, pictures of their children in the nude while the children are clowning around in the bathtub. Many museums proudly display statues of nude children created throughout history. A number of important artists have created images of children in the nude. These images include the works of Italian Renaissance artists—for example, Verrocchio, Botticelli, and Leonardo. Professional photographers who have photographed children in the nude include Jock Sturges, Sally Mann, David Hamilton, Jacques Bourboulon, Garo Aida, and Bill Henson.

ethically sensitive, reasonable persons, no matter what social conventions have supported or dictated those practices.

Social Mores Vary across Cultures

Cultural diversity derives from the fact that there are an unlimited number of ways for social groups to satisfy their needs and fulfill their desires. Over time, these traditional ways of living within a social group or culture take on the force of habit and custom. Social customs are handed down from one generation to another. To individuals in a given group, these social conventions seem to be the *only* way, or the only *reasonable* way, to do things. And, of course, these social customs sometimes have ethical implications. Social habits and customs answer questions such as:

> All social practices that violate human rights should be rejected—and have been rejected by ethically sensitive, reasonable persons, no matter what social conventions have supported or dictated those practices.

- How should marriage take place? Who should be allowed to marry, under what conditions, and with what ritual or ceremony? Once married, what role should the male play? What role should the female play? Are multiple marriage partners possible? Is divorce permissible? Under what conditions?

> Schools traditionally function as apologists for conventional thought; those who teach often inadvertently foster confusion between conventions and ethical principles, because they themselves have internalized the conventions of society.

- Who should care for the children? What should they teach the children as to proper and improper ways to act? When children do not act as they are expected to act, how should they be treated?
- When should children be accepted as adults? When should they be considered old enough to be married? Whom should they be allowed to marry?
- When children develop sensual and sexual desires, how should they be allowed to act, given these desires? With whom, if anyone, should they be allowed to engage in sexual exploration and discovery? What sexual acts are considered acceptable and wholesome? What sexual acts are considered perverted or sinful?
- How should men and women dress? To what degree should their body be exposed in public? How is nudity treated? How should those who violate nudity and dress codes be treated?
- How should food be obtained, and how should it be prepared? Who is responsible for obtaining food? Who for preparing it? How should it be served? How eaten?

- What individuals or groups will hold power in the society? What belief system is used to justify the distribution of goods and services, and the ways in which rituals and practices are carried out?
- If the society develops enemies or is threatened from without, how will it deal with those threats? How will it defend itself? How does the society relate to the concept of war? How does the society engage in war, or does it?
- What sorts of games, sports, or amusements will be practiced in the society? Who is allowed to engage in them?
- What religions are taught or allowable within the society? Who is allowed to participate in the religious rituals, or to interpret divine or spiritual teachings to the group?
- How are grievances settled in the society? Who decides which parties are right and which are wrong? How are violators treated?

When answering the questions above, it is essential for societies to be able to distinguish between questions that entail an ethical dimension and those that illuminate mere culture preferences.

Schools traditionally function as apologists for conventional thought; those who teach often inadvertently foster confusion between conventions and ethical principles, because they themselves have internalized the conventions of society. Education, properly so called, should foster the intellectual skills that enable students to distinguish between cultural mores and ethical precepts, between social commandments and ethical truths. In each case, when social beliefs and taboos conflict with ethical principles, ethical principles should prevail.

Examples of Social Conventions Being Confused With Ethics:

- Many societies have created taboos against showing various parts of the body, and have severely punished those who violated such taboos.
- Many societies have created taboos against giving women the same rights as men.
- Many societies have socially legitimized religious persecution.
- Many societies have socially stigmatized interracial marriages.

These practices seem (wrongly) to be ethically obligatory to those indoctrinated into accepting them.

Critical thinkers recognize that social conventions and rules may or may not be based in ethical concepts and principles. They therefore do not confuse ethics with social ideologies. They may go along with social conventions and rules for any number of reasons, but this doesn't mean they agree with them. Critical thinkers work toward the cultivation of societies in which social conventions and rules having ethical implications are based in ethical concepts and principles. Critical thinkers allow people to choose their own social preferences where ethics are not relevant.

Test the Idea

On page 122, look at the categories of examples of social conventions that are often confused with ethics. For each category, articulate two actual examples from your society.

Taboos Are Prevalent in Human Societies

The term "taboo" is now widely used throughout human cultures to mean that which is prohibited in accordance with social customs. Taboos may or may not be connected with ethics, though the term is more often used in reference to behaviors forbidden by arbitrary social rules.

Social taboos are often connected with strong emotions. People are frequently disgusted when others violate a taboo. Their disgust signals to them that the behavior is unethical. They forget that what is socially repugnant to us may not violate any ethical principle but, instead, may merely reflect deep indoctrination into arbitrary social ideologies. Social doctrines regarding human sexuality are often classic examples of conventions expressed as if they were ethical truths. Social groups frequently establish strong sanctions for unconventional behavior involving the human body. For example, some social groups inflict unjust punishments on women who do no more than appear in public without being completely veiled, an act considered in some cultures to be indecent and sexually provocative. But sexual behaviors should be considered unethical only when they result in unequivocal harm or damage (or when they are intended to cause harm).

> Taboos are so much a part of human societies, so entrenched in our worldviews as humans, so deeply embedded in our collective psyches that most people have little or no notion that they are being driven by taboos at all.

Taboos are so much a part of human societies, so entrenched in our worldviews as humans, and so deeply embedded in our collective psyches that most people have little or no notion that they are being driven by taboos at all; they have little to no understanding of the pervasive role that taboos play in their thought and action. Humans are so accustomed to uncritically adhering to prescribed rules and admonishments, from such a young age, that they fail to notice even the most significant, most absurd, most dangerous, most far-reaching taboos. Taboos are intrinsically received by individuals in a society as if they had been critically analyzed before being accepted, when no such analysis typically occurs.

Because people take them for granted, taboos tend to operate at the unconscious level. The majority of people assume them to be reasonable; thus, rarely are they questioned. Certainly, when brought to their attention, people tend to recognize and even find amusing some of the more trivial taboo violations—like facing away from the door in the elevator when everyone else is facing forward, or skipping rather than walking in the office. But when confronted with more substantial taboos, people tend to become uncomfortable, threatened, or even hostile. This is, of course, natural, given the many ways in which societies indoctrinate people into uncritical acceptance of taboos.

Reasonable persons would agree that unethical behaviors should be avoided in human societies. But as has been pointed out, when people routinely confuse ethics with social rules and conventions, many behaviors will seem unethical that are, in fact, merely socially unacceptable. When people uncritically accept the norms, traditions, and taboos of their culture, and when people are taught that to question social rules is disloyal and unpatriotic, they have difficulty distinguishing practices that should be avoided (because such behaviors violate the rights of others) from practices that should be allowed and even encouraged (because they don't violate anyone's rights, and may even help someone). To identify taboos in a culture, one might ask:

> What are some behaviors, forbidden in this culture, that do not, in and of themselves, cause harm? In other words, what are some behaviors people are not allowed to engage in, but which do not actually cause harm to someone else?

Due to the prohibited nature of taboos, to even speak or write about the most significant ones might get one into trouble, even in many so-called democracies that tout the importance of freedom of speech. It should be noted that even in universities, open discussion of taboos is often taboo. In an article in the *Chronicle of Higher Education* (December 11, 2009), Donald Livingston, a political philosopher at Emory University, is quoted as saying, "The university should be the place where the unthinkable can be thought and the unspeakable said as long as it is backed by civil conduct and argument. It is not that today."

If we go back in time, we can engage in an analysis of taboos less likely to "offend" than an analysis of current-day taboos is likely to do, simply because society no longer views the taboos in the same way. Consider the following taboo having to do with the roots of virginity throughout human societies (Sumner, 1906; 1940):

> The university should be the place where the unthinkable can be thought and the unspeakable said as long as it is backed by civil conduct and argument. It is not that today.
>
> — *Donald Livingston*

> In the development of the father family, fathers restricted daughters in order to make them more valuable as wives. Here comes in the notion of virginity and pre-nuptial chastity. This is really a negative and exclusive notion. It is an appeal to masculine vanity, and is a

singular extension of the monopoly principle. His wife is to be his from the cradle, when he did not know her. Here, then, is a new basis for the sex honor of women and the jealousy of men. Chastity for the unmarried meant—no one; for the married—none but the husband. The mores extended to take in this doctrine, and it has passed into the heart of mores of all civilized peoples, to whom it seems axiomatic or "natural." (p. 359)

In illustrating the arbitrary nature of dress and customs in human societies, and the taboos that become connected with them, Sumner gives these examples, among hundreds of others:

Humans are so accustomed to uncritically adhering to prescribed rules and admonishments, from such a young age, that they fail to notice even the most significant, most absurd, most dangerous taboos.

The dresses of Moslem women, nuns, and Quaker women were invented in order to get rid of any possible question of decency. The attempt fails entirely. A Moslem woman with her veil, a Spanish woman with her mantilla or fan, a Quakeress with her neckerchief, can be as indecent as a barbarian woman with her petticoat of dried grass.

It would be difficult to mention anything in Oriental mores which we regard with such horror as Orientals' feel for low-necked dresses … Orientals use dress to conceal the contour of the form. The waist of a woman is made to disappear by a girdle. To an Oriental a corset, which increases the waist line and the plasticity of the figure, is the extreme of indecency—far worse than nudity.

Perhaps the most instructive case of all is that of the Tuareg men, who keep the mouth always covered. The cloth has a utilitarian purpose—to prevent thirst. … A Tuareg would think that he committed an impropriety if he should remove his veil, unless it was in extreme intimacy or for a medical investigation. … Evidently we have here a case of an ancient fact that men are never seen with the mouth uncovered, which has produced a feeling that a man ought never to be seen with it uncovered.

Ethnographical studies have established the fact that things were first hung on the body as amulets or trophies, that is, for superstition or vanity, and that the body was painted or tattooed for superstition or in play. The notion of ornament followed. … When all wore things attached to the body a man or woman did not look dressed, or "right," without such attachments. He or she looked bare or naked. They were ashamed. This is the shame of nakedness.

In some places the Yakuts attach great importance to the rule that young wives should not let their husband's male relatives see their hair or their feet. In mediaeval Germany a respectable woman thought it a great disgrace if a man saw her naked feet.

The back and navel are sometimes under a special taboo of concealment, especially the navel, which is sacred ... in connection with birth. Peschel quotes private information that a woman in the Philippine Islands put a shirt on a boy in order to cover the navel and nothing more. In her view nothing more needed to be covered. Many peoples regard the navel as of erotic interest.

Taboos can emerge from virtually any custom or practice and proceed in virtually any direction.

It is very improper for a Chinese woman who has compressed feet to show them.

An Arab woman, in Egypt, cares more to cover her face than any other part of her body, and she is more careful to cover the top or back of her head than her face. (pp. 426–434)

In many places throughout his catalogue of customs, mores, taboos, and traditions, Sumner discusses how taboos can emerge from virtually any custom or practice and proceed in virtually any direction. In focusing on concealment and "decency" taboos, he says, "It appears that if any part of the body is put under a concealment taboo for any reason whatever, a consequence is that the opinion grows up that it ought never to be exposed. Then interest may attach to it more than to exposed parts, and erotic suggestion may be connected with it ... the whole notion of decency is held within boundaries of habit" (p. 435).

Sumner also illuminates behaviors considered taboo in many parts of the world today, but which in times past were often norms (with no logical basis):

Every well-to-do man of the Bassari, in Togo, has three wives, because children are suckled for three years. This follows from the fact that "in primitive society women are laborers and the industrial system is often such that there is an economic advantage in having a number of women to one man." In such societies, "women welcome more wives to help do the work and do not quarrel" ... a Spartan who had a land allotment was forced to marry. His younger brothers lived with him and sometimes were also husbands to his wife. Wives were also lent out of friendship or in order to get vigorous offspring. (p. 351)

Today, many of the examples of taboos uncovered by Sumner more than a century ago seem to border on the bizarre. But we need not look far to find similar examples in current customs and practices. Consider, for example, childhood sexuality. For more than half a century, it has been well understood among scholars of sexuality that humans are naturally sexual at all ages, and that it is not only normal but healthy for children to have sexual thoughts and engage in sexual behavior. Yet, in the United States and in many other countries today, sexual exploration among children is often considered perverted or even dangerous. Children at younger and younger ages are being watched by criminal systems as potential "sexual predators." Increasing numbers of states include consensual childhood sexuality in their battery of sex "offenses." These laws emerge out of the fact that sexual activity between and among children and youths is, at present, taboo in our culture. The harm that follows from this taboo, the punishment and shame attending it, and the effects on the future sexuality of these youths can only be imagined.

Test the Idea

If you haven't already answered this question, answer it now: what are some behaviors, forbidden on "ethical" grounds in your culture, which do not cause harm in and of themselves? In other words, what are some behaviors people are not allowed to engage in (taboos), but which do not actually cause harm to another?

Be on the lookout for examples in the news.

Other inhibiting cultural taboos now prevalent (and safe to mention) include public nudity, nude bathing among adults and children, nudity in the home with children present, the use of illegal drugs for recreational purposes, interracial marriage, and marriage between people of widely differing ages.

Though conventional "wisdom" sometimes seems to imply that humans are progressing with time, that we are "naturally" becoming more rational, a full view of the evidence doesn't support this notion. Indeed, close examination of cultural taboos illuminates the fact that in many ways humans have regressed, not progressed, as thinkers. Some of our sex laws, for instance, are increasingly draconian.

In 1948, the book *Sexual Behavior in the Human Male*, written by Alfred Kinsey and his research colleagues, detailed their remarkably revealing scientific study on sexuality. At the time of its publication, this book was more widely known to the public than any other book in the twentieth century (Jones, 1997). It represented a culmination of years of research in which Kinsey set out to understand human sexuality in as many of its modes and manifestations as possible. For nearly two decades, he and his colleagues interviewed more than 18,000 people in attempting to better understand human sexuality in all of its multiplicities. An entomologist by training, Kinsey was more interested in, and impressed by, the differences that exist between and among humans (just as he had been when studying other animals) than by their similarities. He hypothesized that normal human sexual activity was widely divergent, a view his study corroborated. In his view, Puritanical ideologies caused untold suffering, because these belief systems generate and support crude sexual laws and taboos. He thought that if the public could properly perceive human sexual experiences as widely diverse, they would become less judgmental about sexuality, more sexually free, and therefore more healthy. He dedicated most of his professional life to understanding sexuality from an unbiased empirical viewpoint and reporting on what he found. In 1953, *Sexual Behavior in the Human Female* was published, a sequel to the male volume. One of his biographers (Jones, 1997)[41] notes:

> *From the outset of his research, Kinsey correctly divined that Americans were awash in secrets. His research was designed to uncover what people actually thought and did in their private lives. Kinsey was supremely confident that he could shatter the conspiracy of silence that kept intimate matters enshrouded in taboo, and until the last few years of his life he remained optimistic that his discoveries would spell the end of what one reformer called "hush and pretend." (p. xi)*

More than a half century after his two studies were published, some taboo sexual behaviors that Kinsey's studies debunked as actually quite common (such as homosexuality and premarital sex) are by many people no longer considered taboo; other sexual practices are still considered as taboo now as they were then.

Test the Idea

If you haven't already done so, answer this question: what are some sexual behaviors, forbidden in your culture, which do not cause harm in and of themselves? Look for examples in news stories.

In sum, rules, conventions, and taboos of any particular time period and within any particular culture are just as likely to be arbitrary as not. Because people are indoctrinated into the ideologies of the culture before they have much, if any, developed capacity for critical thought, they naturally take these beliefs to be "correct."

Critical thinkers do not assume that taboos are based in ethical concepts and principles. They recognize that some behaviors people are not allowed to engage in are perfectly fine from an ethical perspective. Critical thinkers realize that every society and every group has taboos, and hence are on the lookout for these taboos. Critical thinkers judge for themselves, using intellectual standards, whether a given taboo is based in sound reasoning. They recognize that it may be dangerous to go against taboos. They often determine that defying a given taboo wouldn't be worth it, given the price. Critical thinkers work toward cultivating societies in which taboos are based in ethics, not in arbitrary social conventions and ideologies.

---

41 The Jones biography of Kinsey, though replete with interesting details of Kinsey's life, should be read with caution as it reveals a number of prejudices about sexuality on the part of the biographer. Moreover, the biographer often perceives as "facts" what are merely his inferences.

SOME ACTS ARE UNETHICAL IN AND OF THEMSELVES

For any action to be unethical, it must deny another person or creature some inalienable right. The following classes of acts are unethical in and of themselves. Any person or group that violates them is properly criticized from an ethical standpoint:

Slavery: Owning people, whether individually or in groups.

Genocide: Deliberately and systematically killing with the attempt to eliminate a whole nation or an ethnic, political, or cultural group.

Torture: Inflicting severe pain to force information, get revenge, or serve some other irrational end.

Sexism: Treating people unequally (and harmfully) in virtue of their gender.

Racism: Treating people unequally (and harmfully) in virtue of their race or ethnicity.

Murder: The pre-meditated killing of people for revenge, pleasure, or to gain advantage for oneself.

Assault: Attacking an innocent person with intent to cause grievous bodily harm.

Rape: Forcing an unwilling person to engage in sexual acts.

Fraud: Intentional deception that causes someone to give up property or some right.

Deceit: Representing something as true one knows to be false in order to gain a selfish end that is harmful to another.

Intimidation: Forcing a person to act against his or her interest, or deterring a person from acting in his or her interest, by threats or violence.

Wrongful imprisonment: Putting persons in jail without telling them the charges against them or providing them with a reasonable opportunity to defend themselves; putting persons in jail, or otherwise punishing them, solely for their political or religious views.

CHAPTER FIVE
SOCIOCENTRIC THINKING AND EGOCENTRIC THINKING IN INTERRELATIONSHIP

Thus far our focus has been on the problem of sociocentricity as a barrier to the development of human societies. Some significant manifestations and categories of sociocentric thinking have been exemplified. But to understand how sociocentricity works, it is important to understand its sometimes intimate connection with egocentricity. (Sociocentricity entails inappropriate relationships with other humans; egocentricity entails an inappropriate relationship with oneself.) Let us then begin to reveal, in this chapter, some foundational links between sociocentricity and egocentricity.[42]

> Though humans are intrinsically egocentric and sociocentric, we have the capacity to develop into reasonable, ethical persons.

It is helpful to begin with this understanding—that humans largely see the world from these two overlapping and interactive sets of tendencies:

1. Our native *egocentrism*: "to view everything in the world in relationship to **oneself**, to be self-centered" (*Webster's New World Dictionary*); to view the world in self-validating or selfish terms.

2. Our native *sociocentrism*: to view everything in relationship to **one's group**; to be group-centered; to attach ourselves to others and together create beliefs, rules, and taboos to which those in the group are expected to adhere, and against which the behavior of those outside the group are judged; to view the world in group-validating or groupish terms.

Of course, though humans are intrinsically egocentric and sociocentric, we do often behave reasonably and have the capacity to develop into characteristically ethical persons. While egocentric and sociocentric thought perhaps should be considered "first-order" orientations of the mind, humans can and do develop their rational capacities to greater or lesser degrees. Selfishness and its equivalent in group thought seem to come more naturally to the mind, while reasonability,

---

42 For a deeper understanding of egocentric thought, see *The Thinker's Guide to Taking Charge of the Human Mind* by Linda Elder and Richard Paul, 2015, Dillon Beach: Foundation for Critical Thinking Press, www.criticalthinking.org. See also: *Critical Thinking: Tools for Taking Charge of Your Professional and Personal Life* by Richard Paul and Linda Elder. 2014, Upper Saddle River, New Jersey: Financial Times Prentice Hall, chapter 10.

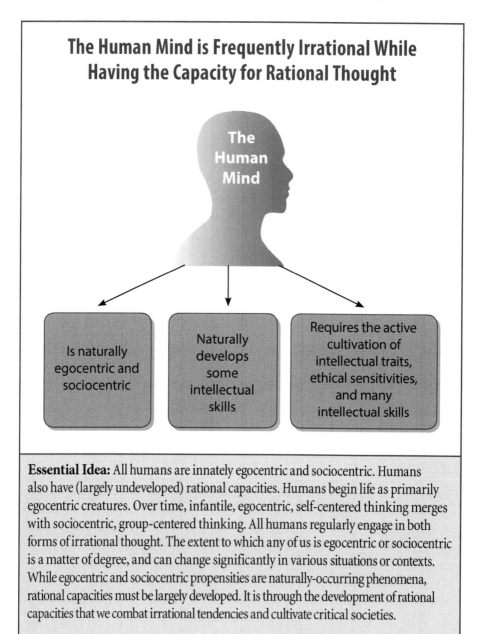

The Human Mind is Frequently Irrational While Having the Capacity for Rational Thought

The Human Mind

Is naturally egocentric and sociocentric

Naturally develops some intellectual skills

Requires the active cultivation of intellectual traits, ethical sensitivities, and many intellectual skills

Essential Idea: All humans are innately egocentric and sociocentric. Humans also have (largely undeveloped) rational capacities. Humans begin life as primarily egocentric creatures. Over time, infantile, egocentric, self-centered thinking merges with sociocentric, group-centered thinking. All humans regularly engage in both forms of irrational thought. The extent to which any of us is egocentric or sociocentric is a matter of degree, and can change significantly in various situations or contexts. While egocentric and sociocentric propensities are naturally-occurring phenomena, rational capacities must be largely developed. It is through the development of rational capacities that we combat irrational tendencies and cultivate critical societies.

ethical sensitivities, and disciplined thought require cultivation.[43, 44]

To diminish the power of selfishness, groupishness, self-deception, and the like requires that we actively develop our raw intellectual and ethical capacities—that we cultivate in ourselves intellectual habits or traits of mind. To come at this from the opposite angle, as people become more rational and reasonable, they become less egocentric and sociocentric.

HUMANS ARE FREQUENTLY EGOCENTRIC

Egocentric thought is the native propensity to see things from one's own narrow, self-serving, self-validating perspective. It leads people to uncritically accept that which makes them feel good, and that which serves their selfish desires. To understand egocentric thinking is to begin with the assumption that the human mind is naturally trapped in pathological ways of looking at the world. Instead of being openminded, we (naturally) tend to be narrowminded. Instead of seeing situations fairmindedly, we (naturally) tend to see them from our own selfish perspectives. Instead of recognizing that complex issues require complex reasoning, we (naturally) oversimplify them.

> Rules, conventions, and taboos of any particular time period, and within any particular culture, are just as likely to be arbitrary as not.

Though egocentric tendencies may be encouraged or discouraged in human societies, they seem to be *implicit* in the mind at birth. As children, we naturally see ourselves as the center of the universe. Everything revolves around "me." This tendency manifests itself in simple, obvious ways at first. But as we age, we increasingly learn to hide our egocentricity, since blatant selfishness won't as easily get us what we want as

---

43 To understand the raw intellectual capacities of the human mind, it is useful to consider the tendencies of young children to be very curious about their world and how it works, to ask questions about the nature of things, and so on. In fairminded critical societies, these healthy tendencies would be encouraged, but in today's societies and schools, intellectual development is largely discouraged. This raw capacity of the human mind to develop intellectually is never fully cultivated, since the mind can continue to develop throughout a lifetime. But in most people this capacity is cultivated only to a small degree—largely because of the power of egocentricity and sociocentricity in the human mind, and the precedence it tends to take in human cultures. Perhaps it goes without saying that people tend not to see much of their egocentric or sociocentric nature, and thus overrate their own rational tendencies.

44 There is much debate as to whether, and to what extent, some people are intrinsically more predisposed (let us say genetically) to empathize with others—to think more fairmindedly and the like, or, conversely, to be more selfish, more intellectually arrogant, and more closeminded. As far as I can tell in reading the research extant today, there are indeed genetic predispositions in one versus another of these directions. But, though it may be easier or more difficult to develop as a thinker due to our "genes," the work involved is, in essence, the same. The fact that some people may be predisposed to empathize with others doesn't mean they will, or that they will when it matters most. At the same time, the fact that other people are less inclined to empathize, from a genetic perspective, doesn't mean that they can't develop as empathic persons (or that they will be less empathetic than those who are genetically inclined in this direction).

manipulative, nuanced, disguised selfishness. In short, as we grow into adulthood, we don't necessarily become less egocentric; we just become more sophisticated in our egocentricity. We learn to hide it better.

TWO PRIMARY TENDENCIES OF EGOCENTRIC THOUGHT

Human egocentricity, although complex, can be organized in terms of two primary tendencies. One is to see the world in *self-serving* terms, i.e., to constantly seek what makes "me" feel good—what I selfishly want—without regard to the rights and needs of others. The second is the desire to maintain "my" beliefs. This latter tendency entails *rigidity of thought*. When I am rationalizing my irrational beliefs, I see them as obviously reasonable.

The first tendency, selfishness, is intuitive to most people. It makes sense that I would want to get what I think is "best" for me, what serves me, what I like and want. The second tendency may seem less intuitive. Why would the mind be naturally rigid? Look at it this way: All the beliefs you have taken in or generated through the years of your life seem to make perfect sense to you—yes? Otherwise, you would have changed them. And no doubt you have changed many of your beliefs. But the beliefs you now hold seem true to you. This would be true for any given period of your life. Egocentrically, we want to "protect" beliefs we hold at the moment. People typically would far rather hold onto their beliefs (however irrational) than to have to deal with the discomfort that accompanies changing them. We are creatures of mental habit.

The long and short of it is that to the extent that we protect our beliefs out of sheer habit, and to the extent that we are closed to new ways of looking at things, we are rigid egocentric thinkers. One caveat to this is that when people are being egocentric, they may be skilled at flexible thought in certain narrow ways to serve their selfish interests. (Highly successful business people and politicians are often paradigm cases of this point.) In other ways they would be egocentrically rigid, or intellectually arrogant.

SOCIOCENTRICITY CAN BE DIRECTLY LINKED TO EGOCENTRIC THOUGHT

Sociocentric thinking may be conceptualized as an extension of egocentric thinking—or as a pathological orientation that interlocks directly with egocentricity. This is evidenced in the fact that sociocentric thought seems to operate from at least two primary tendencies of egocentric thought:

1. Seeking to get what it (or its group) wants without regard to the rights and needs of others; and

2. Maintaining a rigid belief system that serves (or is perceived as serving) the group's interests.

Test the Idea

Complete the following statements. See how many examples you can come up with for each (some of these examples will overlap with those you identified previously in working through these activities).

1. The following examples illuminate the problem of egocentric selfishness...
2. The following examples illuminate the problem of sociocentric groupishness...
3. The following examples illuminate the problem of egocentric validation...
4. The following examples illuminate the problem of sociocentric validation...

From a conceptual viewpoint, all four forms of sociocentric thought—groupishness, group validation, group control, and group conformity—seem intimately connected with egocentric thought. Individuals are often selfish due to their egocentricity; groups are often groupish due to their sociocentricity. Individuals often (egocentrically) validate their narrow or self-serving views; groups often (sociocentrically) validate their group-serving views. Individuals often (egocentrically) dominate others; groups often (sociocentrically) dominate other groups, certain members within, and/or individuals exterior to the group. Individuals often (egocentrically) submit to others who dominate them; groups often (sociocentrically) submit or conform to the views of the group.

Egocentrism intrinsically leads to bias, prejudice, self-glorification, distortion, rigidity, intolerance, intellectual arrogance, hypocrisy, and so on. These and related dysfunctional tendencies of the mind are seen in sociocentric thought as well. More on the connection between egocentric and sociocentric thought presently.

Distinguishing Rational from Egocentric and Sociocentric Thoughts

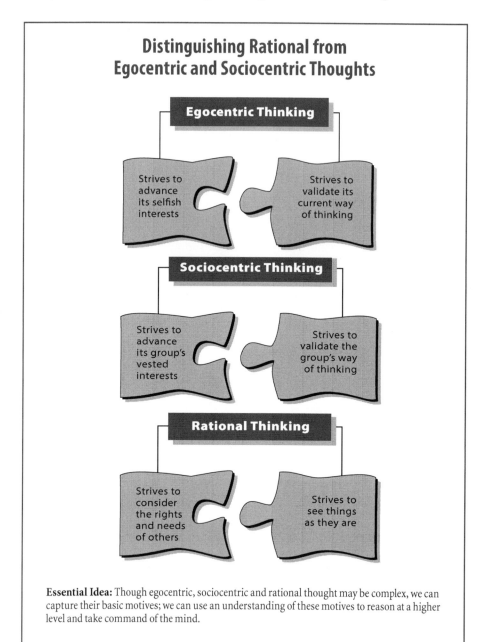

Egocentric Thinking

Strives to advance its selfish interests

Strives to validate its current way of thinking

Sociocentric Thinking

Strives to advance its group's vested interests

Strives to validate the group's way of thinking

Rational Thinking

Strives to consider the rights and needs of others

Strives to see things as they are

Essential Idea: Though egocentric, sociocentric and rational thought may be complex, we can capture their basic motives; we can use an understanding of these motives to reason at a higher level and take command of the mind.

SELF-DECEPTION PLAYS A PRIMARY ROLE IN SOCIOCENTRIC THOUGHT

Take self-deception as a primary driving force for sociocentric thought. This force, as I understand it, ultimately derives from native, self-deceptive, egocentric thought.

Humans are nothing if not self-deceived. Indeed, humans might best be described as *the self-deceived and self-deceiving animal.* The natural inclination toward self-deception, intrinsic to the human mind, is found in phenomena such as rationalization, stereotyping, distortion, egocentric memory, intellectual arrogance, hypocrisy, closed mindedness, and partiality (see diagram, page 103). Methods of self-deception, evident even in young children, become more sophisticated as we grow and age.[45]

Humans can deceive themselves into believing virtually anything—that beating someone is good for them, that torture is justifiable, that locking people up in prisons over minor infractions for long periods of time is reasonable, that slavery is acceptable, that stealing land from native persons is justifiable, that the planet is indestructible, etc. There seem to be almost no limits to the human capacity for maintaining beliefs contradictory to *readily-available* evidence.

In his book *How We Know What Isn't So,* Thomas Gilovich (1991) focuses on, among other things, "the tendency for people to believe, within limits, what they want to believe" (p. 76). He says:

> One of the most documented findings in psychology is that the average person purports to believe extremely flattering things about him or herself—beliefs that do not stand up to objective analysis. We tend to believe that we possess a host of socially desirable characteristics, and that we are free of most of those that are socially undesirable. For example, a large majority of the general public thinks that they are more intelligent, more fairminded, less prejudiced, and more skilled behind the wheel of an automobile than the average person. This phenomenon is so reliable and ubiquitous that it has come to be known as the "Lake Wobegon effect," after Garrison Keillor's fictional community where "the women are strong, the men are good-looking, and all the children are above average." (p. 77)

What this reveals, among other things, is that people are adept at telling themselves things that simply aren't true in order to see themselves in a certain light. This intrinsic phenomenon naturally extends to groups and manifests itself in any number of ways.

---

45 See the work of Piaget for detailed analyses of the child's native egocentricity, which is often manifested in self-deception. Also see the work of Sigmund Freud and Anna Freud on self-deception and the defense mechanisms—for example, *The Psychopathology of Everyday Life* and *Ego and the Mechanisms of Defense.*

Laurence Gonzales (Oct. 2008), in focusing on the problem of groupthink and self-deception, targets the loss of two space shuttles by NASA, which cost the lives of 14 crew members:

> NASA defined itself as technically excellent—"the perfect place," as one researcher called it. They put a man on the moon, and it was hard to argue with success. The insidious message was: We know what we're doing. The corollary to that is: You can't tell me anything I don't already know. … The official report on the crash of Columbia said, "External criticism and doubt … reinforced the will to "impose the party line vision … not to reconsider it …" This in turn led to "flawed decision making, self deception, introversion and diminished curiosity about the world outside the perfect place." (p. 28)

Humans are nothing if not self-deceived. Indeed, humans might best be described as *the self-deceived and self-deceiving animal.*

Through complex ideologies, groups routinely deceive themselves into believing they are taking the moral high ground when in fact they are caught up in narrow, parochial views. Consider the case of Bertrand Russell, a preeminent philosopher, who, in 1941, was prevented from teaching at the College of the City of New York due to his writings on marriage and the family. In these writings, he took the view that homosexuality is neither immoral nor unhealthy, that childhood masturbation is natural and thus shouldn't be discouraged, that sex outside of marriage should be considered a private matter, and that married couples should decide for themselves whether they want to (and can find a reasonable way to) engage in sexuality with people other than their marriage partners.

After it became known publicly that Russell had been invited to teach at the college (specifically to teach courses in logic, mathematics, and the relations of pure and applied sciences to philosophy), a number of groups known for their interest in "education" protested the appointment, including "the Sons of Xavier, the New York Branch of the Catholic Central Verein of America, the Ancient Order of Hibernians, the Knights of Columbus, the Guild of Catholic Lawyers, the St. Joan of Arc Holy Name Society, the Metropolitan Baptist Ministers' Conference, the Midwest Conference of the Society of New England Women, and the Empire State Sons of the American Revolution" (Edwards, 1957, p. 211).

Bishop Manning of the protestant Episcopal Church wrote a letter to all New York newspapers in which he said, "What is to be said of colleges and universities which hold up before our youth as a responsible teacher of philosophy … a man who is a recognized propagandist against both religion and morality, and who specifically defends adultery?" (Edwards, 1957, p. 210). Further quoting from

Edwards, "The Bishop's letter was the signal for a campaign of vilification and intimidation unequaled in American history since the days of Jefferson and Thomas Paine. The ecclesiastical journals, the Hearst press, and just about every Democratic politician joined the chorus of defamation. Russell's appointment, said *The Tablet*, came as a 'brutal, insulting shock to old New Yorkers and all real Americans'" (p. 210).

All these groups, propped up by narrow religious and Puritanical belief systems and their accompanying sense of righteousness, systemically deceived themselves into believing they had to protect students from the views of Russell. In fact, 1) none of Russell's views on marriage and the family were relevant to the specific courses he was slated to teach at the college; 2) even if they had been, the views espoused by Russell were far more enlightened than both the views of his detractors and the mainstream views at the time; and 3) it was the views not of Russell, but of the religious zealots who attacked him, that were in fact harmful to students and the general public. These religious groups fancied themselves champions of ethics when, in fact, they were calling for and exemplifying its opposite. Group self-deception, aided by group validation, made this possible. We might label this phenomenon "in-group deception."[46]

Whenever people behave unethically, they likely do so for one of two reasons: 1) they are sincerely attempting to do the right thing but don't know what the right thing is (thus are making a mistake in thinking), or 2) they are deceiving themselves into thinking they are doing the right thing when they aren't. In the second case, self-deception enables people to avoid seeing what they are actually thinking and doing when they behave unethically.[47]

Because humans have the raw capacity to reason ethically, to be concerned with the rights and needs of others, it stands to reason that we can (at least theoretically) develop this raw capacity in ourselves. And it seems that, to a large extent, people want to live an ethical life. We want, as it were, to "do the right thing." But we must contend with the largely unconscious, lurking tendencies within our minds that are focused on gratifying personal desires and/or maintaining existing beliefs. When faced with an ethical dilemma, we often experience direct conflict between what we know is ethically obligatory and what our irrational tendencies would lead us toward. The mind seems at times unable to deal directly with this conflict— unable to take command of irrational tendencies through

> Self-deception… enables people "justify" (in bad faith) what cannot (in good faith) be justified.

---

46 As with the term selfishness (in reference to my use of the term "groupishness"), the term self-deception, when focused on group thought, seems inadequate. "In-group deception" might be a better term for capturing the problem of groups deceiving themselves into believing that which is false.

47 Depending on how one conceptualizes the mind, there might be other reasons why people behave unethically. There may be people, for instance, who just don't care whether they do the right thing. Or we might say that sociopaths are simply incapable of knowing what the right thing is. In either case, however, one might argue that these people still think they are doing the right thing and are self-deceived. In other words, they believe their actions to be justified in the context.

reasonable, disciplined self-command. At the same time, we want to experience our thoughts as cohesive, as logical. In other words, we humans dislike conflicting thoughts. So we quite simply engage in self-deception to avoid the conflict. The mind tells itself that what is unethical is actually ethical. This routine form of self-deception enables people to maintain selfish or narrow viewpoints with little or no discomfort. It enables them to "justify" (in bad faith) what cannot (in good faith) be justified. It enables people to sleep soundly at night even when committing the most atrocious acts.

When groups deceive themselves into believing that some unethical act is reasonable, there are no limits to the pain and suffering they might cause. During the Inquisitions of the sixteenth and seventeenth centuries, Christians of different stripes (and nonbelievers as well) were beheaded, burned at the stake, and boiled alive in tar—all in the name of God. Catholic leaders in Rome, under the direction of the Pope, collectively deceived themselves into believing that the only way to save the souls of the Protestants, or "dissenters," and keep others from rejecting the Catholic Church was to imprison or execute them. Protestant leaders followed suit. Through elaborately-developed religious ideologies, all convinced themselves they were carrying out the will of God.

Through "in-group deception," human groups are responsible for the needless pain and suffering each year of millions of animals labeled "livestock." Most of these animals are denied their most fundamental rights. They are deprived of the basic necessities and living conditions for a reasonable quality of life. Many are locked away their entire lives in cages that prohibit movement, waiting and suffering until deemed "big enough" or "fat enough" to be killed for human consumption.

In sum, throughout history and to the present day, sociocentric thinking, enabled through "in-group deception," has led directly to the pain and suffering of innocent persons and creatures in the billions.[48] This has been possible because human groups, unaware of or unconcerned with the problem of sociocentric thought, often use power in unethical ways. Once they internalize a group-serving ideology, they can then act in ways that flagrantly contradict their announced "morality" while conveniently hiding from their own contradictions or inconsistencies.

> Sociocentric thinking, largely enabled by self-deception, has led directly to the pain and suffering of innocent persons and creatures in the billions.

In-group deception is so powerful a force in the mind of humans, so naturally a part of our makeup, and so essential to the dysfunctional group beliefs that guide and control much of our behavior, that unless we train

---

48 Support for this claim can be easily achieved by knowing that roughly half the world's population lives in absolute poverty, meaning they lack the basic necessities (food, shelter, and medical care) for a reasonable quality of life. Since there are more than 7 billion people in the world, more than 3 billion live in absolute poverty, almost all of which is enabled or directly caused by sociocentric thought. Further, somewhere near 100 million animals are used in experimentation each year, almost all of whom are then killed.

our minds to notice this propensity and actively correct for it, we have very little chance of reaching our potential as ethical persons or of creating an ethical world.

Critical thinkers are keenly aware of the problem of self-deception and in-group deception, both in their own thought and that of others. They focus on their own self-deception because they understand that it is only their thinking which they have any real control over. They realize that self-deception operates at the unconscious level and makes irrational or absurd beliefs seem reasonable. Thus critical thinkers realize that they must look underneath the surface of their thought to identify when they are deceiving themselves. When they do catch themselves in an act of self-deception, they target the problems in their thinking that they would rather avoid. They try not to allow themselves "off the hook." They find pleasure in detecting and correcting problems in their thinking, including acts of self-deception. They recognize these as essential learning opportunities.

Test the Idea

Look for examples of self-deception and *in-group deception* in your life. Look for it in the thinking of others. Look for it in articles and books you read; look for it on the internet, in movies, and in TV programs.

MANY COMPLEX RELATIONSHIPS EXIST BETWEEN AND AMONG EGOCENTRIC, SOCIOCENTRIC, AND RATIONAL THOUGHT

A natural marriage exists, then, between egocentric and sociocentric thought; both are rooted in:

1. the inherent tendency to seek what one wants—either working alone or in groups;
2. the inherent tendency to hold onto and validate one's beliefs—either individually or in groups.

Not withstanding these shared connections between egocentric and sociocentric thought, sociocentrism seems to be more than just egocentric thinking manifest in groups. And the relationships between these two sets of tendencies are complex; they become increasingly so over time as people grow from childhood to adulthood.

Let us see if we can begin to sketch out this complex set of relationships between egocentric and sociocentric thought. At birth, we seek what we want without any sense that we are doing so. We want food, so we cry for food. We want to be held, so we cry to be held. We are sleepy and tired, so we go to sleep (or cry because we are too tired to go to sleep). We are completely centered in ourselves, consummately egocentric. We are automatically wired into our own needs and desires, *but with the sense that others are wired into them as well.* At the

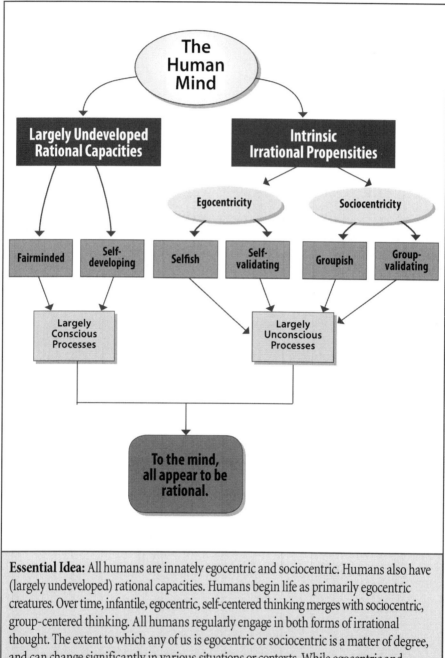

Essential Idea: All humans are innately egocentric and sociocentric. Humans also have (largely undeveloped) rational capacities. Humans begin life as primarily egocentric creatures. Over time, infantile, egocentric, self-centered thinking merges with sociocentric, group-centered thinking. All humans regularly engage in both forms of irrational thought. The extent to which any of us is egocentric or sociocentric is a matter of degree, and can change significantly in various situations or contexts. While egocentric and sociocentric propensities are naturally-occurring phenomena, rational capacities largely must be largely developed. It is through the development of rational capacities that we combat irrational tendencies and cultivate critical societies.

base of thinking is the unconscious, infantile belief that the world is here to serve "me." This seems one of the barest roots of egocentric thought.

But at some point we realize 1) that there are others in the world besides us, and 2) that those others will not necessarily always give us what we want. To get what we want, we sometimes have to do what others want us to do, which often means heeding *group expectations*. This is a routine pattern in early relationships between children and parents. The logic of this early phenomenon of getting along in the world might be understood as follows:

1. The child intrinsically pursues her perceived needs and desires (primarily egocentric).
2. But in this pursuit, she might run up against group (i.e., family) expectations (which are likely a combination of reasonable and unreasonable expectations).
3. Further, the child has an intrinsic need to be accepted by others (the group), which at this point is both necessary to survival and sociocentric in nature.
4. The group (usually the family) systematically rewards, punishes, and/or reasons with the child (through a mixture of egocentric, sociocentric, and rational influences).
5. The child seeks ways and means of satisfying her needs and desires that are socially acceptable through a mixture of rational, egocentric, and sociocentric thought.
6. Thus, the child must forge a balance between pursuing her needs and desires (which may be egocentric, sociocentric, or rational in nature) and shaping her behavior to survive in the group (the group expectations being a mixture of rational and sociocentric thought).

> Mutually-validating relationships can be found between egocentric and sociocentric thought in many parts of human life. We see it exemplified when group beliefs and customs validate individual self-serving desires, and when individual egocentric beliefs align neatly with group goals and purposes.

This analysis helps us begin to see the complex relationship that exists among egocentric, sociocentric, and rational forces in human thought and action.[49] This analysis also explains why, from a very young age, children become habituated to a large number of expectations, rules, and taboos.[50] Then, as children move beyond the family into schools, peer groups, specialized groups (such as clubs, organizations, sports, etc.), and the broader culture, they take on the views of

---

49 It is likely that this complex set of interrelationships and dynamic processes has never been fully examined or understood.

50 A big part of why groups can so easily influence the mind of a child is because children have little or no developed critical capacities. Children take on group ideologies because they can't see through them—and because they have a vested interest in accepting them (i.e., survival within the group).

those groups as well—largely without questioning them. Where conflict exists between or among the beliefs of these groups, some compartmentalization is employed to hide the contradictions. And still, at times, people pursue their own individual agendas, which will entail some combination of egocentric thought and rational thought.

Mutually-validating relationships can be found between egocentric and sociocentric thought in many parts of human life. We see it exemplified when group beliefs and customs validate individual self-serving desires, and when individual egocentric beliefs align neatly with group goals and purposes. In a culture, for example, where greed is fostered, egocentric individuals will be able to pursue their own (intrinsic) greedy desires, relatively untrammeled, and will be sociocentrically validated by the group for doing so. In a culture where group dogmatism (sociocentrism) is the norm, individual dogmatism (egocentrism) will be expected and tacitly encouraged (as long as individual beliefs don't undermine group beliefs).

More often than not, people come to uncritically hold the dominant beliefs of society, and then fiercely protect and defend those beliefs. Their egocentric tendency to protect and validate their individual beliefs is funneled into protecting and validating group beliefs. At the same time, they see themselves as openminded. They think they have good reason to hold these beliefs. They see no problems in their thinking, or in the thinking of the groups to which they belong. They think in these ways because of the power of self-deception.

Though egocentric and sociocentric tendencies are often mutually reinforcing (or "compatible" in any case), they are frequently in conflict with one another. And when this occurs, each one vies for power. We naturally want to do that which is in our selfish interest; but, we also naturally want to fit into the groups with which we identify, and into which we have been thrust. We want to pursue what feels good to us as individuals, but we also want to be accepted and validated by the groups that are important to us. We want to have our individual beliefs validated, but we want our group beliefs validated too. Accordingly, at times what we (as individuals) want will not coincide with what "the group" expects of us. And then (thankfully), at times, we are relatively rational, reasonable, empathic creatures.[51]

---

51 It is possible that, at any given moment, we might be egocentric, sociocentric, or rational—or engaging in some combination of these three modes of thought. We may even move among the three in any particular circumstance—for instance, first by being egocentric, then sociocentric, then with rational thoughts attempting to influence our actions, only to be pushed out by sociocentric and/or egocentric forces. For instance, imagine the business manager who, during a meeting, introduces a new idea to his colleagues for their consideration—an idea that has negative implications he can't see. His colleagues point out problems with the idea. The manager, egocentrically stuck in a rigid orientation to the idea, merely wants his views to be accepted and becomes very pushy with his colleagues. A few days after the meeting, he notices that he is getting the cold shoulder from them, so he adjusts his behavior to fit into the group, not wanting to be ostracized by them. He may even recognize that he behaved irrationally during the meeting, and that his thinking was perhaps overly rigid. So at first, he is egocentric (in presenting and pressing his ideas), then sociocentric (in needing validation from the group), then, finally, rational (in recognizing problems in his behavior).

Test the Idea

Come up with examples from your own life in which there is, or has been, conflict between your egocentricity, your sociocentricity, and your rational self. Actively begin looking for these conflicts within yourself every day.

SOCIOCENTRIC THOUGHT CAN BE MORE DANGEROUS THAN EGOCENTRIC THOUGHT

Though the patterns of dysfunctional thinking are similar for egocentric and sociocentric thinking, there is at least one critical distinction between the two: groups have more power. Certainly, egocentric thinking is potentially dangerous. Through self-deception, individuals can justify the most egregious of actions, but individuals operating alone are usually more limited in the amount of harm they can do. Conversely, groups engaging in sociocentric thinking can typically do greater harm to greater numbers of people. During the Spanish Inquisition, the state, controlled by the church, executed thousands of reputed heretics. Under Hitler's leadership, the Germans tortured and murdered millions of Jews, as well as other ethnic groups. Under U.S. leadership, the Vietnam war led to horrific suffering. Under the direction of Israel (supported by the U.S. government), misery among masses of Palestinians has continued for more than 50 years. Under the direction of the Rwandan government, in 1994, an estimated 800,000 people were murdered.

We can look more closely at any such example, of which there are an unlimited number. For instance, consider the fact that the "founders" of the Americas, presumably guided by the "hand of God," enslaved, murdered, or tortured millions of Native Americans and Africans. The heinous crimes committed by Columbus and his lot are now well documented. In his book *A People's History of the United States* (1980; 2006), Howard Zinn chronicles the sad fate of native peoples in the Americas during the seventeenth century. Here is a brief excerpt that gives us a sense of the enormity of the atrocities committed by Columbus and his men:

> The Indians, Columbus reported, "are so naïve and so free with their possessions that no one who has not witnessed them would believe it. When you ask for something they have, they never say no. To the contrary, they offer to share with anyone. ... " He concluded his report by asking for a little help from their Majesties, and in return he would bring them from his next voyage "as much gold as they need ... and as many slaves as they ask." He was full of religious talk: "Thus the eternal God, our Lord, gives victory to those who follow His way over apparent impossibilities." ... Because of Columbus's exaggerated report and promises, his second expedition was given seventeen ships and more than twelve hundred men. The aim was clear: slaves and gold.

They went from island to island in the Caribbean, taking Indians as captives ... In the province of Cicao on Haiti, where he and his men imagined huge gold fields to exist, they ordered all persons fourteen years or older to collect a certain quantity of gold every three months. When they brought it, they were given copper tokens to hang around their necks. Indians found without a copper token had their hands cut off and bled to death ... Trying to put together an army of resistance, the Arawaks faced Spaniards who had armor, muskets, swords, horses. When the Spaniards took prisoners they hanged them or burned them to death ... Among the Arawaks, mass suicides began ... Infants were killed to save them from the Spaniards. In two years, through murder, mutilation, or suicide, half of the 250,000 Indians on Haiti were dead. (pp. 3–5)

In short, people within groups often work together in any number of unethical ways, validating thinking which is faulty, yet which appears perfectly reasonable within the logic of pathological groupthink.

Test the Idea

Think of an example of sociocentric thought that you consider to be dangerous. Complete these statements:

1. The example is as follows...
2. This thinking and behavior is a problem because...

CONVINCING PARALLELS BETWEEN EGOCENTRIC AND SOCIOCENTRIC THOUGHT

Sociocentric thought has, it seems to me, a life of its own beyond the propensities it shares with egocentric thought. Still, to best understand sociocentric thought, it may help to further explore the foundational tendencies it holds in common with egocentric thought, and how these tendencies are manifest differently in sociocentric thought. Let us now consider some of these connections.

Egocentric Dominating and Submissive Tendencies Are Often Transformed into Sociocentric Domination and Submission

Two unreasonable ways to gain and use power are given in these distinct forms of egocentric thinking: 1) the art of dominating others (a direct means to getting what one wants), and 2) the art of submitting to others (an indirect means to getting what one wants). In other words, insofar as we are thinking egocentrically, we seek to satisfy our egocentric desires either directly or indirectly by exercising power and control over others, or by submitting to those who can act to serve our interests. To put it crudely, egocentric behavior often either bullies or grovels.

Either it threatens those weaker, subordinates itself to those more powerful, or oscillates between the two in subtle maneuvers and schemes.

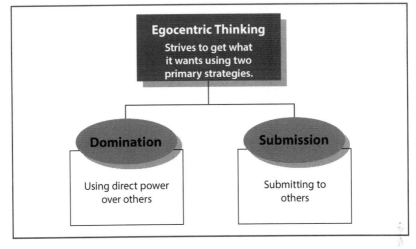

These same tendencies are prevalent in sociocentric thought, and can be visualized as follows:

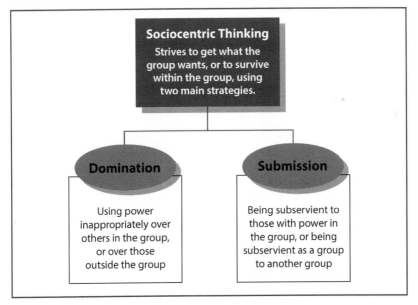

These sociocentric motives help explain the logic of group control and conformity discussed in the opening chapter. In most groups, there are people who dominate and people who submit to those in power. Bureaucrats tend to dominate those they are intended to serve. Teachers sometimes dominate students. Police officers frequently bully citizens. Governments tend to tyrannize the people they have been entrusted to protect and support. Religious groups often covertly control their members. Domination can take many forms, from the overt (coercing, bullying, and intimidating) to the covert (manipulating, inculcating, indoctrinating, brainwashing, and "recruiting"). Domination, in the sense used here—either by groups or individuals—refers to the use of power to control others in ways that deny or violate their interests.

Of course, domination works only if there are willing "submitters." Hence, the submitter is the natural and necessary counterpart to the dominator. The two fit together but don't complement one another in the high sense of the word, as both sets of tendencies are dysfunctional. Where the control is complete—for instance where people have been successfully brainwashed by their "controllers"—they may be wholly compliant and "feel" relatively satisfied. Those who exhibit blind patriotism to their country, or blind faith in religion, exemplify this phenomenon.

Egocentric and sociocentric domination are found in a multitude of forms through countless examples in human life. People may be dominators in one context while being submitters in another. For instance, a man may dominate his wife while submitting to his supervisor at work. A woman may submit to her husband and dominate her children. A mother may dominate her son until he is of a certain age, at which time he may become her dominator.

The dangers inherent in egocentric and sociocentric domination and submission seem apparent. For instance, millions of soldiers throughout history have been willing to sacrifice their lives in wars being fought for reasons of which they were in complete ignorance. Millions of people have supported war through blind allegiance to their country. The dangers of these dysfunctional modes of thought can also be found in conformity to laws that are unethical and unjust.

When submitters go along with dominators, they may appear to be living together peacefully. But in addition to the dangers implicit in blind loyalty, submitters are frequently resentful of their "controllers." They may seem content in their subservient role while privately fuming. When the fuming erupts, the formerly "passive" behavior becomes "aggressive"—hence the phrase "passive-aggressive behavior."

In sum, irrational domination and submission are intrinsic human tendencies. They manifest themselves in human life in a multitude of forms—both egocentric and sociocentric.

> Millions of soldiers throughout history have been willing to sacrifice their lives in wars being fought for reasons of which they were in complete ignorance. Millions of people have supported war through blind allegiance to their country.

Critical thinkers avoid dominating or submitting to others for egocentric reasons. When they believe their views are best in a situation, they try always to use reasoning to convince others, rather than controlling others through force, coercion, or manipulation. At the same time, critical thinkers do not egocentrically submit to others who try to irrationally control them. In some situations, it isn't easy to tell whether you must go along with those in power or whether you have a choice. Sometimes, especially in dangerous situations, rational people choose to go along with those who wield power over them. On the other hand, there are many times when people may think they must submit in a situation when, in fact, they have other choices. It is common, for instance, for people to feel trapped in a job—and to therefore feel that they must be subservient to the irrational whims of supervisors—when, in fact, they do have other options. Similarly, people often trap themselves in irrational marriages, submitting to the domination of an overbearing or manipulative spouse. These people trap themselves through their own dysfunctional habits of thought.

Test the Idea

Come up with examples from your own life in which egocentric or sociocentric domination or submission have been a problem. Complete these statements:

1. I tend to be egocentrically dominating in the following types of situations ...
2. I tend to be egocentrically submissive in the following types of situations ...
3. These dysfunctional tendencies have caused problems for me in the following ways ...
4. In one group in which I am a member, I can see sociocentric domination as a problem in the following ways ...
5. I can see sociocentric submission as a problem in this group in the following ways ...

People Often Use Egocentric Standards for Determining What to Believe

Because people are largely egocentric, they often use egocentric standards to determine what to accept and what to reject. At the same time, they are unrealistically confident that they have fundamentally figured out *the way things actually are*, and that they have done so objectively. They naturally *believe* in their *intuitive perceptions*—however inaccurate. Here are the most commonly-used egocentric standards in human thinking:

"IT'S TRUE BECAUSE *I* BELIEVE IT." *Innate intellectual arrogance:* I assume that what I believe is true, even though I have never questioned the basis for many of my beliefs or carefully examined them.

"IT'S TRUE BECAUSE I *WANT* TO BELIEVE IT." *Innate wish fulfillment:* I believe what "feels good," what supports my other beliefs, what does not require me to change my thinking (or my life) in any significant way, and what does not require me to admit that I have been wrong. I believe in accounts of behavior that put me in a positive rather than a negative light, even though I have not seriously considered the evidence for the more negative account.

"IT'S TRUE BECAUSE I *HAVE ALWAYS* BELIEVED IT." *Innate self-validation:* I have a strong desire to maintain beliefs I have long held, even though I have not seriously considered the extent to which those beliefs are justified, given the evidence.

"IT'S TRUE BECAUSE IT IS *IN MY SELFISH INTEREST* TO BELIEVE IT." *Innate selfishness:* I hold fast to beliefs that justify my getting more power, money, or personal advantage, even though these beliefs are not grounded in sound reasoning or evidence.

Test the Idea

Come up with examples for each of the categories above. Complete these statements, focusing on problems in your own thinking as much as possible:

1. The following examples illustrate the problem of innate intellectual arrogance . . .
2. The following examples illustrate the problem of innate wish fulfillment . . .
3. The following examples illustrate the problem of innate self-validation . . .
4. The following examples illustrate the problem of innate selfishness . . .

Sociocentric Standards for Determining What to Believe Are Linked with Egocentric Standards

Just as humans use egocentric standards to determine what to believe, they use sociocentric standards as well. Consider the following parallels between egocentric and sociocentric "standards" of thought. These pathological standards are routinely used in human life:

Egocentric standard: "It's true because I believe it."

Related sociocentric standard: "It's true because we believe it." *Innate group intellectual arrogance*: We assume our group beliefs to be true, even though we have never questioned the basis for many of them.

Egocentric standard: "It's true because I want to believe it."

Related sociocentric standard: "It's true because we want to believe it." *Innate group wish fulfillment*: We believe what "feels good" to our group, what supports our other beliefs, what does not require us to change our thinking in any significant way, and what does not require us to admit we have been wrong. We believe in, for example, accounts of behavior that put our group in a positive rather than a negative light, even though we have not seriously considered the evidence for the more negative account.

Egocentric standard: "It's true because I have always believed it."

Related sociocentric standard: "It's true because we have always believed it." *Innate group-validation*: We have a strong desire to maintain beliefs we have long held, even though we have not seriously considered the extent to which those beliefs are justified, given the evidence.

Egocentric standard: "It's true because it's in my selfish interest to believe it."

Related sociocentric standard: "It's true because it's in our vested interest to believe it." *Innate groupishness*: We hold fast to beliefs that justify our group getting more power, money, or personal advantage, even though these beliefs are not grounded in sound reasoning or evidence.

Given our four forms of sociocentric thought, we can add these two sociocentric standards for thought:

"It's true because we tell you it's true." *Innate group control*: We expect group members to accept uncritically the beliefs and values of those dominant in the group (which is usually "us"). We are the "dominators" in the group.

"It's true because we have been told it's true." *Innate group conformity*: We are indoctrinated into the ideologies of the group, and therefore often uncritically accept group beliefs, norms, customs, and taboos. We are the "submitters" in the group.

All of these pathological standards naturally lie at the unconscious level of human thought. They illuminate some of the parallels that exist between egocentric and sociocentric thought. Just as individuals deceive themselves through egocentric thinking, groups deceive themselves through sociocentric thinking. Just as egocentric thinking functions to serve one's selfish interest, sociocentric thinking functions to serve groupish interests. In the same way that egocentric thinking operates to validate the uncritical thinking of the individual, sociocentric thinking operates to validate the uncritical thinking of the group.

Piaget's Insights on Egocentricity Can Be Linked to Sociocentric Thought

Jean Piaget (1976) identified specific patterns of egocentricity in the thought and actions of children. It has been pointed out that these same tendencies are found in adult thought. Further, Piaget's characterizations of egocentric tendencies have significant application, with appropriate translation, to sociocentric thinking. Consider Piaget's characterizations of the egocentric thinker, then note my formulation of each phenomenon's sociocentric parallel:

Egocentrism of thought necessarily entails a certain degree of unconsciousness, with the egocentric thinker "in a perpetual state of belief ... "

Sociocentrism of thought necessarily entails a certain degree of unconsciousness, with the sociocentric thinker in a perpetual state of belief (i.e., a perpetual state of uncritical acceptance of one's own beliefs).

The egocentric thinker is confident in his own ideas ...

The sociocentric thinker is confident in the ideas of his group.

The egocentric thinker is naturally … [untroubled] about the reasons and motives which have guided his reasoning process …
The sociocentric thinker is naturally untroubled about the reasons and motives that guide the reasoning of his social group.

The egocentric thinker [seeks] to justify himself in the eyes of others … only under the pressure of argument and opposition …
The sociocentric thinker seeks to justify his group in the eyes of other groups, or of people external to the group, only under the pressure of argument and opposition.

The egocentric thinker is incapable either by introspection or retrospection of capturing the successive steps … [his] mind has taken …
The sociocentric thinker is incapable, either by introspection or retrospection, of capturing the successive steps his group has taken in formulating its beliefs.

The egocentric thinker suffers from illusions of perspective …
The sociocentric thinker suffers from illusions of group perspective.

The egocentric thinker is ignorant of his own ego, takes his own point of view to be absolute, and fails to establish … that reciprocity which alone would ensure objectivity …
The sociocentric thinker is ignorant of his group's sociocentric nature, takes his group's point of view to be absolute, and fails to establish that reciprocity among and between perspectives which alone would ensure objectivity.

The egocentric thinker [uses] thought … at the service of personal desire …
The sociocentric thinker uses thought at the service of group desire.

The egocentric thinker simply believes … without trying to find the truth …
The sociocentric thinker simply believes group ideologies without trying to find the truth.

The egocentric thinker assimilates everything he hears to his own point of view …
The sociocentric thinker assimilates everything he hears to his group's point of view.

The egocentric thinker does not try to prove whether such and such of his idea does or does not correspond to reality. When the question is put to him, he evades it. It does not interest him, and it is even alien to his whole mental attitude …
The sociocentric thinker does not try to prove whether such and such of his group's ideas do, or do not, correspond to reality. When the question is put to him, he evades it. It does not interest him, and is even alien to his whole mental attitude.

In sum, for each characterization of egocentric thought identified by Piaget, one can find a ready parallel in sociocentric thought. These parallels can easily be exemplified in many human social groups; hence, they illuminate the strong connection between egocentric and sociocentric tendencies.

Test the Idea

For each pattern on pages 151 and 152, see how many real-life examples you can identify—either the egocentric or sociocentric versions. Try to target your own thinking with examples from your life.

Sociocentric Pathological Tendencies Are Common in Human Life

There are multiple interrelated sociocentric dispositions that emerge out of egocentric tendencies. All of us, insofar as we are sociocentric, embody these pathological dispositions (as well as others that would cluster with them). Critical thinkers are keenly aware of these tendencies and consistently seek to counter them with fairminded reasoning. As you read through these dispositions, ask yourself whether you recognize them as processes that take place regularly in your own mind (if you conclude "not me!"—think again):

- *sociocentric memory:* the natural group tendency to "forget" evidence and information that does not support their thinking, and to "remember" evidence and information that does.
- *sociocentric myopia:* the natural group tendency to think in an absolutist way within a narrow "groupish" viewpoint.
- *sociocentric righteousness:* the natural group tendency to feel that "our group" is superior in light of our confidence that "we" inherently possess the truth.
- *sociocentric hypocrisy:* the natural group tendency to ignore flagrant inconsistencies between what a group professes to believe and the actual beliefs implied by its members' collective behavior, or between the standards to which they hold their group members and those to which they expect other groups to adhere.
- *sociocentric oversimplification:* the natural group tendency to ignore real and important complexities in the world in favor of simplistic, group-interested notions when consideration of those complexities would require the group to modify its beliefs or values.
- *sociocentric blindness:* the natural group tendency not to notice facts and evidence that contradict the group's favored beliefs or values.
- *sociocentric immediacy:* the natural group tendency to over-generalize immediate group feelings and experiences so that when one significant event, (or a few such events), is experienced by the group as highly favorable or unfavorable, this feeling is generalized to the group's overall outlook on the world (or view of other groups).
- *sociocentric absurdity:* the natural group tendency to fail to notice group-thinking that has "absurd" consequences or implications.

Test the Idea

See how many of the sociocentric pathologies on page 153 you can "prove" with examples from life—either from your own life or from news articles, books, blogs, people you know, etc.

Test the Idea

Look back at any of the examples of sociocentric thought used thus far in this book, and see how many of the pathological tendencies on page 153 you can identify in them.

Sociocentric Pathological Tendencies Can Be Challenged

It is not enough to recognize abstractly that the human mind has predictable sociocentric pathologies. If we want to live rational lives and create rational societies, we must take concrete steps to correct these pathologies. Routinely identifying these tendencies in action needs to become habitual for us. Those who take this challenge seriously recognize that it is a long-term process, never complete. To some extent, it is analogous to stripping off onion skins. After we remove one layer, we find another beneath it. Therefore, each of the following admonitions should not be taken as simple suggestions that any group could immediately, and effectively, put into action, but rather as strategic formulations of long-range goals. Every group can perform these corrections, but only over time and with considerable practice.

Correcting sociocentric memory. We can take steps to correct the natural tendency of our group to "forget" evidence that does not support our group's thinking and "remember" evidence that does by overtly seeking evidence and information that does not support the thinking of the group, and by directing explicit attention to that information. We should especially seek information and evidence that does not place our group in a positive light—information the group would rather forget or not be faced with. (If you "try" but cannot find such evidence, you should probably assume that your sociocentric tendencies are standing in the way of finding it.)

Correcting sociocentric myopia. We can take steps to correct our natural group tendency to think in an absolutistic way within an overly-narrow, group point of view by routinely thinking within points of view that conflict with our group's viewpoint. For example, if we are "liberals," we can read books by insightful conservatives. If we are "conservatives," we can read books by insightful liberals. If we are North Americans, we can study a contrasting

South American point of view, or a European, Far-Eastern, Middle-Eastern, or African point of view. (If you don't discover significant group prejudices in your thought through this process, you should question whether you are acting in good faith in trying to identify your group's prejudices.)

Correcting sociocentric righteousness. We can take steps to correct our natural sociocentric tendency to feel superior in light of our confidence that our group possesses *the truth*. We can do this by regularly reminding ourselves of how little our group actually knows. To do so, we can explicitly state the unanswered questions that our group has never openly reasoned through (though our group behavior would imply that we have *the truth* in answer to those questions). (If, in this process, you don't discover that your group knows far less than its behavior would imply, you should question the manner in which you pursued these questions.)

Correcting sociocentric hypocrisy. We can take steps to correct the natural tendency of our group to ignore flagrant inconsistencies between what it professes to believe and the actual beliefs its behavior implies. We can uncover inconsistencies between the standards we impose on group members and those we require of those outside the group. We can do this by regularly comparing the criteria and standards by which we judge others with those by which we judge our own group. (If you don't find many flagrant inconsistencies in your group's thinking and behavior, you should doubt whether you have dug deeply enough.)

Correcting sociocentric oversimplification. We can take steps to correct our group's natural tendency to ignore real and important complexities in the world by regularly focusing on those complexities, formulating them explicitly in words, and targeting them. We can look for instances when it is in our group's interest to simplify the complex in order to maintain a particular view, or to pursue some particular group interest. (If you don't discover over time that your group has oversimplified many important issues, you should question whether you have really confronted the complexities inherent in the issues.)

Correcting sociocentric blindness. We can take steps to correct our natural tendency to ignore facts or evidence that contradict our group's favored beliefs or values, by explicitly seeking out those facts and that evidence. We can look for situations when it is in our group's interest to ignore information it would rather not see or have to face. (If you don't find yourself experiencing significant discomfort as you pursue these facts, you should question whether you are taking this process seriously. If you discover that your group's traditional beliefs were all correct from the beginning, you probably moved to a new and more sophisticated level of self-deception.)

Correcting sociocentric immediacy. We can help correct our natural tendency to overgeneralize our group's immediate feelings and experiences by developing the habit of putting them into a larger perspective. We can look for examples of times in the past when our group has overgeneralized some event or set of events, whether positive or negative, then examine the consequences of our group having done so. We can consider the implications of our doing so again, should we face similar events in the future. We can strive to avoid group distortions of any kind. (If, in seeking examples of group or sociocentric immediacy, you come up short, you need to look more closely at your group's history.)

Correcting sociocentric absurdity. We can take steps to correct our natural tendency to ignore groupthink that has absurd implications by making the important implications of our group's thinking explicit, then assessing them for their desirability and realism. This requires that we frequently trace the implications of our group beliefs and the consequences of our group's behavior. For example, we should frequently ask ourselves: "If we really believed this, how would we act? Do we really act that way? Do we want to act that way? Is it ethical for us to act that way?" (If, after what you consider to be a serious search, you find no sociocentric absurdity in the thinking of your groups, think again. You are likely deceiving yourself.)

Groups Routinely Use Sociocentric Defense Mechanisms

Sociocentric thought is connected to a number of well-established defense mechanisms. Defense mechanisms tend to be understood in terms of individual thought—the individual person as in denial, the individual as engaging in identification, projection, and repression, and so on. But defense mechanisms that apply to individual thought are commonly used in pathological group thought. All are connected with "in-group deception"; they interact with the sociocentric pathological tendencies described in the last section.

Consider the following ***sociocentric defense mechanisms***:

sociocentric denial: when a group refuses to believe indisputable evidence or facts in order to maintain a favorable group image, or a favored set of group beliefs. Members of a basketball team, for example, may deny that they collectively have significant weaknesses which the opposing team lacks. "Patriots" in a given country may deny—in the face of clear-cut evidence— that their country ever violates human rights or acts unjustly.

sociocentric identification: when people within a group accept, as their own, the values and ideals of the group. Through connection with the group, its members elevate their sense of worth. For instance, football fans often experience an inner sense of triumph when "their" team wins; parents often experience a sense of "puffed up" success when their children perform well (or even relatively well) at something; citizens often feel smug when their nation's armed forces make a "clean sweep" or assassinate someone.

sociocentric projection: when, to avoid unacceptable thoughts and feelings, a group attributes to another group what they themselves are doing; by avoiding these thoughts and feelings, they can successfully avoid facing their own actions and changing them. For instance, "country A" may accuse "country B" of terrorism, when "country B" is merely defending itself against "country A." In this case, it is really "country A" that is terrorizing "country B." "Country A" avoids having to face responsibility for its actions by falsely accusing "country B" of what it (country A) is, in fact, doing. (Perhaps you might suggest possibilities for countries "A" and "B"?)

sociocentric repression: when thoughts, feelings, or memories unacceptable to the group are prevented from reaching consciousness. This often occurs when groups do not want to face something disagreeable they have done or are doing. For hundreds of years in the United States, for instance, the vast majority of people repressed the fact that Christopher Columbus engaged in egregious acts against native peoples during the "discovery" of the Americas (and is therefore not the hero he is often portrayed to be). In the United States today, the often horrific treatment of native peoples during "colonialism" is still, to a large extent, repressed (as are its accompanying consequences that last to this day).

sociocentric rationalization: when members of a group give reasons (sometimes good reasons) for their behavior—but not the real reasons, because they cannot consciously face their actions. Farmers who don't care about the effects of dangerous pesticides on animals, and people rationalize their behavior by saying they have no reasonable alternatives to control pests (when, in fact, they often do).

sociocentric stereotyping: when a group lumps together people exterior to the group based on some perceived common (usually negative) characteristics. The in-group forms a rigid, biased perception of the out-group. One form of stereotyping comes from cultural bias, wherein people assume the practices and beliefs in their culture to be superior to those in other cultures. They take their group to be the measure of all groups and people. For instance, those who argue for public-nudity rights are sociocentrically stereotyped by many western cultures as perverted and unethical, whereas in many cultures throughout history this practice has seemed only natural.

sociocentric scapegoating: when groups attempt to avoid criticism of their practices by blaming persons outside their group, or blaming the circumstance, etc., for their own mistakes or faults. A group of teachers criticized for failing to foster critical thinking in the classroom may try to avoid responsibility for this failure through scapegoating—by blaming the school system, the parents, or the curriculum—when in fact they could do far more to foster critical thinking.

sociocentric sublimation: when groups divert instinctive, primitive, or socially unacceptable desires into socially acceptable activities. A group of sexually-unfulfilled prison guards may well sublimate their sexual energy through aggressive and dominating behavior toward prisoners, and may encourage one another in this egregious behavior.

sociocentric wishful thinking: when those within a group unconsciously misinterpret facts in order to maintain their beliefs. Wishful thinking leads to false expectations, and usually involves seeing things more positively than is reasonable in a given situation. Military leaders who ignore relevant data that implies little chance of success in a military battle, and who send their troops to fight anyway (while merely hoping for the best), are engaging in sociocentric wishful thinking.

Test the Idea

See how many of these sociocentric defense mechanisms you can "prove" with examples from life—either from your own life or from news articles, books, people you know, etc.

Test the Idea

Look back at the examples used in this book thus far, and see if you can identify (potentially) any of these sociocentric defense mechanisms in those examples.

INTRINSIC COGNITIVE PROCESSES CAN SERVE RATIONAL, EGOCENTRIC, OR SOCIOCENTRIC AGENDAS

We can better understand egocentric and sociocentric thinking when we understand that many naturally-occurring cognitive processes can, on the one hand, enable us to do many things with our minds and, on the other hand, can work against us. For instance, humans have a remarkable capacity for figuring things out and working through highly complex issues. To do this, the mind naturally formulates assumptions upon which we can build our thinking; we must be able to take certain things for granted in order to figure other things out. When a builder is hired to build a house and receives blueprints from the architect or engineer, he takes a number of things for granted—that the owners have approved the house as designed, that the blueprints have been prepared using proper methods of design and calculation, that the slope of the land upon which the house will be built has been taken into account, and so on.

But just because we naturally generate assumptions doesn't mean we naturally generate *reasonable* or *justifiable* ones. We frequently generate assumptions that are faulty or biased. Building a space shuttle requires hundreds, if not thousands, of assumptions—about how the technology works that will be used in the shuttle, about the humans who will be operating it, about natural forces that may affect it, and so on. When a shuttle explodes without intention, some assumptions held when designing and/or deploying it will have been faulty. Something will have been taken for granted that should have been questioned.

As mentioned, we often generate assumptions that are egocentric in orientation, and that enable us to hold onto a viewpoint that feels comfortable (assumptions such as: *It's true because I believe it. It's true because I want to believe it*). This natural egocentric tendency to generate assumptions that shield us from seeing unpleasant realities is an inherent part of sociocentric thinking as well. In groups, we often generate assumptions that are unreasonable or unjustifiable. We validate one another in holding to these assumptions and the viewpoints they engender. Many of these assumptions have been the focus of this book. Here are some we have already considered, as well as some new ones:

- It's true because we want to believe it.
- It's true because it makes our group look good.
- It's true because it leads to our group getting what we want.
- It's true because everyone in my group believes it.
- If I go along with those in power, I will be taken care of.
- If I dissent from the group, I will be ostracized, which I can't tolerate.
- If we want to be in control, we must keep the people ignorant.
- My self-worth comes from being validated by others.

In addition to the mind naturally generating assumptions, it engages in many other cognitive processes. At any given moment, any of these processes can be under the "direction" of egocentric, sociocentric, or rational thought. These processes include: making inferences and coming to conclusions, gathering information, formulating purposes and questions, thinking through implications, formulating concepts and theories, interpreting ideas, synthesizing ideas, contrasting and comparing ideas, and so on.[52]

---

52 In this book I have dealt primarily with barriers to good reasoning or rational thought. To learn more about how to intervene in thought and thereby improve it, see *Critical Thinking: Tools for Taking Charge of your Professional and Personal Life* by Richard Paul and Linda Elder (2014). Also see *The Thinker's Guide to Analytic Thinking* by Linda Elder and Richard Paul (2016); Tomales, CA: Foundation for Critical Thinking Press.

CHAPTER SIX
ENVISIONING CRITICAL SOCIETIES

As I have heretofore pointed out, though human thought naturally tends toward egocentricity or sociocentricity, it is possible to cultivate rational, reasonable thought. By implication, it is possible to create fairminded critical societies. A fairminded critical society is a community of people who live in harmony through mutual respect and concern for the welfare of all its members. Those living in such societies seek not only the good for their own members, but that of the broader civilization, other species, and the earth. They recognize critical thinking as necessary to the creation and maintenance of critical societies. Critical societies are cultures that continually develop and improve, because people within these societies routinely question practices and customs in seeking ever-more rational and reasonable ways of living. A distinguishing characteristic of critical societies is recognizing that *critical thinking— clear, accurate, fairminded thinking*—is essential to emancipating the mind, to advancing just practices, and to preserving and enhancing life on Earth.

> A distinguishing characteristic of critical societies is recognizing that *critical thinking— clear, accurate, fairminded thinking*—is essential to emancipating the mind, to advancing just practices, and to preserving and enhancing life on Earth.

If we are to achieve critical societies, it is important to consider a host of interrelated realities. In this section, I will deal in some detail with these realities, and in so doing will begin to lay out a conception of a critical society for your consideration. Of course, this conception needs to be developed, and will be developed, should such societies actually emerge over time. In any case, we should not expect them to emerge in the next century to any significant degree, given the natural tendencies of the human mind and the current state of human affairs.

CULTIVATING CRITICAL THINKING IS THE KEY TO FAIRMINDED CRITICAL SOCIETIES

To envision a critical society, imagine a world in which problems are routinely solved through reasoning based on openmindedness and mutual respect, rather than on vested interest and power. Imagine a world that protects maximum freedoms and liberties, a world free from hunger and homelessness, a world in which people work to understand the viewpoints of others, especially those with whom they disagree. Imagine a world in which people are encouraged to think for themselves, rather than to mindlessly conform.

To comprehend these possibilities, we must also be able to imagine a world in which, from the beginning of life, people are intensely and routinely focused on understanding the faults in thinking that cause most of the problems we face—in our relationships, in our work, and in every other part of our lives. We must begin to take thinking seriously, each of us, as a routine matter of fact. When we do so, we can begin to systematically foster critical societies. We can begin to emancipate the mind.

The long and the short of it is that to fix the problems looming before us, there is one thing we must get command of—our thinking. Everything we do is determined, usually to a large extent, by our thinking. Consider these implications of thinking: When we divert waterways for irrigation, we do so because we *think* the positive implications of doing so outweigh its negative implications. When we dump pollutants into the oceans, we do so because we *think* the oceans can absorb the waste. When we create unjust laws, we do so because we *think* that being tough on crime significantly deters it. When we send our children to schools that fail to teach them basic intellectual skills, we do so because we *think* that teachers know best. When we send our parents and grandparents to end their lives in nursing homes, we do so because we *think* there are no other feasible options. When we torture for state purposes (or for "security," "liberty," or any other manufactured reason), we do so because we *think* the agenda of the state precedes the ethical rights of those being tortured (and because we *think* it will produce reliable information).

> If we are ever to create critical societies, thinking and the problematics of thinking must become routine objects of our thought.

Critical societies can and will emerge only to the extent that people take a *primary interest* in their own thinking, and in the thinking of others. Critical societies will emerge when people come to recognize thinking as a complex phenomenon that must be routinely illuminated, discussed, and critiqued in every relationship, family, business, organization, field, discipline, and indeed in every part of human life.

In short, because the human mind is naturally riddled with problems, the creation of critical societies depends on people within societies taking thinking seriously, studying its problems, its tricks and stratagems, its weaknesses and strengths, its native tendencies, and its rational capacities.

If we are ever to create critical societies, then, thinking and its problematics must become routine objects of our thought.

CRITICAL THINKING IS LARGELY IGNORED IN TODAY'S SOCIETIES

Since thinking is at the heart of every human action (because everything we do is either determined or influenced by our thinking), there is no more important set of skills, abilities, and dispositions to develop than those of the critical mind. To create critical societies we must begin—as a species, across countries, religions, genders, and races—to take thinking seriously. We must begin to address it as we address the development of complex skill sets in any domain of life, such as training as an athlete, learning to play an instrument, and other areas of life requiring disciplined, routine, committed practice to achieve a given skill set. We must assume that improvement will occur only incrementally, throughout many years, and will depend on daily practice driven by sheer grit and determination.

> People with untrained minds should no more expect to think clearly and logically than those people who have never learnt and never practiced can expect to find themselves good carpenters, golfers, bridge-players, or pianists.
>
> —*A.E. Mander*

At present, little attention is given to the *thinking* that underlies our decisions, actions, emotions, and desires. Though every field and subject of study presupposes skilled, disciplined thought, few people within any field *think about the thinking* at the heart of their disciplines. Few explicitly concern themselves with the thinking that determines the questions they ask and the assumptions at the root of their thinking; few are aware of the concepts that determine the information they consider and the conclusions they draw; few realize they have developed points of view from which they examine issues within their fields of study and that, hence, those viewpoints might be reasonably questioned like any other.

20 BARRIERS TO CRITICAL SOCIETIES

To illustrate the fact that we as humans tend not to take thinking seriously in today's cultures, consider the following 20 barriers to critical societies. Most people:

1. are only superficially aware of critical thinking.
2. cannot clearly articulate the ideal of critical thinking, know of it only as a positive buzz term, and, in any case, habitually violate its standards, and in multiple ways. Most humans, in other words, have not aspired to the ideal of critical thought, and most who have done so (having only an implicit idea of it) have succeeded only modestly.
3. uncritically accept the traditional, mainstream views and beliefs of their culture.
4. are "culture bound" (enslaved within social conventions).
5. uncritically accept the views of authority figures.
6. are not aware of, and do not attempt to explicitly use, intellectual standards in their thinking.
7. do not understand human thinking (their own or others') or the impediments to reasonability.
8. (unconsciously) believe much that is arbitrary or irrational.
9. uncritically accept bureaucratic rules, procedures, and formulas.
10. accept a variety of forms of authoritarianism (such as blindly following a religious ideology).
11. are uncreative and unoriginal.
12. are trapped in their social class.
13. never come to think well within any subject, and have no sense of what it is to think beyond subject-matter compartments.
14. do not believe in freedom of thought and speech, or in a wide range of other inalienable freedoms.
15. are biased on questions of gender, culture, species, and politics.
16. use their intellects only superficially.
17. have little command over their primitive emotions and desires; rather, they tend to be at the mercy of their own irrational impulses and passions.
18. do not value true spontaneity, naturalness, or artlessness.
19. are unable and/or unwilling to think within the viewpoints of others who hold a different worldview.
20. are unable to achieve self-actualization, self-command, or enlightenment, because they lack command of their thoughts and understanding of the relationship between thoughts and emotions.

Test the Idea

Go through the above list of barriers to critical societies and ask yourself this question: to what extent do you, or those in your group(s), fall prey to these barriers?

Test the Idea

See if you can add to my list of barriers to critical societies.

In 1936, in a book titled *Clearer Thinking*, A. E. Mander (1936; 1938) conceptualized the development of thinking as requiring training and discipline, and as entailing skills that must be practiced over time. He says:

> *Thinking is skilled work. It is not true that we are naturally endowed with the ability to think clearly and logically—without learning how, or without practicing than those people who have never learnt and never practiced can expect to find themselves good carpenters, golfers, bridge-players, or pianists. Yet our world is full of people who apparently do suppose that thinking is entirely unskilled work; that thinking clearly and accurately is so easy and so "natural" that "anybody can think"; and that any person's thinking is quite as reliable as any other person's. This accounts for the fact that, as a people, we are so much less efficient in this respect than we are in our sports. For nobody assumes that any game is so easy that we are all first-class players "naturally," without having to learn how to play or without practice (p. vii).*

Thus the first and most important characteristic of a critical society is that thinking is taken seriously and studied carefully. Consistently high-quality reasoning is understood to entail an integrated, agreed-upon, explicit set of skills, abilities, and traits that must be developed over time through committed practice.[53]

CRITICAL SOCIETIES SUPPORT MAXIMUM FREEDOMS

Because humans will always be social creatures, what we need is what might be termed a *socio-egalitarian* orientation—a worldview that values and affirms equal rights for all, that does not favor one's own group over others, and that

---

53 For an overview of the explicit tools in a substantive conception of critical thinking, see Richard Paul and Linda Elder's *The Miniature Guide to Critical Thinking Concepts and Tools* (2014), and *The Thinker's Guide to Analytic Thinking* (2016), Tomales, CA: Foundation for Critical Thinking Press.

consistently and actively pursues fair treatment of any and all creatures. We might juxtapose the term sociocentric with *criticocentric*, the latter referring to groups that truly and deeply value critical thinking.

Critical societies, then, take seriously the importance of human freedoms. Such societies simultaneously cultivate and systematically reward many forms of freedoms, including freedom of thought, freedom of speech, freedom of religion, freedom of movement, political freedom, economic freedom, intellectual freedom, freedom to learn, freedom to dissent, academic freedom, freedom of peaceful assembly and association, freedom to participate in government, sexual freedom, freedom from inhumane treatment, and the freedom to maintain one's own privacy. Each of these freedoms supports one another. And most are presupposed in the others. Their coexistence becomes a powerful underlying dynamic for moving from the narrow provincialism now prevalent in human societies to cosmopolitan internationalism, and from the vulgar dogmatic worldviews now pervasive to cultivated ethical worldviews now so rare.

> If we cannot freely and openly discuss ideas of every kind—ideas that critique the way things are in our societies, ideas that call into question mainstream views, ideas that may even undermine the status quo—it cannot be said that we live in a free society.

One of the most valued characteristics of critical societies is freedom of thought. Freedom of thought presupposes freedom of speech. If we cannot freely and openly discuss ideas of every kind—ideas that critique the way things are in our societies, ideas that call into question mainstream views, ideas that may even undermine the status quo—it cannot be said that we live in a free society. If we cannot dissent without being stereotyped, typecast, pigeon-holed, and marginalized—if we cannot openly disagree with, oppose, contest, and resist irrational and unfair laws and rules—we are not a free society.

In the early nineteenth century, H. L. Mencken (1923), arguably the most distinguished journalist in U.S. history, illuminated the importance of allowing maximum individual freedoms. He said:

> *I believe in liberty. And when I say liberty, I mean the thing in its widest imaginable sense—liberty up to the extreme limits of the feasible and tolerable. I am against forbidding anybody to do anything, or say anything, or think anything so long as it is at all possible to imagine a habitable world in which he would be free to do, say, and think it. The burden of proof, as I see it, is always upon the policeman, which is to say, upon the lawmaker, the theologian, the right-thinker. He must prove his case doubly, triply, quadruply, and then he must start all over and prove it again. The eye through which I view him is watery and jaundiced. I do not pretend to be "just" to him—any more than a Christian pretends to be just to the devil. He is the enemy of everything I admire and respect in this world—of everything*

that makes it various and amusing and charming. He impedes every honest search for the truth. He stands against every sort of good-will and common decency. His ideal is that of an animal trainer, an archbishop, a major general in the army. I am against him until the last galoot's ashore.

John Stuart Mill feared the conformity prevalent among the majority of people—what he saw as sheeplike uniformity that imposed narrow, parochial views and arbitrary rules on those more enlightened. On Mill's view, a critical society would entail freedom of thought, freedom of speech, and the protection of other fundamental human rights. In speaking of human freedom, in his classic essay *On Liberty*, Mill (1859; 1997) writes:

It comprises, first, the inward domain of consciousness; demanding liberty of conscience in the most comprehensive sense; liberty of thought and feeling; absolute freedom of opinion and sentiment on all subjects, practical or speculative, scientific, moral, or theological. The liberty of expressing and publishing opinions ... is practically inseparable from it. Second, the principle requires liberty of tastes and pursuits; of framing the plan of our life to suit our own character; of doing as we like, subject to such consequences as may follow; without impediment from our fellow-creatures, so long as what we do does not harm them, even though they should think our conduct foolish, perverse, or wrong ... No society in which these liberties are not, on the whole respected, is free, whatever may be its form of government; and none is completely free in which they do not exist absolute and unqualified. The only freedom which deserves the name is that of pursuing our own good in our own way, so long as we do not attempt to deprive others of theirs, or impede their efforts to obtain it.

Intellectual freedom—the freedom to think for oneself, to determine what to believe and what to reject on one's own, using disciplined thought—is a hallmark of the critical society.

If all mankind minus one were of one opinion, and only one person were of the contrary opinion, mankind would be no more justified in silencing that one person, than he, if he had the power, would be justified in silencing mankind ... the peculiar evil of silencing the expression of an opinion is, that it is robbing the human race; posterity as well as the existing generation; those who dissent from the opinion, still more than those who hold it. If the opinion is right, they are deprived of the opportunity of exchanging error for truth; if wrong, they lose, what is almost as great a benefit, the clearer perception and livelier impression of truth, produced by its collision with error.

We can never be sure that the opinion we are endeavoring to stifle is a false opinion; and if we were sure, stifling it would be an evil still. First: the opinion which it is attempted to suppress by authority may possibly be true. Those who desire to suppress it, of course, deny its truth; but they are not infallible. They have no authority to decide the question for all mankind, and exclude every other person from the means of judging. To refuse a hearing to an opinion, because they are sure it is false, is assuming that their certainty is the same thing as absolute certainty. All silencing of discussion is an assumption of infallibility ... on any matter not self-evident, there are ninety-nine persons incapable of judging of it for one who is capable; and the capacity of the hundredth person is only comparative; for the majority of the eminent men of every past generation held many opinions now known to be erroneous, and did or approved numerous things which no one will now justify (p. 50–56).

Bertrand Russell (1957) emphasized the importance of open and free inquiry to rational societies. He stressed the need to create education systems that foster the fairminded pursuit of knowledge and warned of the dangers implicit in dogmatic ideologies:

The conviction that it is important to believe this or that, even if a free inquiry would not support the belief, is one which is common to almost all religions and which inspires all systems of state education. ... A habit of basing convictions upon evidence, and of giving to them only that degree of certainty which the evidence warrants, would, if it became general, cure most of the ills from which the world is suffering. But at present, in most countries, education aims at preventing the growth of such a habit, and men who refuse to profess belief in some system of unfounded dogmas are not considered suitable as teachers of the young. ... The world that I should wish to see would be one freed from the virulence of group hostilities and capable of realizing that happiness for all is to be derived rather from cooperation than from strife. I should wish to see a world in which education aimed at mental freedom rather than at imprisoning the minds of the young in a rigid armor of dogma calculated to protect them through life against the shafts of impartial evidence. The world needs open hearts and open minds, and it is not through rigid systems, whether old or new, that these can be derived. ...

I do not think there can be any defense for the view that knowledge is ever undesirable. I should not put barriers in the way of the acquisition of knowledge by anybody at any age. A person is much less likely to act wisely when he is ignorant than when he is instructed ... (pp. vi–vii, 27–29).

CRITICAL SOCIETIES ENCOURAGE INTELLECTUAL AUTONOMY AND RESPONSIBILITY

The creation of critical societies presupposes not only maximum freedoms, but an explicit and pervasive emphasis on disciplining the mind, including fostering individual responsibility and intellectual autonomy.

In his book *Ideas and Opinions*, Albert Einstein (1954) discusses the importance of intellectual autonomy to the creation of critical societies, and the problem of mindless conformity to group influences:

> *Only the individual can think, and thereby create new values for society, nay, even set up new moral standards to which the life of the community conforms. Without creative personalities able to think and judge independently, the upward development of society is as unthinkable as the development of the community. … In politics not only are leaders lacking, but the independence of spirit and the sense of justice of the citizen have to a great extent declined. … In two weeks the sheeplike masses of any country can be worked up by the newspapers into such a state of excited fury that men are prepared to put on uniforms and kill and be killed … the present manifestations of decadence are explained by the fact that economic and technologic developments have highly intensified the struggle for existence, greatly to the detriment of the free development of the individual … there is such a thing as a spirit of the times, an attitude of mind characteristic of a particular generation, which is passed on from individual to individual and gives its distinctive mark to a society. Each of us has to do his little bit toward transforming this spirit of the times. … Let every man judge by himself, by what he has himself read, not by what others tell him (pp. 15, 29–30).*

> In two weeks the sheeplike masses of any country can be worked up by the newspapers into such a state of excited fury that men are prepared to put on uniforms and kill and be killed …
>
> — *Albert Einstein*

In an open letter to the *Society for Social Responsibility in Science*, Einstein (1954) emphasized the importance of independence of mind to living an ethical life and creating a civilized world, even when this means defying the laws or expectations of society:

> *The problem of how man should act if his government prescribes actions or society expects an attitude which his own conscience considers wrong is indeed an old one. It is easy to say that the individual cannot be held responsible for acts carried out under irresistible compulsion, because the individual is fully dependent upon the society in which he is living and therefore must accept its rules. But the very formulation of this idea*

makes it obvious to what extent such a concept contradicts our sense of justice. External compulsion can, to a certain extent, reduce but never cancel the responsibility of the individual. In the Nuremberg trials this idea was considered to be self-evident. Whatever is morally important in our institutions, laws, and mores, can be traced back to interpretation of the sense of justice of countless individuals. Institutions are in a moral sense impotent unless they are supported by the sense of responsibility of living individuals. An effort to arouse and strengthen this sense of responsibility of the individual is an important service to mankind (p. 27).

Intellectual freedom—the freedom to think for oneself, to determine what to believe and what to reject on one's own using disciplined thought—is essential to the critical society. It requires open access to, and free exchange of, information. It enables us to see through indoctrination and propaganda. It requires a host of interrelated freedoms that must be protected.

CRITICAL SOCIETIES ENTAIL THE FOLLOWING SIX HALLMARKS

We can now summarize six hallmarks of a critical society. Critical societies will develop only to the extent that these dimensions are present. Each overlaps with, and illuminates, all the others.

1. **Critical thinking is highly valued when people in the culture:**

> Critical societies protect maximum freedoms, while fostering the development of autonomous intellectual skills and abilities.

- see critical thinking as essential to living reasonably, rationally, and fruitfully.
- come to understand, from an early age, that, generally speaking, the development of their thinking takes precedence over their development in every other skill area, because the quality of every part of their life, and their ability to live peacefully with other people, depends on the quality of their thinking.
- continue to develop the skills, abilities, and traits of the disciplined mind throughout life.
- understand that the development of critical thinking occurs in stages and in accordance with one's level of commitment and willingness to practice.
- are committed to becoming increasingly more skilled at fairminded critical thinking over time.
- recognize the importance of all people in societies learning to think critically, and work together to help one another develop intellectually.

2. The problematics in thinking are an abiding concern when people in the culture:

- recognize that everyone falls prey to mistakes in thinking, and therefore are constantly on the lookout for problems in their own thinking and in the thinking of others.
- systemically discourage closedmindedness and systematically encourage openmindedness.
- recognize egocentric and sociocentric thinking as significant barriers to critical thought.
- routinely study and diminish irrational thought.
- avoid manipulating, controlling, or using others to serve their selfish interests; avoid being manipulated, controlled, or used by others.
- recognize and guard against the natural tendencies of the human mind toward self-deception, rationalization, hypocrisy, conformism, intellectual arrogance, and other related pathologies.

3. Intellectual virtues are consistently fostered when people in the culture:

- think for themselves and avoid uncritically accepting the thinking or behavior of others.
- regularly and routinely enter the viewpoints of those with whom they disagree, in order to understand those viewpoints and to acknowledge any merit that might be found in them.
- encourage and foster multicultural worldviews; consider themselves citizens of the world, just as concerned with the well-being of all people on the planet as they are with the well-being of their own families, neighbors, societies, and countries.
- routinely and willingly engage in open, free discussion when reasoning through issues and problems.
- do not fear new ideas and ways of looking at things. Rather, they regularly think within ideas that may at first seem "strange" or "dangerous" in order to understand them.
- are not trapped in ideological systems.
- systematically apply the same standards to themselves as they do to others, expecting as much (or more) from themselves as they do of others.
- regularly seek and willingly admit to problems in their reasoning.
- regularly distinguish between what they know and don't know.
- believe deeply in the idea that their interests, and those of society, are best served by giving the freest play to reason.
- regularly examine their beliefs and are willing to publicly disagree with others on issues they have deeply thought through.
- persevere through the difficulties in issues and problems, using their best reasoning abilities; do not give up when faced with complexities in thought.
- communicate and relate with others through civility and mutual respect.

4. **Ethical reasoning is systematically fostered when people in the culture:**
- treat the rights and needs of others as equal to their own.
- do not use other people to serve their selfish interests.
- are routinely encouraged and expected to question the rules, mores, requirements, and taboos of the culture.
- are taught the important distinctions between ethics, social rules, laws, and religious belief systems.
- do not confuse theological beliefs and social rules with ethics.
- do not see their groups as superior to other groups in terms of fundamental human rights.
- do not perceive the rights of humans as superior to the rights of other sentient creatures.
- use intellectual skills and abilities for the betterment of people and sentient creatures across the world, not to serve power and vested interests.
- recognize the intimate connections between how we live today, the health of the planet, and the well-being of future generations.

5. **The analysis and assessment of reasoning are routinely used as primary tools for determining what to believe when people in the culture:**
- recognize the predominant role of reasoning in human thought—the fact that the main activity of the human mind is reasoning.
- recognize that all reasoning contains eight elements: it targets *purposes*, formulates *questions*, pursues *information*, makes *inferences*, begins with *assumptions*, is shaped by *concepts*, is guided by a *point of view*, and leads to *implications*.
- are skilled at analyzing thinking; routinely analyze their own and others' thinking in order to assess its quality.
- continually improve their ability to take thinking apart in order to better understand it and find potential flaws in it.
- routinely assess reasoning using universal intellectual standards such as *clarity, accuracy, relevance, breadth, depth, logic, precision,* and *fairness.*
- are keenly aware of the relationship between uses of language and the mind's conceptualizations, and routinely study connections between the two.
- do not use language to manipulate other people; do not allow other people to manipulate them through their use of language.
- recognize the important role of questions in living a rational life; recognize that thinking is driven by questions, that significant questions lead to significant understandings, and that superficial questions lead to superficial understandings.
- recognize that their points of view, assumptions, and conceptualizations guide the ways in which they interpret information and influence the conclusions they come to.

6. **Freedom of thought and action are protected when people in the culture:**

- work together to protect the maximum freedoms for all people.
- work together to minimize the number of laws in the society.
- do not allow irrational power—through systems of justice, the police, or government—to undermine human freedoms.

Hopefully it is apparent that the characteristics laid down in this section are merely a beginning place. When deeply understood, they serve as organizers for a much broader and more detailed conceptualization, yet to be developed, of a critical society. These understandings provide the scaffolding. Perhaps as significantly, they illuminate the distance between current thinking (and practices) and those that would exist in critical societies.

CONCEPTUALIZING EVERYDAY WAYS OF THINKING IN CRITICAL SOCIETIES

Human thinking is frequently a fundamental problem in human life. Yet this understanding is very little appreciated today. How would thinking be treated in critical societies? How would people relate to their own thinking? What role would self-reflection play in daily life? How would people cultivate their thinking? What would typical conversation entail?

Since thinking is at the heart of every human action, there is no more important set of skills, abilities, and dispositions to develop than those of the critical mind.

To begin, people in enlightened, fairminded critical societies would be keenly aware of the problems of egocentric and sociocentric thought in human life. Hence, they would be consistently on the lookout for these pathological tendencies in themselves. People would everyday be watchful for selfishness, self-deception, biases, and prejudices in their own thinking. In other words, people would look first to themselves for the roots of problems before pointing their fingers at others. Where truth was relevant, people would always attempt to seek it, wherever it might lead and however painful it might be to face. People would combat intrinsic pathologies of their own minds by creating and actively using intellectual strategies.

People would develop the ability to make "powerful intellectual moves" to achieve their goals, while also being deeply concerned with the well-being of the global village. People would routinely engage in disciplined, self-reflective analysis and assessment using the tools of critical thought. To improve their reasoning abilities, they would create inner dialogues that would help them better adhere to intellectual standards such as logicalness, reasonability, and fairness. People would bring to these dialogues a rich understanding of "pathologies of thought" in order to guard against them. People would routinely target the "elements of thought" to analyze their thinking. They would cultivate, within and among themselves, a deep commitment to living the examined life as Socrates perceived it.

Consider this example of the type of inner dialogue I envision. Imagine a situation in which you are arguing with your spouse. In a critical society, instead of assuming yourself to be correct, you would actively pursue potential problems in your thinking. Instead of automatically defending yourself as "in the right," you would recognize your defensiveness to be likely irrational. You would engage in this sort of self-reflective questioning consistently, perhaps many times a day:

> *Here is what I understand the issue to be. But am I seeing the information clearly? Am I failing to notice some information I don't want to see? Am I distorting what my spouse is saying in order to maintain my viewpoint? What will I gain by maintaining this position, this way of looking at the situation? What will I have to give up if I acknowledge information I would rather evade? What will I have to face about myself that I would like to hide from myself? What will I have to reveal to my spouse about myself that I would rather hide from him or her? What is the most truthful, disinterested, honest view of the situation? Why can't I seem to accept this truth? What if the problem is really my way of looking at the situation, not my spouse's?*

In critical societies, this process of self-reflection would be one of many strategies routinely used for combatting egocentric and sociocentric thought in everyday life. In such societies, people would understand that each of us is responsible for our thoughts and actions, and that to command one's mind entails developing unique strategies for oneself. When procrastinating on important matters, we would develop strategies for getting ourselves moving. When we were envious of others, we would face our envy, attempt to deeply understand it, and actively work to counteract it. When we were greedy, we would want to recognize our greed and then work to check this tendency. All of us share typical egocentric and sociocentric patterns; in critical societies, people would realize that these patterns can be played out in many different ways across the domains of their lives. They would look for the broad patterns that are problematic in all of us. They would seek the specific egocentric and sociocentric tendencies within themselves.

In critical societies, people would openly and honestly discuss thinking—their own thinking, the thinking of others, the thinking of authors, the thinking of politicians, the thinking of conservatives, the thinking of liberals, the thinking behind religious beliefs, and the thinking behind their fears, motivations, and actions. Imagine a situation in which a husband and wife disagree on how their children should be raised. In today's societies, in such circumstances, it is often the case that one or both parents become irrational in discussing parental issues. In critical societies, parents would frankly and fairmindedly discuss the issues; they would follow the evidence closely and carefully. Today, when one parent becomes unreasonable, the other often follows suit. This can lead to accusations, posturing, and blaming. In fairminded critical societies, people seek a better way of dealing with such conflicts, such as backing off and allowing the spouse time to reflect, or giving a counterargument based in sound reasoning while showing empathy for the spouse who is—at least at the moment—less rational and less in control of herself or himself.

Dialogical and dialectical reasoning would be the norm in critical societies. Richard Paul (1990; 2012) argues for the importance of such reasoning in schooling if we are to cultivate open minds. He says,

> Dialogical and dialectical thinking involves dialogue or extended exchange between different points of view or frames of reference. Both are multilogical (involving many logics) rather than monological (involving only one logic) because in both cases there is more than one line of reasoning to consider, more than one "logic" being formulated. Dialogue becomes dialectical when ideas or reasonings come into conflict with each other and we need to assess their various strengths and weaknesses. (p. 310)

Paul explains his conception of dialogical reasoning:

> Whenever students discuss their ideas, beliefs, or points of view with other students or the teacher; whenever students have to role play the thinking of others; whenever students have to use their thinking to figure out the thinking of another (say, that of the author of a textbook or of a story); whenever students have to listen carefully to the thoughts of another and try to make sense of them; whenever students, whether orally or in writing, have to arrange their thoughts in such a fashion as to be understood by another; whenever students have to enter sympathetically into the thinking of others or reason hypothetically from the assumptions of others, they are reasoning dialogically. (pp. 309-310)

Dialogical and dialectical reasoning, held to the perfections of thought such as clarity, accuracy, relevance, breadth, depth, logicalness, significance, sufficiency, and fairness, would run throughout daily discourse in fairminded critical societies. At present, very little attention is given to these standards.

Language and its role in human perceptions and actions would be a primary focus. People would realize that whenever they use language, they make conceptual decisions. If you say to a reasonable person, "every time you speak to me, you are rude," you are using language in a way that is sloppy and, hence, inaccurate. You make the decision to say "every time" rather than "some of the time" or "most of the time," either of which would likely be more accurate. By using the words "every time," you decide to stereotype the person. This enables you to discount what he or she says, and therefore avoid examining yourself and changing anything in your own behavior.

Rational dissent in critical societies would be encouraged. People would realize that open, honest, routine dialogue is essential is to the creation of fairminded critical societies. People would therefore not only be comfortable with reasoned disagreement, but encourage and seek it. They would have confidence in reason, or in other words, would assume that, in the final analysis, humans are best served by following the evidence objectively.

In sum, critical thinking would be the core concept in fairminded critical societies. The problematics in thinking would be a predominant and abiding concern. Thinking would be routinely discussed, in all contexts, to understand where it is going wrong and where it needs to be improved. People would study their own everyday use of language and begin to see how the words they formulate, and the sentences they use to explain situations and experiences, largely determine their perceptions of reality. People would at all times try to adhere to educated uses of words. People would study their neurotic, pathological tendencies and develop unique strategies for dealing with them. People would create inner dialogues and assess their inner thoughts using universal intellectual standards, rather than egocentric or sociocentric ones. People would encourage reasonable alternative ways of looking at situations and issues. People would recognize the difficulties in addressing complex issues, and would therefore avoid simplistic answers to complex problems.

These thoughts are only a beginning place for conceptualizing a world in which critical societies are encouraged and honored. Many issues would need to be worked out using our best collective thinking. Recognizing and addressing problems in thinking will not lead to a less complex world. Such complexities will have to be reasoned through, debated, and argued over, but always in a spirit of disinterested search for the truth—for the most egalitarian, the most emancipatory, and the most progressive ways to think and live.

USING THE TOOLS OF CRITICAL THINKING TO EMANCIPATE THE MIND

To cultivate the mind and develop as rational persons, we need tools—conceptual tools that we deeply internalize and use in everyday discourse, and in reasoning through everyday problems. To this point we have focused primarily on intrinsic barriers to fostering critical societies, namely, sociocentric and egocentric thought. When we deeply understand these barriers and are using these understandings to live better throughout life, we have cultivated, in our minds, intellectual tools for self-improvement. Hence, any powerful idea is a potential "tool" for intellectual development, but only if taken seriously.

Thus far, we have targeted a number of potential "tools" for emancipating the mind, mainly clustering around the constellations of egocentricity and sociocentricity. And, we have discussed some hallmarks of critical societies, all of which directly connect with specific tools for self-development and the cultivation of group thought.

All of the concepts targeted to this point represent essential understandings if one is to develop one's criticality, or one's capacity for critical or rational thought. But though deeply understanding egocentric and sociocentric tendencies is essential to the cultivation of critical societies, once these are identified, what then? How do we deal with these neurotic tendencies within us? How do we intervene in thought? What tools of mind are essential to human enlightenment? What intellectual tools must we cultivate in ourselves if we are to effectively interface with this complex, pathological, and often frightening world that humans have created?

It seems to me that the answer is critical thinking and a fierce passion to cultivate it in oneself. In this section, we will therefore consider, briefly, some further foundational concepts in critical thinking relevant to the advancement of fairminded critical societies. These ideas are the original work of Richard Paul, enhanced and developed by other Paulian scholars in critical thinking, including myself. They are presented on page 179 in diagrammatical form.

Why Critical Thinking?

The Problem: Everyone thinks; it is our nature to do so. But much of our thinking, left to itself, is biased, distorted, partial, uninformed, or down-right prejudiced. Yet the quality of our life and that of what we produce, make, or build depends precisely on the quality of our thought. Shoddy thinking is costly, both in money and in quality of life, as well as in terms of advancing fairminded critical societies. Excellence in thought, however, must be systematically cultivated.

A Definition: Critical thinking, in a rich sense of the term, is self-guided disciplined thought which attempts to reason at the highest level of quality in a fairminded way. People who think critically consistently attempt to live rationally, reasonably, and empathically. They are keenly aware of the inherently flawed nature of human thinking when left unchecked. They strive to diminish the power of their egocentric and sociocentric tendencies. They use the intellectual tools that critical thinking offers—concepts and principles that enable them to analyze, assess, and improve thinking. They realize that no matter how skilled they are as thinkers, they can always improve. They recognize that at times, they will fall prey to mistakes in reasoning—to irrationality, prejudices, biases, distortions, uncritically-accepted social rules and taboos, self-interest, and vested interest. They avoid thinking simplistically about complicated issues, and they strive to appropriately consider the rights and needs of others. They embody the Socratic principle: *the unexamined life is not worth living.* They are concerned with their own intellectual development, while taking into account and advancing the rights and needs of others. They want to contribute to the emancipation of all people and other sentient creatures.

The Result: A well-cultivated critical thinker:

- raises vital questions and problems, formulating them clearly and precisely;
- gathers and assesses relevant information, using abstract ideas to interpret it effectively;
- comes to well-reasoned conclusions and solutions, testing them against relevant criteria and standards;

- thinks openmindedly within alternative systems of thought, recognizing and assessing, as need be, their assumptions, implications, and practical consequences; and
- communicates effectively with others in figuring out solutions to complex problems.

Critical thinking is, in short, self-directed, self-disciplined, self-monitored, and self-corrective thinking. It requires rigorous standards of excellence and mindful command of their use. It entails effective communication and problem-solving abilities, and a commitment to overcoming our native egocentrism and sociocentrism.

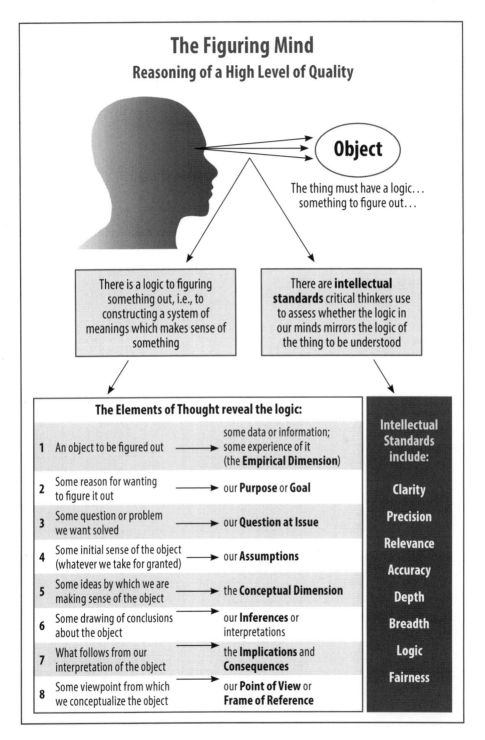

The Figuring Mind
Reasoning of a High Level of Quality

Object

The thing must have a logic…
something to figure out…

There is a logic to figuring something out, i.e., to constructing a system of meanings which makes sense of something

There are **intellectual standards** critical thinkers use to assess whether the logic in our minds mirrors the logic of the thing to be understood

The Elements of Thought reveal the logic:

1 An object to be figured out ⟶ some data or information; some experience of it (the **Empirical Dimension**)

2 Some reason for wanting to figure it out ⟶ our **Purpose** or **Goal**

3 Some question or problem we want solved ⟶ our **Question at Issue**

4 Some initial sense of the object (whatever we take for granted) ⟶ our **Assumptions**

5 Some ideas by which we are making sense of the object ⟶ the **Conceptual Dimension**

6 Some drawing of conclusions about the object ⟶ our **Inferences** or interpretations

7 What follows from our interpretation of the object ⟶ the **Implications** and **Consequences**

8 Some viewpoint from which we conceptualize the object ⟶ our **Point of View** or **Frame of Reference**

Intellectual Standards include:

Clarity

Precision

Relevance

Accuracy

Depth

Breadth

Logic

Fairness

Why the Analysis of Critical Thinking Is Important

If we want to think well, we must understand at least the rudaments of thought—the most basic structures out of which all thinking is created. We must learn how to take thinking apart.

All Thinking Is Defined by the Eight Elements That Make It Up

Eight basic structures are present in all thinking: Whenever we think, we think for a purpose, within a point of view, based on assumptions, leading to implications and consequences. We use concepts, ideas, and theories to interpret data, facts, and experiences in order to answer questions, solve problems, and resolve issues.

Thinking, then:

* generates purposes

* raises questions

* uses information

* utilizes concepts

* makes inferences

* makes assumptions

* generates implications

* embodies a point of view

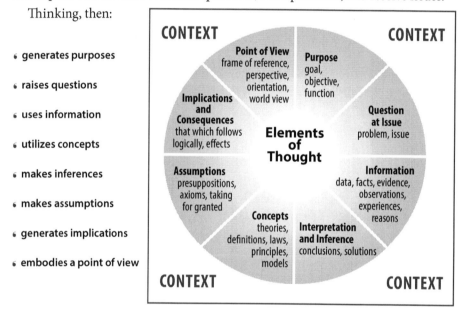

Each of these structures has implications for the others. If you change your purpose or agenda, you change your questions and problems. If you change your questions and problems, you are forced to seek new information and data. If you collect new information and data...

The Elements of Thought and Questions They Imply

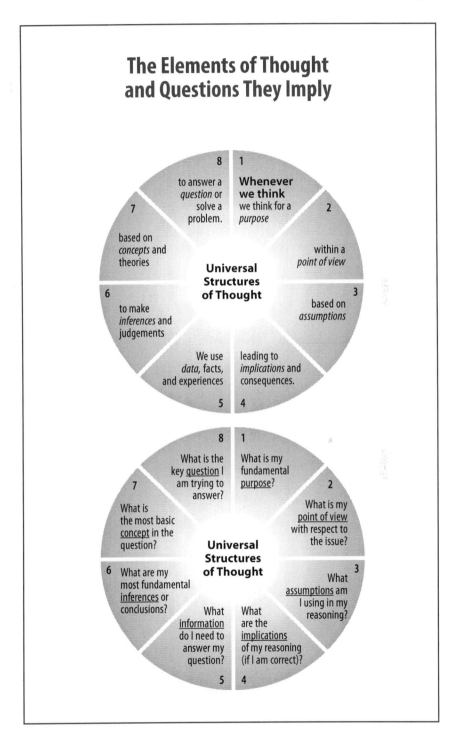

Universal Structures of Thought

1. Whenever we think we think for a *purpose*
2. within a *point of view*
3. based on *assumptions*
4. leading to *implications* and consequences.
5. We use *data*, facts, and experiences
6. to make *inferences* and judgements
7. based on *concepts* and theories
8. to answer a *question* or solve a problem.

Universal Structures of Thought

1. What is my fundamental purpose?
2. What is my point of view with respect to the issue?
3. What assumptions am I using in my reasoning?
4. What are the implications of my reasoning (if I am correct)?
5. What information do I need to answer my question?
6. What are my most fundamental inferences or conclusions?
7. What is the most basic concept in the question?
8. What is the key question I am trying to answer?

To Evaluate Thinking We Must Understand and Apply Intellectual Standards

Reasonable people judge reasoning through intellectual standards. When you internalize these standards and explicitly use them in your thinking, your thinking becomes more clear, accurate, precise, relevant, deep, broad and fair.* You should note that we focus here on a selection of standards. Among others are credibility, sufficiency, reliability, and practicality. Some powerful questions that employ these standards are listed on the following page.

Clarity:
understandable; the meaning can be grasped

Accuracy:
free from errors or distortions; true

Precision:
exact to the necessary level of detail

Relevance:
relating to the matter at hand

Depth:
containing complexities and multiple interrelationships

Breadth:
encompassing multiple viewpoints

Logic:
the parts make sense together; no contradictions

Significance:
focusing on the important; not trivial

Fairness:
justifiable; not self-serving or one-sided

* For a deeper look at intellectual standards, see *The Thinker's Guide to Intellectual Standards* by Linda Elder and Richard Paul (2008), Tomales, CA: Foundation for Critical Thinking Press.

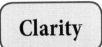

Clarity
Could you elaborate further?
Could you give me an example?
Could you illustrate what you mean?

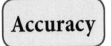

Accuracy
How could we check on that?
How could we find out if that is true?
How could we verify or test that?

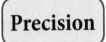

Precision
Could you be more specific?
Could you give me more details?
Could you be more exact?

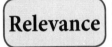

Relevance
How does that relate to the problem?
How does that bear on the question?
How does that help us with the issue?

Depth
What factors make this a difficult problem?
What are some of the complexities of this question?
What are some of the difficulties we need to deal with?

Breadth
Do we need to look at this from another perspective?
Do we need to consider another point of view?
Do we need to look at this in other ways?

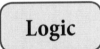

Logic
Does all this make sense together?
Does your first paragraph fit in with your last?
Does what you say follow from the evidence?

Significance
Is this the most important problem to consider?
Is this the central idea to focus on?
Which of these facts are most important?

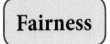

Fairness
Do I have any vested interest in this issue?
Am I sympathetically representing the viewpoints of others?

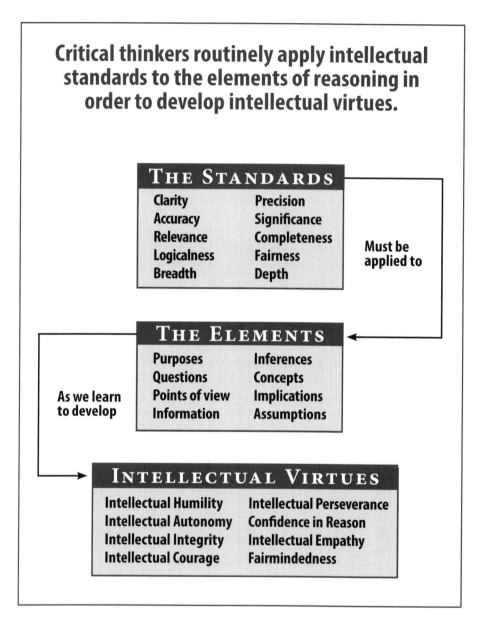

Critical Thinkers Commit Themselves to the Development of Intellectual Virtues

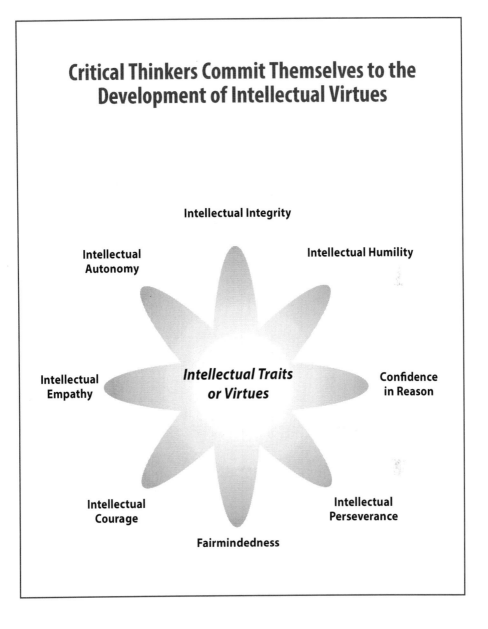

Essential Intellectual Traits

Intellectual Humility   vs Intellectual Arrogance

Having consciousness of the limits of one's knowledge, including a sensitivity to circumstances in which one's native egocentrism is likely to function self-deceptively; sensitivity to bias, prejudice, and the limitations of one's viewpoint. Intellectual humility depends on recognizing that one should not claim more than one actually knows. It does not imply spinelessness or submissiveness. It implies the lack of intellectual pretentiousness, boastfulness, or conceit, combined with insight into the logical foundations, or lack of such foundations, of one's beliefs.

Intellectual Courage   vs Intellectual Cowardice

Having consciousness of the need to face and fairly address ideas, beliefs, or viewpoints toward which we have strong negative emotions and to which we have not given a serious hearing. This courage is connected with the recognition that ideas considered dangerous or absurd are sometimes rationally justified (in whole or in part), and that conclusions and beliefs inculcated in us are sometimes false or misleading. To determine for ourselves which is which, we must not passively and uncritically "accept" what we have "learned." Intellectual courage comes into play here, because inevitably we will come to see some truth in some ideas considered dangerous and absurd, and distortion or falsity in some ideas strongly-held in our social group. We need courage to be true to our own thinking in such circumstances. The penalties for nonconformity can be severe.

Intellectual Empathy   vs Intellectual Narrowmindedness

Having consciousness of the need to imaginatively put oneself in the place of others in order to genuinely understand them, which requires awareness of our egocentric tendency to identify truth with our immediate perceptions of long-standing thought or belief. This trait correlates with the ability to reconstruct accurately the viewpoints and reasoning of others, and to reason from premises, assumptions, and ideas other than our own. This trait also correlates with the willingness to remember occasions when we were wrong in the past despite an intense conviction that we were right, and with the ability to imagine our being similarly deceived in a case-at-hand.

Intellectual Autonomy   vs Intellectual Conformity

Having rational control of one's beliefs, values, and inferences. The ideal of critical thinking is to learn to think for oneself, to gain command over one's thought processes. It entails a commitment to analyzing and evaluating beliefs on the basis of reason and evidence, to questioning when it is rational to question, to believing when it is rational to believe, and to conforming when it is rational to conform.

Intellectual Integrity   vs Intellectual Hypocrisy

Recognition of the need to be true to one's own thinking, to be consistent in the intellectual standards one applies, to hold one's self to the same rigorous standards of evidence and proof to which one holds one's antagonists, to practice what one advocates for others, and to honestly admit discrepancies and inconsistencies in one's own thought and action.

Intellectual Perseverance   vs Intellectual Laziness

Having consciousness of the need to use intellectual insights and truths in spite of difficulties, obstacles, and frustrations; firm adherence to rational principles despite the irrational opposition of others; a sense of the need to struggle with confusion and unsettled questions over an extended period of time to achieve deeper understanding or insight.

Confidence in Reason   vs Distrust of Reason and Evidence

Confidence that, in the long run, one's own higher interests and those of humankind at large will be best served by giving the freest play to reason, by encouraging people to come to their own conclusions through development of their own rational faculties; faith that, with proper encouragement and cultivation, people can learn to think for themselves, form rational viewpoints, draw reasonable conclusions, think coherently and logically, persuade each other by reason, and become reasonable persons, despite deep-seated obstacles in the native character of the human mind and in society as we know it.

Fairmindedness   vs Intellectual Unfairness

Having consciousness of the need to treat all viewpoints alike, without reference to one's own feelings or vested interests, or the feelings or vested interests of one's friends, community, or nation; implies adherence to intellectual standards without reference to one's own advantage or the advantage of one's group.

The Mind's Three Distinctive Functions

The mind has three basic functions:
thinking, feeling, and wanting.

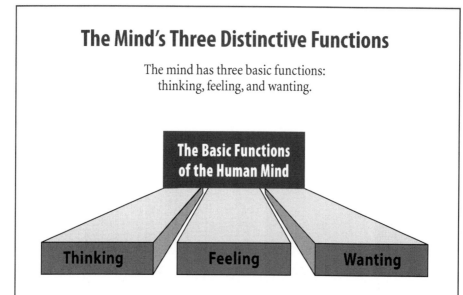

- <u>Thinking</u> is the part of the mind that figures things out. It makes sense of life's events. It creates the ideas through which we define situations, relationships, and problems. It continually tells us: "This is what is going on." "This is what is happening." "Notice this and that."

- <u>Feelings</u>* are created by thinking — evaluating whether the events of our lives are positive or negative. Feelings continually tell us: "This is how I should feel about what is happening in my life. I'm doing really well." Or, alternatively, "Things aren't going well for me."

- Our <u>desires</u> allocate energy to action, in keeping with what we define as desirable and possible. It continually tells us: "This is worth getting. Go for it!" Or, conversely, "This is not worth getting. Don't bother."

---

* When I speak of feelings, I am not referring to emotions caused by dysfunctional biological processes such as problems in brain chemistry. When emotions are caused by imbalances in brain chemistry which people cannot control themselves, clinical help may be needed. When I speak of feelings, I am also not referring to bodily sensations, though feelings often accompany bodily sensations. For instance being "cold" might cause you to feel irritable. Recognizing the feeling of irritability might lead you to do something about being cold, like putting on a jacket. Finally, though the terms "feelings" and "emotions" might be used in some cases to refer to different phenomena, I use these terms interchangeably in this guide.

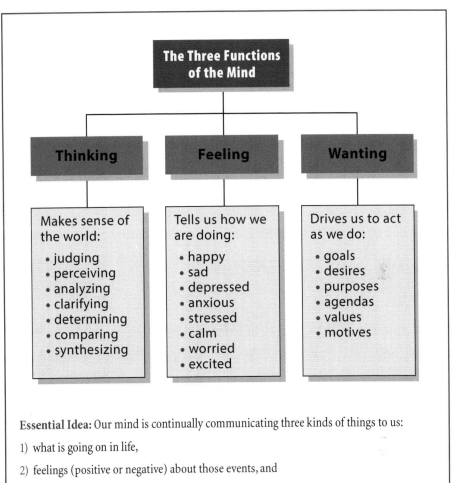

The Three Functions of the Mind

Thinking

Makes sense of the world:
- judging
- perceiving
- analyzing
- clarifying
- determining
- comparing
- synthesizing

Feeling

Tells us how we are doing:
- happy
- sad
- depressed
- anxious
- stressed
- calm
- worried
- excited

Wanting

Drives us to act as we do:
- goals
- desires
- purposes
- agendas
- values
- motives

Essential Idea: Our mind is continually communicating three kinds of things to us:

1) what is going on in life,

2) feelings (positive or negative) about those events, and

3) things to pursue, i.e., where to put our energy (in light of 1 and 2).

Thinking as the Key to Feelings and Desires

Though thoughts, feelings, and desires play equally important roles in the mind, continually influencing and being influenced by one another, thinking is the key to command of feelings and desires. To change a feeling is to change the thinking that leads to the feeling. To change a desire is to change the thinking that underlies the desire.

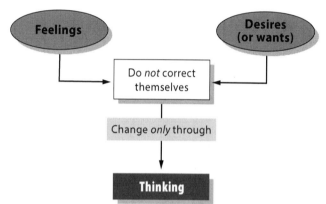

If I feel angry because my child is behaving disrespectfully toward me, I can't simply replace anger with satisfaction, for example. To change the anger to a more positive emotion, I must change the thinking I am doing in the situation. Perhaps I need to think about how to teach my child to behave respectfully towards me, and then behave in accordance with that new thinking. Perhaps I need to think about the influences in my child's life that might be causing the rude behavior, and then try to eliminate those influences. In other words, I get control of my emotional state through my thinking.

Similarly, we can't change a desire without changing the thinking that causes the desire. Suppose two people, Jan and John, have been in a romantic relationship, but John has broken off the relationship. Yet, Jan still wants to be in the relationship. Suppose her desire comes from thinking (perhaps unconsciously) that she needs to be in the relationship to be emotionally stable, and that she won't be able to function without John. Clearly this thinking is the problem. Jan must therefore change her thinking so she no longer wants a relationship with John. In other words, until she thinks that she does not need John to be OK, that she can function satisfactorily without him, and that she doesn't need to be in a relationship with a person who doesn't want to be with her, she will want to be in the relationship with John. Unless her thinking changes, her desire won't change. She must defeat the thinking that is defeating her.

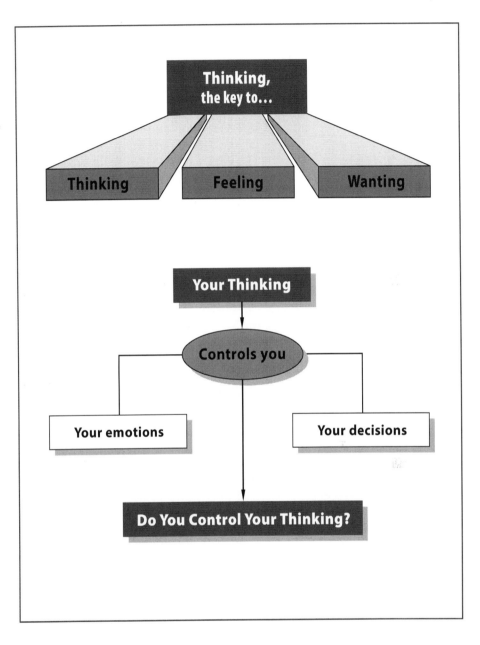

CONCLUSION:
SOME ELEMENTS OF CRITICAL SOCIETIES CAN BE FOUND THROUGHOUT HUMAN HISTORY

Threads of criticality can be traced to the beginning of recorded history. From an anthropologic view, evidence of critical thought goes back much further, tens of thousands of years and more (consider the complex tools humans crafted long before the development of written language). Among the earliest written documents, the Homeric poems (circa 8th century BCE) reveal some beginning links to fairminded criticality. For instance, in *The Iliad*, Achilles, a mythological Greek hero of the Trojan war, "saw the Achaeans in their deathroes and had compassion upon them." In another passage, Achilles "scowled at [Agamemnon] and answered, 'You are steeped in insolence and lust of gain.'" [54] These passages reveal that more than 2,500 years ago, at least some people were distinguishing compassionate from uncompassionate thought and action, insolence from respect, and greed from moderation—all of which are important distinctions in ethical reasoning (and hence fairminded critical thought).

Still, much of what we find in these poems is connected not with ethical reasoning, but with attempts by people to live in accordance with a mythological god's wishes in order to reap some "benefit" bestowed by the god—like getting more land and wealth through expansionist wars, accumulating more people for slave labor, or capturing wives of foreign warriors and handing them out as prizes to the home ("valiant") warriors.

In short, much of what is found in these earliest Homeric poems advances a conception not of fairminded, or *strong-sense,* critical thinking, but of *weak-sense* critical thinking—on getting "more for me and my group" through any means possible, including and most especially the gods. Hesiod, in *Works and Days* (circa 7th or 6th century BCE), says: "Zeus himself ordained law for mankind. As for fishes and beasts and winged fowls, they may feed on one another without sin, for justice is unknown to them. But to man he gave the law of justice." In this passage, Hesiod implies that humans, unlike other animals, have been given laws by which to live justly or fairly. Notwithstanding the fact that these laws have been "given" by the god Zeus, still the reference to justice in this passage is significant; it illuminates early discussions on ethics, however primitive.

Multiple forces contributed to advancements in critical thought beginning around the 5th century BCE. Greece was experiencing the first democratic process in recorded history. Citizens of Athens (excluding slaves and women) were encouraged to openly express their views, to discuss and debate, and to argue and disagree. Men voted on issues large and small. From this fledgling democracy emerged a way of life that stimulated people to take command of their own government through dialogical and dialectical reasoning. People began to more

---

54 Both quotes from *The Iliad, Book I*, as found in *Great Books of the Western World*, Chicago: Encyclopaedia Britannica, Inc. 1952, pp. 3-4.

openly question nature and how it worked, the received views on the mythological gods, and the decisions of their rulers. With a growing political tolerance for dialogue and open debate, "scholars" in various parts of Greece began teaching the Homeric poems and Hesiodic texts, encouraging various interpretations of them. Small groups of scholars sprang up around Greece. Once recorded, the Homeric and Hesiodic texts would, we can infer, begin to be more closely scrutinized than when in oral form.

The Pre-Socratics (6th and 5th centuries BCE), among the Greeks' earliest intellectuals, were predominantly concerned with questions about the universe, about nature, and about mathematics and its relationship with the natural world. These philosophers are remembered through fragments of their own writing and that of later philosophers. Though much of these works focus on metaphysics, often amalgamated with mathematics, science, and what we now term astrology, we can find among these works some important references to ethical thought. In Electra, Sophocles appeals to Apollo: " ... I bow before thee and with deep humility beg and implore: aid our deliberations by thy foresight, and reveal to us what is right and what is wrong for men to do."[55] This passage seems to imply a search for clear-cut ethical concepts and principles. Pythagoras prohibited his followers from killing and eating animals because he thought animals, like humans, possess a soul. This is one of the earliest references to the notion that non-human animals have natural rights which are usually reserved for humans.

During the Pre-Socratic era, developments in mathematics and science emerged and began to be articulated more clearly, and developed more fully, than (it seems) ever before. For instance, the concept of mathematics as we know it seems initially to have grown out of Pre-Socratic thought, first for practical reasons and later out of sheer intellectual interest. With the rise of agriculture in the western world, farmers began to see the need for measuring distances— dimensions of a field, length of a given row, and so on. Out of this need grew agreed-upon, though primitive, systems for taking basic measurements; these were often based on properties of the human anatomy such as the length of a foot or a stride. The need to communicate these dimensions to others led to a *standardized* way of conceptualizing measurements. This, then, is an early definitive identification of an intellectual standard—that of accuracy. An accurate way of taking measurements is needed; a system is devised (through human criticality) to achieve it and help people adhere to it. People then begin to think mathematically, to think more systematically, and to see knowledge occurring or existing in logical systems (as in a *mathematical* system) in which all the concepts embedded in it interrelate.[56]

---

55 Referenced in *The PreSocratics*, ed. Philip Wheelwright, 1966, New York: The Odyssey Press, Inc., p. 26.

56 It is invariably true that many peoples before the Hellenic period (circa 500 BCE) used mathematics in figuring things out, most especially in agriculture, but also, one might assume, in daily life (for things like measuring a room, recording time, and so forth). What is most relevant here is that at some point in human history, people began first to implicitly adhere to (and expect others to adhere to) intellectual standards, then to do so explicitly, and then to operationalize the use of such standards.

Roughly speaking, the Pre-Socratic philosophers asked questions like:

- What natural (rather than mythological) explanations can be found for physical occurrences? (Ionians)
- How can we make sense of nature in orderly, mathematical ways? (Pythagorans)
- What is the mechanical structure of the universe? (Democritus)

The Pre-Socratics were beginning to recognize the need to separate religious beliefs from theories about nature and the universe. For the first time in recorded history, it seems, people were beginning to pursue the logical analysis of ideas, to call for the grounding of theory in verifiable evidence, and to search in earnest for "truth." People were attempting to tease apart the religious ideologies that had been handed down for centuries from the facts of real life. In the process, they were incubating concepts, principles, and tools of reason.

Heraclitus, for instance, is purported to have said:[57]

- *"It is hard to fight against impulsive desire; whatever it wants it will buy at the cost of the soul."* (pointing out the importance of inner discipline to living well)

- *"Bigotry is the sacred disease."* (illuminating bigotry, because unethical, as something to be avoided)

- *"Most people do not take heed of the things they encounter, nor do they grasp them even when they have learned about them, although they think they do."* (illuminating intellectual arrogance and self deception as common among people—and hence something to guard against in oneself)

- *"What sort of mind or intelligence have they? They believe popular folktales and follow the crowd of their teachers, ignoring the adage that the many are bad, the good are few."* (illuminating the fact that people tend to blindly conform, rather than being intellectually autonomous; people should therefore guard against this tendency)

- *"The Ephesians had better go hang themselves, every man of them, and leave their city to be governed by youngsters, for they have banished Hermadorus, the finest man among them, declaring 'Let us not have anyone among us who excels the rest; if there should be such a one, let him go and live elsewhere.'"* (highlighting the fact that there are often significant implications of jealousy—thereby implying that people should be careful not to let jealousy guide their thoughts and actions)

Many Sophists (who lived at the time of Socrates) turned away from speculation about the universe, thinking that ultimate knowledge about the universe was unintelligible to humans. Instead they concerned themselves

---

57 Referenced in *The PreSocratics*, ed. Philip Wheelwright, 1966, New York: The Odyssey Press, Inc., pp. 73-76.

with cultivating reason in individual and civic life. Sophists traveled from city to city in Greece, teaching grammar, rhetoric, poetry, gymnastics, music, and mathematics. Many believed it possible to formulate just laws and policies. They argued that the law, as it stood, merely benefited those in power, and was made for their good rather than that of the people. Some Sophists also attacked the predominant tradition of moderation and self-discipline, encouraging people to maximize pleasure and disregard cultural traditions that restricted them from pursuing their desires. Importantly, most of the Sophists did not believe in universal standards of ethics.

By the time of Socrates (c. 470-399 BCE), people in Greek society had become increasingly more sophisticated in terms of critical thought and ethical reasoning. But it is Socrates who emerged as perhaps the most important all-time exemplar of fairminded critical thinking. Like the Sophists, Socrates agreed that human energy should be used first to pursue questions, not about the universe and nature, but about human thought and human decisions. Unlike many of the Sophists, Socrates did not believe in relativism. Further, he perceived many of the Sophists to be teaching people, through rhetoric, to gain what they could for themselves without concern for the rights and needs of others. This was troubling to Socrates, who spent more than 50 years attempting to pursue thought at the highest level of ethical reasoning and criticality. He questioned the views of "teachers," "scholars," and authorities who set themselves up as exemplary thinkers. In the end, he walked the streets of Athens, conversing with people, questioning them and himself, and inviting others to develop their minds through questioning. He embodied, as far as any living example probably could, the intellectual virtues—intellectual humility, intellectual integrity, and confidence in reason.

Socrates was fundamentally focused on understanding the human mind; he wanted to investigate human reason to improve human reason. Concerned with bettering life conditions, he believed our ultimate focus should be on comprehending not the astronomical or mathematical world, but the world of the human mind. He wanted people to use their intellectual energy to highlight problems in human thought and develop methods for intervention. In effect, he studied how thinking works, how it can go wrong, and how we can best intervene in thinking to raise it to a higher level of quality. Socrates was not afraid to openly question everything. He believed it his responsibility and his right to question human thought, especially when it seemed to go awry.

Socrates not only developed his own questioning and reasoning abilities. He encouraged others to question. He stimulated people to take command of their conception of the gods, to pay attention to what they attributed to these gods, to question what the gods would reasonably ask of people. He taught people to question what seemed illogical or unreasonable, to question their uses of words, to follow out the implications of their thoughts and potential actions, and to compare what they said they believed with what their actions implied. At a time when unethical critical thought was prevalent and largely unquestioned by Greek culture and society—when critical thinking was primarily at the command of vested and selfish interests—Socrates attempted to encourage and lead people to a radically different, more ethical way of thinking and living. He encouraged his students to think in a disinterested way about real questions concerning real life. Importantly, he emphasized the crucial distinction between ethics and other domains of thought, specifically religion and social ideology. He recognized the intrinsic fallibility of human thought in a way, it seems, never before recognized. Socrates sought a method for identifying and correcting problems in thought, and he publicly opposed those Sophists who taught people to twist meanings to fit their agendas.

Aristotle (384–322 BCE), among other contributions, developed important conceptual underpinnings for scientific thinking. He significantly advanced our understanding of living forms, laying the foundations for what would later become biology. Like Socrates, he approached ethics as something for all to strive toward as a way of living, rather than merely as an object of abstract study. He thought that to be happy, people needed good character, and that good character required ethical virtue.

Of course, much of Greek thought was largely lost for hundreds of years through the fall of the Roman empire, and throughout the dark ages. However, in the Middle Ages, these early texts were beginning to be rediscovered. Thomas Aquinas (*Summa Theologica*, 1485) argued for the importance of cultivating reason, and for objectively considering opposing viewpoints when forming one's own views. Francis Bacon (1561-1626) laid the foundations for modern science. Further, in *Novum Organum*, he illuminated systematic problems in human thinking, calling them *idola tribus*—translated, "idols of the tribe." He says

> *The idols of the tribe are inherent in human nature and the very tribe or race of man; for man's sense is falsely asserted to be the standard of things … the human mind resembles those uneven mirrors which impart their own properties … from which rays are emitted and distort and disfigure them.*
> —Novum Organum, Aphorism XLI, p. 8 [58]

Through these "idols of the tribe," Bacon called attention to the fact that most people develop bad habits of thought that lead them to believe what is false or misleading. Further, he conceptualized "Idols of the Market-Place," focusing attention on the ways we misuse words, and "Idols of the Theater," illuminating our tendency to become trapped in conventional systems of thought.

An emphasis on science, rather than superstition, became increasingly more prominent in the 17th, 18th, and 19th centuries with the contributions of Copernicus, Galileo, Darwin, and others. At the same time, literature became more sophisticated, increasingly illuminating problems in human thought and culture, and contributing to our conception of the critical person (consider

---

58   Bacon, F. (1620; 2019). *Novum Organum*, Aphorism XLI. Whithorn England: Andodos Books., p. 8.

the works of Jane Austen, George Eliot, the Brontës, Charles Dickens, Leo Tolstoy, Émile Zola, and Oscar Wilde, among many others). Simultaneously, philosophical thought continued to add to our emerging conception of critical thinking through the work of such thinkers as John Locke, Immanuel Kant, René Descartes, John Henry Newman, Thomas Paine, and others.

In the later part of the 20th century and through today, many scholars have continued to enrich our conception of fairminded critical societies from a multiplicity of disciplines and traditions. An early use of the term "critical thinking" can be traced to the first methodologically-disciplined study of critical thinking, conducted in 1941 by Edward Glaser and entitled, "An Experiment in the Development of Critical Thinking." In this study, Glaser lays out a foundational explanation of critical thinking still highly relevant today:

> [critical thinking] … calls for persistent effort to examine any belief or supposed form of knowledge in the light of the evidence that supports it and the further conclusions to which it tends … [It] requires ability to recognize problems, to find workable means for meeting those problems, to gather and marshal pertinent information, to recognize unstated assumptions and values, to comprehend and use language with accuracy, clarity, and discrimination, to interpret data, to appraise evidence and evaluate arguments, to recognize the existence (or non-existence) of logical relationships … to draw warranted conclusions and generalization at which one arrives, to reconstruct one's patterns of beliefs on the basis of wider experience, and to render accurate judgments about specific thinking and qualities in everyday life. (p. 182)

The state of critical thinking in human societies today is mixed. Since the 1980's, when critical thinking was emerging as a force be reckoned with in education, people have increasingly used the term to reference what schools should be doing and what societies should be cultivating. In 1993, in *Critical Thinking: What Every Person Needs to Survive in a Rapidly Changing World*, Richard Paul argued:

> Because we do not come to our experience with a blank slate for a mind, because our thinking is already, at any given moment, moving in a direction, because we can form new ideas, beliefs, and patterns of thought only through the scaffolding of our previously formed thought, it is essential that we learn to think critically in environments in which a variety of competing ideas are taken seriously. There is no way around the need for minds to think their way to knowledge. Thought is the key to knowledge. Knowledge is discoverable by thinking, assessed by thinking, organized by thinking, transformed by thinking, assessed by thinking, and most importantly acquired by thinking … (p. xi)

In short, we can identify elements of critical societies traceable to the beginning of recorded history (and beyond) and intimately connected with the rich conception of critical thinking emerging today. And again, given the intrinsic human capacity for critical thought, it stands to reason that there have perhaps always been some (or many) enlightened "ordinary" people at every period in history, however repressive the conditions.

Enlightened people throughout history have worked to improve conditions in whatever ways they could during their lifetimes, given the periods in history to which they were respectively bound and however imperfect their own thinking might have been. But these improvements have not always taken root in human thought and action. (For instance, where in today's societies do we encounter the criticality that Socrates was committed to advancing, and for which he gave his life?) Examples of criticality continue to emerge, but often within narrow specialties rather than in ways that would truly advance human civilizations. And though these specialties are frequently very important (such as those in technology and medicine), they cannot substitute for the cultivation of generalizable intellectual skills necessary for reasoning through everyday life problems, and accessible to people living in all human societies.

We are a very long distance from the realization of critical societies. We are a long way from emancipating the mind. For the most part, any one of us has only limited influence. We cannot, as individuals, change the world. But we can change ourselves, and we can positively influence others through measured, reasonable, rational thought. When the majority of us are doing this, critical societies will emerge. Unfortunately, the problems being created by sociocentric and egocentric thought have such far-reaching and significant consequences, and are pressing down upon us to such a degree, that we can only hope critical societies will emerge before we, as it were, self-destruct.

AFTERWORD

In writing a book on sociocentric thought, Linda Elder is taking on a challenging task. On the one hand, most everyone will agree that unthinking conformity is an obvious and common problem in human thought. Groupthink—who would claim to be free of it? We see it in multiple dimensions of our thought: in our religious beliefs, our national loyalties, our gender—influenced prejudices, our social, political, and cultural ideologies. We all live in a sea of unquestioned presuppositions. Most of us are willing to admit this—in a highly general and non-specific way. Yet, the more specific a sociocentric belief, the more intense is its emotional charge, the more intertwined with our identity, the less willing are we to question it, and the more we greet those who do question it with scorn and derision. To an irrational person, a rational person is irrational.

To the extent that I am right, Linda Elder is bravely (or foolishly) flying into a host of hornets' nests. Hornets' nest number one: RELIGION. Two: SEX. Three: CAPITALISM. Four: HUMAN-INFLICTED SUFFERING TO INNOCENT ANIMALS. Five: UNJUST LAWS. All these domains of life and thought (along with others mentioned in this book) are taboo-infested.

I suspect that Elder will become persona non grata to those who inhabit the nests she is stirring up—to all those who believe and uncritically accept the received views of society. One unfortunate consequence of Elder's decision to target (very hot) manifestations of deep sociocentric thought is that she may well lose many of the readers she seeks to gain, namely those who do not presently question the most destructive beliefs into which they have been deeply socially indoctrinated. Still, Elder may say in her own defense, "Someone must open Pandora's box—if we are to see and transcend what is in it. Someone must model critical thinking in a strong sense—if we are to actually construct the critical societies to which we say we are committed." I certainly hope she is correct. There are some things about which all reasonable people hope to be wrong.

Richard Paul
Dillon Beach, 2013

REFERENCES

Abusive G.I.'s not pursued, survey finds. (2006, February 23). *New York Times*, p. A8.

Arum, R. & Roksa, J. (2011). *Academically Adrift: Limited learning on college campuses.* Chicago: University of Chicago Press.

Asch, S. (1963). Effects of group pressure upon the modification and distortion of judgments. In H. Guetzkow, *Groups, leadership and men.* New York: Russell and Russell, pp. 177-190.

Bazelon, E. (February 6, 2012). Shaken. *New York Times Magazine.*

Beauvoir, S. de. (1974; 1949). *The second sex: The classic manifesto of the liberated woman.* New York: Random House.

Bekoff, M. (2002). *Minding animals: Awareness, emotions and heart.* New York: Oxford University Press.

Bion, W. (1961). *Experiences in groups.* London: Tavistock Publications.

Bosman, J. (2007, May 4). Plan for Arabic school in Brooklyn arouses protests. *New York Times*, p. A22.

Broder, J. (2010, October 21). Skepticism on climate change is article of faith for Tea Party. *New York Times*, pp. A1, A4.

Campbell, S., ed. (1976). *Piaget sampler: An introduction to Jean Piaget through his own words.* New York: John Wiley & Sons.

Carter, L. A. (2008, July 14). Sonoma sex offender challenges 200-year prison term. *Press Democrat.*

Cartwright, D., & Zander, A. (1968). *Group dynamics: Research and theory* (3rd ed.). New York: Harper & Row.

Center on Budget and Policy Priorities. (2010, June 25). *Income gaps between very rich and everyone else more than tripled in last three decades, new data show.* Retrieved from http://www.cbpp.org/files/6-25-10inc.pdf

Chaplin, J. P. (1985). *Dictionary of psychology.* New York: Dell.

Park, A. (2010, December 13). Lab report: Child abuse. *Time*, briefing page.

Christy, B. (2010, January). The kingpin. *National Geographic*, 84–105.

Clark, A. (1984) *Einstein: The life and times.* NY: Avon Books.

Coleman, L. (1984). *Reign of error.* Boston: Beacon Press.

Cook, J. (1821). *The three voyages of Captain James Cook round the world (Vol. 5).* London: Longman, Hurst, Rees, Orme and Brown, Paternoster-Row.

culture (n.d.). Dictionary.com unabridged (Vol. 1.1). Retrieved from http://dictionary. reference.com/browse/culture

Dineen, T. (1996). *Manufacturing victims.* Montreal: Robert Davies Multi Media Publishing.

Downie Jr., L., & Kaiser, R. (2002). *The news about the news.* NY: Alfred Knopf.

Edwards, P. (1957). "How Bertrand Russell was prevented from teaching at the College of the City of New York." In *Why I am not a Christian* by Bertrand Russell. New York: Touchstone, Simon and Schuster.

Einstein, A. (1954). *Ideas and opinions.* New York: Random House.

Einstein, A. (1979). *Autobiographical notes.* Chicago, Illinois: Open Court Publishing Company.

Ellmann, R. (1987). *Oscar Wilde.* New York: Penguin Books.

Foucault, M. (1978). *The history of sexuality, volume I: An introduction.* New York: Vintage Books.

Fouts, R. (1997). *Next of kin: My conversations with chimpanzees.* New York: HarperCollins Publishers.

Frank, R. & Cook, P. (1995). *The winner-take-all society.* NY, NY: The Free Press.

Frankl, V. (1959; 1984). *Man's search for meaning.* NY: Washington Square Press.

Fromm, E. (1976). *To have or to be.* New York: Harper and Row Publishers, Inc.

Gilovich, T. (1991). *How we know what isn't so: The fallibility of human reason in everyday life.* New York: The Free Press.

Giroux, H. (1988). *Teachers as intellectuals.* Westport, CT: Bergin & Garvey Publishers.

Glaser, E.M. (1941). An experiment in the development of critical thinking. *Contributions to Education,* 843, 182.

Goldman, E. (1996). *Red Emma speaks: An Emma Goldman reader.* Amherst, NY: Humanity Books.

Gonzales, L. (2008, October). Deep survival: Mob mentality. *National Geographic Adventure.* Carmel: National Geographic Society.

Goodall, J. (2000). *Reason for hope: A spiritual journey.* New York: Grand Central Publishing.

Goode, R. (2011, November 5). Life sentence for possession of child pornography spurs debate over severity. *The New York Times,* p. A9.

Groopman, J. (2007). *How doctors think.* New York: Houghton Mifflin Company.

Haack, S. (1992, December). *Epistemological reflections of an old feminism,* presented at annual meetings of the Eastern division of the American Philosophical Association, Washington, D.C. In C. Sommers (1995). *Who stole feminism? How women have betrayed women.* New York: Simon and Schuster.

Hagen, M. (1997). *Whores of the court.* New York: HarperCollins Publishers.

Hardt, M., & Negri, A. (2000). *Empire.* Cambridge: Harvard University Press.

Harris, G., & Carey, B. (2008, June 8). Researchers fail to reveal full drug pay. *The New York Times.*

Hastorf A., & Cantril H. (1954). They saw a game: A case study. *Journal of Abnormal and Social Psychology,* 49.

Hay, J. (2004, February 7). Ex-Sonoma coach gets 30 years to life in sex. *Press Democrat,* p. 1.

Hill, G. (2013, March 10). Living with a lot less. *New York Times Review.*

Iran cleric blames quakes on promiscuous women. (2011, April 20). *Press Democrat,* p. A6.

Israel flap over, playwright Kushner granted NY degree. (2011, June 4). *Press Democrat,* p. A2.

Janis, I. (1972). *Victims of groupthink; a psychological study of foreign-policy decisions and fiascoes.* Boston: Houghton, Mifflin.

Jenkinson, E. (1979). *Censors in the classroom.* Carbondale: Southern Illinois University Press.

Johnston, D. (2007). *Free lunch: How the wealthiest Americans enrich themselves at government expense (and stick you with the bill).* New York: Penguin Group.

Jones, H. (1997). *Alfred C. Kinsey: A life.* NY: W.W. Norton & Co., Inc (p. 590).

Jones, M. (2007, July 22). How can you distinguish a budding pedophile from a kid with real boundary problems? *New York Times Magazine.*

Kidd, I. G. (1967). *The encyclopedia of philosophy* (volumes 7 and 8, index). NY: McMillan publishing company, Macmillan Publishing Co., & The Free Press.

Kinsey, A. *Sexual behavior in the human male.* Bloomington: Indiana University Press.

Leland, J. (2010, May 3). The other porn addicts. *New York Times,* p. A12.

Lewin, K. (1947). Group decision and social change. In T. Newcomb and E. Hartley (Eds.), *Readings in social psychology.* New York: Holt, pp. 197-211.

Lewis, C. S. (1947). *The abolition of man.* NY: HarperCollins Publishers.

Lincoln, A. (1864, November 21). *From a private letter to Col. William F. Elkins.* In A. H. Shaw (Ed.), *The Lincoln encyclopedia.* New York: Macmillan, 1950.

Loewen, J. (2007). *Lies my teacher told me: Everything your American history textbook got wrong.* NY: Touchstone (pp. 6-7).

Lord, C., Ross, L., & Lepper, M. (1979). Biased assimilation and attitude polarization: The effects of prior theories on subsequent considered evidence. *Journal of Personality and Social Psychology,* 37(11), 2098–2109.

MacDonald, G. (1931; 1959). *50 years of free thought.* NY: Arno Press, p.vii

Mander, A. E. (1936; 1938). *Clearer thinking: Logic for everyman.* (3rd ed.) London: Watts & Co.

Martin A., & Story, L. (2010, September 12). The loneliest analyst. *New York Times,* pp. B1, B9.

Maugham, S. (1938). *The summing up.* New York: Country Life Press.

McGowan, D. (2000). *Derailing democracy: The America the media don't want you to see.* Monroe: Common Courage Press.

McMichael, P. (1996). *Development and social change: A global perspective.* Thousand Oaks, CA: Pine Forge.

Mencken, H. L. (1923, December 5). On liberty. *Nation Magazine.*

Merrill, F., & Merrill, M. (1931; 1933). *Among the nudists.* With an introduction by John Langdon-Davies. New York: Garden City Publishing.

Milgram, S. (1974). *Obedience to authority.* New York: Harper and Row.

Mill, J. S. (1859; 1997). *The spirit of the age, on liberty, the subjection of women.* Alan Ryan (ed.), New York, NY: Norton and Company.

Mills, C. W. (1956). *The power elite.* New York, NY: Oxford University Press.

Neumann, E. (1969; 1973). *Depth psychology and a new ethic.* NY: Harper and Row.

Newman, J. (1852; 1996). *The idea of a university.* London: Yale University Press.

Nordberg, J. (2010, September 21). Where boys are prized, girls live the part: In some Afghan families, a fake son is considered better than none. *New York Times,* p. A1.

Paul, R. (1990; 2012). *Critical thinking: What every person needs to survive in a rapidly changing world.* Tomales, CA: Foundation for Critical Thinking Press.

Paul, R., Elder, L., & Bartell, T. (1997). *California teacher preparation for instruction in critical thinking: Research findings and policy recommendations.* Sacramento, CA: California Commission on Teacher Credentialing.

Payne, P. (2010, October 21). Ex-coach charged in molestation case. *The Press Democrat,* p. B5.

Peters, W. (1987). *A class divided: Then and now.* London: Yale University Press.

Piaget, J. (1962). *The moral judgment of the child.* New York: Collier Books.

Piaget, J. (1976). *Judgment and reasoning in the child.* Totowa, NJ: Littlefield, Adams.

Plato (1960). *The republic and other works.* New York: Dolphin Books.

Plotnicov, L., & Tuden, A. (Eds.) (1970). *Essays in comparative social stratification.* Pittsburgh: University of Pittsburgh Press.

police state (n.d.). *The American Heritage Dictionary of the English language* (4th ed.). Retrieved from http://dictionary.reference.com/browse/police state

Population Reference Bureau. (2010). Female genital mutilation cutting: Data and trends: Update 2010. Retrieved from http://www.prb.org/pdf10/fgm-wallchart2010.pdf

Robinson, W. (2004). *A theory of global capitalism.* Baltimore, MD: The Johns Hopkins University Press.

Rosen, R. D. (1977). *Psychobabble: Fast talk and quick cure in the era of feeling.* New York: Atheneum.

Ross, R., & Trachte, K. (1990). *Global capitalism: The new leviathan.* Albany: SUNY Press.

Rubin, A. (2010, November 8). For Afghan wives, a desperate, fiery way out. *New York Times,* pp. A1, A10.

Russell, B. (1930). *The conquest of happiness.* New York: Horace Liveright.

Russell, B. (1945). *A history of Western philosophy.* New York: Simon & Schuster.

Russell, B. (1957). *Why I am not a Christian.* New York: Simon and Schuster.

Russell, B. (1967). *War crimes in Vietnam.* New York: Monthly Review Press.

Schmitt, E., & Yardley, W. (2012, March 15). Accused G.I. 'Snapped' Under Strain, Official Says. *New York Times,* A1.

Schneider, K. (2011, June 4). Doctor who helped end lives. *New York Times,* pp. A1, A17.

Shermer, M. (1997). *Why people believe weird things.* New York: W. H. Freeman and Company.

Simmel, G. (1971). *On individuality and social forms.* Chicago: University of Chicago Press.

Singer, P. (2000). *Writings on an ethical life.* New York: HarperCollins Publishers.

Smith, A. (1776; 1976). An inquiry into the nature and causes of the wealth of nations. R. H. Campbell & A. S. Skinner (Eds.). 2 vols. *Glasgow edition of the works and correspondence of Adam Smith 2.* Oxford: Oxford University Press.

Smith, T., ed. (1956). *Philosophers speak for themselves: From Aristotle to Plotinus.* Chicago, IL: The University of Chicago Press.

Sommers, C. (1995). *Who stole feminism? How women have betrayed women.* New York: Simon and Schuster.

Sulzberger, A. G. (2010, May 22). Defiant judge takes on child pornography law. *New York Times,* p. A1.

Sumner, W. G. (1906; 1940). *Folkways: A study of the sociological importance of usages, manners, customs, mores, and morals.* New York: Ginn and Co.

taboo (n.d.). *Online etymology dictionary.* Retrieved from http://dictionary.reference.com/browse/taboo

Talaska, R., ed. (1992). *Critical reasoning in contemporary culture.* New York: SUNY Press.

Terris, B. (2009, December 11). Secretive scholars of the Old South. *Chronicle of Higher Education.* (https://www.chronicle.com/article/Secretive-Scholars-of-the-Old/49337)

Unjust and Ineffective. (2009, August 8). *The Economist,* pp. 21-23.

Whyte, W. H., Jr. (1952, March). Groupthink. *Fortune.* pp. 114–117, 142, 146.

Xinran (2011). *Message from an unknown mother: Stories of loss and love.* New York: Scribner.

Yong, W., & Worth, R. (2010, August 12). Iran shows what it says is murder confession by woman condemned for adultery. *New York Times,* p. A8.

Zimbardo, P. (2007). *The Lucifer effect: Understanding how good people turn evil.* New York: Random House.

Zinn, H. (1980; 2006). *A people's history of the United States.* New York: HarperCollins Publishers.

Zinn, H. (2003). *Passionate declarations: Essays on war and justice.* New York: HarperCollins Publishers.

IMAGE SOURCES

p. 6   *By Minnesota Historical Society - https://www.flickr.com/photos minnesotahistoricalsociety/5355384180/sizes/o/in/photostream/, CC BY-SA 2.0, https://commons.wikimedia.org/w/index.php?curid=19183908*

p. 13   Top: *https://images.pexels.com/photos/247763/pexels-photo-247763 jpeg?w=940&h=6 50&auto=compress&cs=tinysrgb*

p. 13   Bottom: *By Capt. Susan Harrington, https://www.pacom.mil/Media Photos/igphoto/2001556746/*

p. 15   *https://pixabay.com/photos/mental-health-depression-anxiety-2211184/*

p. 16   *By Zeynel Cebeci [CC BY-SA 4.0 (https://creativecommons.org/licenses by-sa/4.0)], https://commons.wikimedia.org/wiki/File:Pesticides_ application_01.jpg*

p. 18   Top: *By Анна Нэсси [CC BY-SA 3.0 GFDL], https://commons.wikimedia.org/ wiki/File:Uruguay_fans_Russia_2018.jpg*

p. 18   Bottom: *By Korea.net / Korean Culture and Information Service [CC BY-SA 2.0 (https://creativecommons.org/licenses/by-sa/2.0)], https://commons.wikimedia org/wiki/File:Korea_Fans_Cheers_Team_Korea_20140623_18_(14515373403).jpg*

p. 21   *By Michelangelo Buonarroti [Public domain], https://commons.wikimedia.org wiki/File:The_Creation_of_Adam.jpg*

p. 22   Top: *https://pixabay.com/photos/astronomical-clock-prague-226897/*

p. 22   Bottom left: *By Underwood & Underwood, London & New York [Publi domain], https://commons.wikimedia.org/wiki/File:A_HIGH_CASTE_LADYS_ DAINTY_LILY_FEET.jpg*

p. 22   Bottom right: *By unknown; Frank and Frances Carpenter Collection. [Public domain], https://commons.wikimedia.org/wiki/File:Bound_feet_(X-ray).jpg*

p. 23   *By Pyotr Yevgenyevich Myasoyedov (1867-1913) [1] [Public domain], https:/ commons.wikimedia.org/wiki/File:Avvakum_by_Pyotr_Yevgenyevich Myasoyedov.jpg*

p. 24   Top: *Catechetical Guild [Public domain], https://commons.wikimedia.org/wiki/ File:Is_this_tomorrow.jpg*

p. 24   Bottom: *Anticommunist_Literature_1950s.tiff: Myron Coureval Faganderivative work: Comte0 [Public domain], https://commons.wikimedia.org/ wiki/File:Anticommunist_Literature_1950s.png*

p. 29   Top left: *By Alex Proimos from Sydney, Australia [CC BY 2.0 (https:/ creativecommons.org/licenses/by/2.0)], https://commons.wikimedia.org/wiki/ File:Beach_couple_2352352.jpg*

p. 29   Top right: *https://pixabay.com/photos namibia-woman-himba-nature-african-495697/*

p. 29   Bottom: *https://commons.wikimedia.org/wiki/File:Nambassa_festival_1978.jpg*

p. 33   Far left: *Nambassa Trust and Peter Terry [CC BY-SA 3.0 (https:// creativecommons.org/licenses/by-sa/3.0)], https://commons.wikimedia.org/wiki/ File:Kutia_kondh_woman_3.jpg*

p. 33   Second from left: *Lirongfrau mit lang ausgedehnten Ohrläppchen.jpg: Haabetderivative work: Nicor [Public domain], https://commons.wikimedia.org/ wiki/File:Lirongfrau_mit_gedehnten_Ohrl%C3%A4ppchen.jpg*

p. 33   Second from right: *By JoeInQueens from Queens, USA [CC BY 2.0 (https:// creativecommons.org/licenses/by/2.0)], https://commons.wikimedia.org/wiki/ File:DSC_0558 (7333963394).jpg*

p. 33   Far right: *By Punya at ne.wikipedia [CC BY-SA 3.0 (https://creativecommons.org licenses/by-sa/3.0)], https://commons.wikimedia.org/wiki/File:Tharu_Mahila.jpg*

p, 35   *By Powhusku from Laramie, WY, USA [CC BY-SA 2.0 (https:// creativecommons.org/licenses/by-sa/2.0)], https://commons.wikimedia.org/ wiki/File:Black_Friday_by_Powhusku.jpg*

p. 37   *By John Owens (VOA) - SourceSource article, Public Domain, https://commons wikimedia.org/w/index.php?curid=58873776*

p. 42   *User:Thiste [CC BY-SA 2.5 (https://creativecommons.org/licenses/by-sa/2.5)], https://commons.wikimedia.org/wiki/File:Age_of_Consent.png*

p. 46   *By VIRIN: 080129-F-1234G-111.JPG, https://www.af.mil/News/Photos/ igphoto/2000661406/*

p. 47   *By Jastrow (2005), Louvre Museum [Public domain], https://en.wikipedia.org wiki/File:Letter_Luenna_Louvre_AO4238.jpg*

p. 58   *By Md. Tanvirul Islam [GFDL (http://www.gnu.org/copyleft/fdl.html) or GFDL (http://www.gnu.org/copyleft/fdl.html)], https://commons.wikimedia.org/wiki/ File:Street_Child,_Srimangal_Railway_Station.jpg*

p. 69   *https://www.maxpixel.net Learn-Study-Students-Education-Children-Books-3835935*

p. 70   Smithsonian Institution Photographed by Watson Davis [Public domain], https://commons.wikimedia.org/wiki/File:John_t_scopes.jpg

p. 73   By The Photographer [CC BY-SA 3.0 (https://creativecommons.org/licenses/by-sa/3.0)] https://commons.wikimedia.org/wiki/File:Chimpance_en_Zoologico_de_Barquisimeto.jpg

p. 74   Screen shot taken from https://www.youtube.com/watch?v=FRlUJrEUn0Y

p. 76   The original uploader was Ernst Stavro Blofeld at English Wikipedia. [Public domain], https://commons.wikimedia.org/wiki/File:George_Curzon_with_his_wife_posing_with_a_hunted_Bengal_tiger,_1903.jpg

p. 78   Screen shot taken from https://www.youtube.com/watch?v=9mLbp2jA-sQ

p. 79   Screen shot taken from https://www.youtube.com/watch?v=1mcCLm_LwpE

p. 81   U.S. Government copyright [Public domain], https://commons.wikimedia.org/wiki/File:Iraqis_tortured_wp-f.jpg

p. 83   Screen shot taken from https://www.youtube.com/watch?v=rdrKCilEhC0

p. 91   Fair use, https://en.wikipedia.org/w/index.php?curid=33999659, https://en.wikipedia.org/wiki/File:Candace_Newmaker.jpg

p. 96   en:Theodor de Bry [Public domain], https://commons.wikimedia.org/wiki/File:Columbus_landing_on_Hispaniola.JPG

p. 99   By Ronald L. Haeberle - Copied from Krysstal.com, "The Acts of the Democracies" http://www.krysstal.com/democracy_vietnam_mylai.html, Public Domain, https://commons.wikimedia.org/w/index.php?curid=883801, https://en.wikipedia.org/wiki/File:My_Lai_massacre.jpg

p. 119   Top: By Russell Lee [Public domain], https://commons.wikimedia.org/wiki/File:KidsBathingInASmallMetalTub.jpg

p. 119   Bottom: By Henry Scott Tuke [Public domain], https://commons.wikimedia.org/wiki/File:Tuke%2C_Henry_Scott_(1858%E2%80%931929)%2C_%22The_Bathers%22.jpg

Image of Rodin's The Thinker used throughout: https://pixabay.com/photos/the-thinker-rodin-rodin-museum-489753/

APPENDIX A[56]
SOME BASIC DEFINITIONS

cognitive processes: generally understood as operations of the intellect that are innate or naturally occurring in the human mind.

It is important to understand cognitive processes in human thought—processes such as classifying, inferring, assuming, planning, analyzing, comparing, contrasting, and synthesizing. However, we should not assume that engaging in these processes automatically ensures skilled and disciplined reasoning. For example, whenever we plan, we do not necessarily plan well. Sometimes we plan poorly. The mere fact of planning does not automatically carry with it high-quality cognition. To ensure excellent thought, we need to consistently meet intellectual standards when engaging in (natural) cognitive processes.

critical society: a society which systematically cultivates critical thinking, and hence systematically rewards reflective questioning, intellectual independence, and reasoned dissent.

To begin to conceptualize a critical society, one must imagine a society in which independent critical thought is embodied in the concrete day-to-day lives of individuals. William Graham Sumner, a distinguished anthropologist, explicitly formulated the ideal:

The critical habit of thought, if usual in a society, will pervade all its mores, because it is a way of taking up the problems of life. Men educated in it cannot be stampeded by stump

orators and are never deceived by dithyrambic oratory. They are slow to believe. They can hold things as possible or probable in all degrees, without certainty and without pain. They can wait for evidence and weigh evidence, uninfluenced by the emphasis or confidence with which assertions are made on one side or the other. They can resist appeals to their dearest prejudices and all kinds of cajolery. Education in the critical faculty is the only education of which it can be truly said that it makes good citizens. Sumner, 1906; 1940 (pp. 632, 633).

Until critical habits of thought pervade human societies (which will likely be decades, if not longer, into the future), there will be a tendency for schools as social institutions to transmit the prevailing world view more or less uncritically—to transmit it as reality, not as a picture of reality. Education for critical thinking, requires that schools and classrooms become microcosms of a critical society. There are currently no existing critical societies on a broad scale. Critical societies will develop only to the extent that:

- critical thinking is viewed as essential to living a reasonable and fairminded life.
- critical thinking is routinely taught and consistently fostered.
- the problematics of thinking are an abiding concern.
- closedmindedness is systemically discouraged, and openmindedness systematically encouraged.

---

56 These definitions are taken from *A Glossary of Critical Thinking Terms and Concepts* by Linda Elder and Richard Paul, 2016, Tomales, CA: Foundation for Critical Thinking Press.

- intellectual integrity, intellectual humility, intellectual empathy, confidence in reason, and intellectual courage are everyday social values.
- egocentric and sociocentric thinking are recognized as a bane in social life.
- children are routinely taught that the rights and needs of others are equal to their own.
- a multi-cultural world view is fostered.
- people are encouraged to think for themselves, and are discouraged from uncritically accepting the thinking or behavior of others.
- people routinely study and diminish irrational thought.
- people internalize universal intellectual standards.

See *intellectual traits.*

critical thinking: the most fundamental concept of critical thinking is simple and intuitive. All humans think. It is our nature to do so. But much of our thinking, left to itself, is biased, distorted, partial, uninformed, or down-right prejudiced. Unfortunately, shoddy thinking is costly, both in money and in quality of life. Critical thinking begins, then, when we start thinking about our thinking with a view to improving it.

Beyond this basic conceptualization, there are many ways to begin to explain critical thinking. Here are some:

- The art of analyzing and evaluating thinking with a view to improving it.
- Disciplined, self-directed thinking which meets appropriate intellectual standards within a particular mode or domain of thinking.
- Thinking that commonly displays intellectual skills, abilities, and traits.
- Thinking about your thinking while you are thinking in order to make your thinking better: more clear, more accurate, more reasonable, and so forth.
- Self-guided, self-disciplined thinking which attempts to reason at the highest level of quality in a fairminded way.

In understanding critical thinking, it is useful to recognize that it exists in many forms and manifestations. For example, much critical thinking is one-dimensional; some is global. Much critical thinking is sophistic; some is Socratic. Some is implicit; some is explicit. Some is systematic and integrated; some episodic or atomistic.

See *strong-sense critical thinkers, weak-sense critical thinkers, intellectual traits.*

cultural associations: cultural associations are ideas linked in the mind, often inappropriately, due to societal influences.

Many, if not most, of our important ideas are connected with, or guided by, cultural associations. Media advertising juxtaposes and joins logically unrelated things to influence our buying habits (e.g., if you drink this particular brand of beverage, you will be "sexy"; if you drive this type of car, you will be "attractive" and "powerful"). Raised in a particular country or within a particular group within it, we form any number of mental links which, if they remain unexamined, unduly influence our thinking and behavior.

Of course, not all cultural associations are problematic. Only through disciplined examination can we distinguish between those that are and those that are not.

See *cultural assumption, critical society.*

cultural assumption: unassessed (often implicit) belief adopted by virtue of upbringing in a society and taken for granted.

Raised in a culture, we unconsciously adopt its point of view, values, beliefs, and practices. At the root of each of these are many assumptions. Not knowing that we perceive, conceive, think, and experience within assumptions we have formulated uncritically, we take ourselves to be perceiving "things as they are," not "things as they appear from a cultural perspective." Becoming aware of our cultural assumptions so that we might critically examine them is a crucial dimension of critical thinking. It is, however, a dimension largely missing from the educational process. Indeed, schools, and even colleges and universities, often implicitly and unknowingly foster blind acceptance to group ideologies.

See *sociocentrism, ethnocentrism, social contradiction.*

defense mechanisms: self-deceptive processes used by the human mind to avoid dealing with socially unacceptable or painful ideas, beliefs, or situations.

The human mind routinely engages in unconscious processes that are egocentrically motivated and that strongly influence our behavior. When functioning egocentrically, we seek to get what we want. We see the world from a narrow self-serving perspective. Yet, we also see ourselves as driven by purely rational motives. We therefore disguise our egocentric motives. This disguise necessitates self-deception. Self-deception is achieved by means of defense mechanisms. Through the use of defense mechanisms, the mind can avoid conscious recognition of negative feelings such as guilt, pain, anxiety, etc. The term 'defense mechanisms' is used in Freudian psychoanalytic theory generally to mean psychological strategies used by the unconscious mind to cope with reality and maintain a positive self-image. The theory of defense mechanisms is complex, with some theoreticians suggesting that defense mechanisms may at times be healthy (particularly in childhood). However, when these mechanisms operate in the mind of the normal adult, they pose significant barriers to rationality and the creation of critical societies. All humans engage in self-deception; however, critical thinkers consistently strive to act in good faith, and to minimize their self-deceptive tendencies, to understand these tendencies and work toward diminishing their frequency and power.

Some of the most common defense mechanisms are: denial, identification,

projection, repression, rationalization, stereotyping, scapegoating, sublimation and wishful thinking. See also *egocentrism.*

denial: when a person refuses to believe indisputable evidence or facts in order to maintain a favorable self-image or favored set of beliefs.

Denial is one of the most commonly used defense mechanisms. All humans sometimes deny what they cannot face—for example, some unpleasant truth about themselves or others. A basketball player, for instance, may deny that there are flaws in his game in order to maintain an image of himself as highly skilled at basketball. A "patriot" may deny—in the face of clear-cut evidence—that his country ever violates human rights or acts unjustly.

See *defense mechanisms.*

egocentrism: a tendency to view everything in relationship to oneself, to confuse immediate perception (how things seem) with reality, to be self-centered, or to consider only oneself and one's own interests; selfishness; to distort "reality" in order to maintain a particular viewpoint or perception.

One's desires, values, and beliefs (seeming to be self-evidently correct or superior to those of others) are often uncritically used as the unconscious norm for much judgment and "experience." Egocentrism is one of the fundamental impediments to critical thinking. As one learns to think critically in a strong sense, one learns to become more rational and less egocentric.

See *egocentric domination, egocentric submission, defense mechanisms, human nature, sociocentrism, strong-sense critical thinkers.*

egocentric domination: the egocentric tendency to seek what one wants through the unreasonable use of direct power over, or intimidation of, people (or other sentient creatures).

Egocentric domination of others may be overt or covert. On the one hand, dominating egocentrism can involve harsh, dictatorial, tyrannical, or bullying behavior (e.g., a physically abusive spouse). On the other hand, it might involve subtle messages and behavior that imply the use of control or force if "necessary" (e.g., a supervisor reminding a subordinate, by quiet innuendo, that his or her employment is contingent upon unquestioning obedience). Human irrational behavior is often some combination of dominating and submissive acts. In the "ideal" fascist society, for example, everyone (except the dictator) is submissive to everyone above him and dominating to everyone below him.

See *egocentric submission, egocentrism.*

egocentric submission: the irrational tendency to psychologically join and serve "powerful" people to get what one wants.

Humans are naturally concerned with their interests and motivated to satisfy their desires. In a world of psychological power and influence, people generally learn to "succeed" in two ways: to psychologically conquer or intimidate (subtly or openly) those who stand in their way (through egocentric domination), or, alternatively, to psychologically join and serve more powerful others, who then (1) give them a sense of personal importance, (2) protect them, and (3) share with them some of the benefits of their success. Irrational people use both techniques, though not to the same extent.

When people submit to more powerful others, they are engaging in what can be termed 'egocentric submission.' Those who use overt force and control are engaging in what can be termed 'egocentric domination.' Both of these forms of behavior can be seen publicly, for example, in the relationships of rock stars or sport stars to their admiring followers. Most social groups have an internal "pecking order," with some playing the role of leader and most playing the role

of follower. A fairminded rational person seeks neither to dominate, nor to blindly serve someone else who dominates.

Opposite is *egocentric domination.* See also *egocentrism.*

ethnocentrism: a tendency to view one's own race or culture as superior to all others, and therefore to judge other cultures according to one's own cultural standards.

Ethnocentrism can be understood as a form of egocentrism extended from one's self to one's group. Much uncritical or selfish critical thinking is either egocentric or ethnocentric in nature. (Ethnocentrism and sociocentrism are often used synonymously, though sociocentricity is broader, relating to any group, including, for example, sociocentric identification with one's profession.) The "treatment" for ethnocentrism or sociocentrism is routine empathic thought within the perspective of opposing groups and cultures. Such empathic thought is rarely cultivated in the societies and schools of today. Instead, many people develop an empty rhetoric of tolerance without seriously considering the value in the beliefs and practices of other groups, the meaning of these beliefs to those others, and their reasons for maintaining them.

See *sociocentrism.*

fairmindedness: a cultivated disposition of mind that enables the thinker to treat all perspectives relevant to an issue in an objective manner, without privileging one's own views or the views of one's group.

Fairmindedness implies being conscious of the need to treat all relevant viewpoints alike without reference to one's own feelings or selfish interests, or the feelings or selfish interests of one's friends, community, nation, or species. It implies adherence to intellectual standards without reference to one's own advantage or that of one's group.

There are three primary reasons why people lack this disposition: 1) native egocentric thought, 2) native sociocentric thought, and 3) lack of intellectual skills necessary for reasoning through complex ethical issues.

See *intellectual traits, egocentrism, sociocentrism.*

human mind: that which thinks, perceives, feels, and wills; the seat of conscious as well as unconscious thought.

The mind is an organized set of capacities by which sentient creatures think, feel, and want. These capacities continually interact. Thus, the human mind entails a cognitive dimension (that of thought), as well as an affective dimension (that of feelings and desires).

In recent years, many studies have been conducted to understand the relationships between the cognitive and affective dimensions of the human mind. Yet, much is known about the human mind that cannot yet be connected to precise neurological processes in the brain. For example, one natural mechanism of the human mind is its tendency toward selfishness. This fact can be documented in hundreds of thousands of ways through simple observation. In short, we know much about the mind and comparatively little about the brain.

human nature: the common qualities, instincts, inherent tendencies, and capacities of human beings.

People have both a primary and secondary nature. Our primary nature is spontaneous, egocentric, and subject to irrational belief formation. It is the basis for our instinctual thought. People need no training to believe what they want to believe: what serves their immediate interests, what preserves their sense of personal comfort and righteousness, what minimizes their sense of inconsistency, and what presupposes their own correctness. People need no special training to believe what those around them believe: what their parents and friends believe, what is taught

to them by religious and school authorities, what is repeated often by the media, and what is commonly believed in their nation and culture. People need no training to think that those who disagree with them are wrong and probably prejudiced. People need no training to assume that their own most fundamental beliefs are self-evidently true or easily justified by evidence. People naturally and spontaneously identify with their own beliefs. They often experience disagreement as personal attack. The resulting defensiveness interferes with their capacity to empathize with, or enter into, other points of view.

On the other hand, people need extensive and systematic practice to develop their secondary nature, their implicit capacity to function as rational persons. They need extensive and systematic practice to recognize the tendencies they have to form irrational beliefs. They need extensive practice to develop a dislike of inconsistencies in their thought, a love of clarity, and a passion to seek reasons and evidence as well as to be fair to points of view other than their own. People need extensive practice to recognize that they live inferentially, that they do not have a direct pipeline to reality, and that it is perfectly possible to have an overwhelming inner sense of the correctness of one's views and still be wrong.

See *egocentricity, sociocentrism, rational, intellectual traits.*

indoctrination: instilling within one a (usually) partisan or sectarian opinion, point of view, or principle. The term 'partisan' entails exhibiting blind, prejudiced, unreasoned allegiance. The term 'sectarian' entails (1) adhering to a particular religious faith or limited in character or scope, or (2) a narrow or bigoted person; brainwashing.

Indoctrination is a perennial problem in schooling, since students are typically taught to accept ideas without thinking them through and critically analyzing them. For most children, this begins early in life. In elementary school in the US, for example, students are often expected to sing the "National Anthem"—a song they are rarely, if ever, encouraged to examine in terms of its implications. Similarly, media bias leads to indoctrination when people are given one side of a story as if it were "the whole," when they are given the side of a story that makes the culture look good, or when they are given the side that feeds established social and political biases and prejudices. Indoctrination is a form of propaganda antithetical to critical thinking and an impediment to the development of critical societies.

See *socialization, critical society.*

intellectual traits/dispositions/virtues:
the traits of mind and character necessary for right action and thinking; the dispositions of mind and character essential for fairminded rationality; the virtues that distinguish the narrowminded, self-serving critical thinker from the openminded, truth-seeking critical thinker.

Intellectual traits include, but are not limited to: *intellectual sense of justice, intellectual perseverance, intellectual integrity, intellectual humility, intellectual empathy, intellectual courage, intellectual curiosity, intellectual discipline, confidence in reason,* and *intellectual autonomy.*

The hallmark of the strong-sense critical thinker is the embodiment of, and deep commitment to, these intellectual virtues. Yet, the extent to which anyone lives in accordance with them on a daily basis is a matter of degree, with no actual person achieving that of the hypothetical ideal thinker.

Intellectual traits are interdependent. Each is properly developed only in conjunction with the development of the others, and only through years of commitment and practice. They cannot be imposed from without; they must be cultivated by encouragement and example.

irrational/irrationality:
lacking the power to reason; contrary to reason or logic; senseless; unreasonable; absurd.

Humans are both rational and irrational. We have innate egocentric and sociocentric tendencies that often lead us to do things that are illogical (though they seem to us at the time to be perfectly logical). We don't automatically sense what is reasonable in any given situation. Rather, the extent to which we think and act rationally depends upon how well our rational capacities have been developed. It depends upon the extent to which he have learned to go beyond our natural prejudices and biases—beyond our narrow, self-serving viewpoint—to see what makes most sense to do and believe in a given situation. Critical thinkers are alert to their irrational tendencies. They strive to become rational, fairminded persons.

See *egocentricity, sociocentricity, rationality, national bias.*

rational/rationality:
being guided by the intellect (rather than emotions), or having to do with reason; being consistent with or based on logic; that which conforms to principles of good reasoning, is sensible, shows good judgment, and is consistent, logical, relevant, and sound.

In everyday discourse, there are at least three different common uses of the term 'rational' or 'rationality.' One refers to a person's general ability to think well. A second refers to a person's ability to use his intellect to achieve his purposes (irrespective of whether or not these purposes are ethically justified). A third refers to one's commitment to think and act only in ways that are intellectually and ethically justified. Behind these three uses lie these distinctions: skilled thinker, sophistic thinker, and Socratic thinker. In the first use, we mark the skills only of the thinker. In the second we mark the skills used "selfishly" (as by the Sophists of old). In the third we mark the skills used fairmindedly (as by Socrates).

Critical thinkers, in the strong sense, are concerned with developing their capacities to reason with skill while also respecting the rights and needs of others. They are fairminded in the use of their intellectual skills.

See *intellectual virtues, strong-sense critical thinkers, weak-sense critical thinkers, irrational.*

social contradiction: an inconsistency between what a society "preaches," or professes to believe, and what it practices.

Every society has some degree of inconsistency between its image of itself and its actual character. When a group, for example, professes to be spreading peace throughout the world, while at the same time systematically engaging in unjust wars, it is demonstrating a social contradiction. Social contradiction is typically connected with sociocentric thought and correlated with human self-deception on the part of the group.

See *sociocentrism.*

socialization: a continuing process of learning to conform to the values, norms, traditions, manners, customs, taboos, and ideologies of one's society; assuming social skills appropriate to one's social position.

For the most part, humans live together in groups. Accordingly, they must learn to live together reasonably in those groups, to get along, to respect the rights and needs of others with whom they interrelate and interact. But the process of socialization often goes beyond a defensible conception of living together reasonably. It often leads to oppression and the violation of individual rights. Because humans create complex ideas and ideologies through which they see the world, these ideas are a necessary part of the "socialization process." At a very young age, children within every culture begin to think within these ideas, seeing them not as possible ways to think, but as the right ways to think (e.g., no elbows on the table, napkin in your lap, no nudity allowed, etc.).

Part of the ideology of any culture, then, is the laying down of rules, the creation of customs, and the forbidding of certain behaviors. Accordingly, people living within every culture are expected to uncritically accept the largely arbitrary rules, customs, and taboos of their culture. Every day, very young children in the US, for example, are expected to stand up and pledge allegiance to the flag of the United States of America. In doing so, they have no real sense of what they are pledging, of what it would mean to take their pledge seriously, of what it would mean to critically analyze it, of how to skillfully argue for and against it. This is just one example of many forms of indoctrination that often come hand-in-hand with socialization.

One important part of the socialization process has to do with social stratification. People in modern societies are layered according to a political and economic "pecking order," to put it somewhat crudely. Those at the top have most of the power and advantages. Those in the middle have a low to modest amount of power, and significant advantages. Those at the bottom have very few advantages and very little power. Part of the socialization process of every culture is to pass on the "correct behavior" for one's social status, according to the system of social stratification within the culture.

It is essential to critically analyze the social rules, customs, taboos, and power structure of one's culture so as not to be intellectually imprisoned by them.

See *sociocentrism, indoctrination.*

sociocentrism: the belief in the inherent superiority of one's own group or culture; a tendency to judge alien people, groups, or cultures from the perspective of one's own group.

As social animals, humans cluster together. Indeed, the very survival of the human species depends upon a lengthy rearing process so that all humans survive, in the first instance, because they are cared for within a group. Accordingly, children learn from an early age to think within the logic of the group. This is required for their "acceptance" in the group. As part of this socialization process, they (largely uncritically) absorb group ideologies.

Sociocentricity is based on the assumption that one's own social group is inherently and self-evidently superior to all others. When a group or society sees itself as superior—and so considers its views as correct or as the only reasonable or justifiable views—and perceives all of its actions as justified, it has a tendency to think closedmindedly. Dissent and doubt are considered disloyal, and are rejected. Few people recognize the sociocentric nature of much of their thought.

Sociocentric thought is connected with the term 'ethnocentrism,' though ethnocentrism is often used more narrowly to refer to sociocentric thought within an ethnic group.

See *socialization, egocentrism, cultural associations.*

strong-sense critical thinkers:
fairminded critical thinkers; skilled thinkers characterized predominantly by the following traits: (1) the ability and tendency to question deeply one's own views; (2) the ability and tendency to reconstruct sympathetically and imaginatively the strongest versions of viewpoints and perspectives opposed to one's own; (3) the ability and tendency to reason dialectically (multilogically) in such a way as to determine when one's own point of view is at its weakest, and when an opposing point of view is at its strongest; (4) the ability and propensity to change one's thinking when the evidence would require it, without regard to one's own selfish or vested interests.

Strong-sense critical thinkers are fundamentally concerned with reasoning at the highest level of skill, considering all the important available evidence, and respecting all relevant viewpoints. Their thought and behavior is characterized primarily by intellectual virtues or habits of mind. They avoid being blinded by their own viewpoints. They recognize the framework of assumptions and ideas upon which their own viewpoints are based. They realize the necessity of putting their assumptions and ideas to the test of the strongest objections that can be leveled against them. Most importantly, they can be moved by reason; in other words, they are willing to abandon their own ideas when other ideas prove more reasonable or valid.

Teaching for strong-sense critical thinking entails routinely encouraging students to explicate, understand, and critique their deepest prejudices, biases, and misconceptions, thereby discovering and contesting their egocentric and sociocentric tendencies (for only when we do so can we hope to develop as fairminded persons).

Regularly thinking dialogically about important and personal issues is necessary for developing strong-sense critical thinking. If critical thinking is taught simply as atomic skills separate from the empathic practice of entering into points of view that students are fearful of or hostile toward, they will simply find additional means of rationalizing prejudices and preconceptions, or convincing people that their point of view is the correct one. They will be transformed from vulgar or naïve thinkers to sophisticated (but not strong-sense) critical thinkers.

See *fairmindedness, intellectual traits, weak-sense critical thinkers.*

vested interest:
promoting personal advantage, usually at the expense of others; group pursuit of collective goals, exerting influence that enables the group to profit, often at the expense of others.

One natural implication of sociocentric thought is the problem of group vested interest. Every group potentially falls prey to this native human tendency—to seek more for its own group at the expense of others. For example, many groups that lobby Congress do so to gain money, power, and advantage for themselves by provisions in law that specially favor their group. The term 'vested interest' classically contrasts with the term 'public interest.' A group that lobbies Congress in the public interest is not seeking to gain special advantage for a comparative few but, rather, protection for the majority. Preserving the quality of the air is a public interest. Building cheaper cars by using second-rate material is a vested interest (it makes more money for car manufacturers at the expense of public safety).

The term 'vested interest' has been largely replaced with the term 'special interest' by those seeking vested interests, for they do not want their real agendas to come to light. By advancing the notion that all groups are simply seeking to protect and expand their "special interest," these groups hope to place their selfish agendas on the same footing with those in the public interest.

See *sociocentrism*.

weak-sense critical thinkers: those who use the skills, abilities, and to some extent, the traits of critical thinking to serve their selfish interests; unfair or unethical critical thinkers.

Weak-sense, or unethical, critical thinkers have the following pronounced tendencies:

(1) They do not hold themselves or those with whom they ego-identify to the same intellectual standards to which they hold opponents.
(2) They do not reason empathically within points of view or frames of reference with which they disagree.
(3) They tend to think monologically (within one narrow perspective).
(4) They do not genuinely accept, though they may verbally espouse, the values of fairminded critical thinking.
(5) They use intellectual skills selectively and self-deceptively to foster and serve their selfish interests at the expense of truth.

6) They use critical thinking skills to identify flaws in the reasoning of others, and sophisticated arguments to refute others' arguments before giving those arguments due consideration.
(7) They routinely justify their irrational thinking through highly sophisticated rationalizations.
(8) They are highly skilled at manipulation.

Opposite is *strong-sense critical thinkers*. See also *egocentrism, irrational, strong-sense critical thinkers*.

APPENDIX B:
THE LOGIC OF SOCIOCENTRIC THOUGHT

The four primary forms of sociocentric thought (groupishness, group validation, group control, and conformity) can be understood in terms of their most basic logic seen on the following few pages. Remember that the circle diagram relates to the elements of thought implicit in all human reasoning.[57]

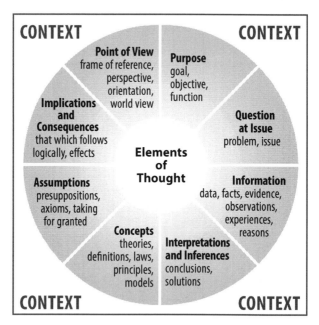

Because sociocentric thought is a form of reasoning, these eight elements are entailed in it. As you read through the following four "logics," note their implicit (rather than explicit) nature. In other words, note that, due to the inherently dysfunctional nature of these forms of reasoning, groups naturally would not admit that these ideas were guiding their thinking and behavior. Or if they admitted to any part of these ideas, they would attempt to justify their thinking through rationalizations. Since sociocentric thought functions at the unconscious level, most people are unaware of its influence.

---

57 For a deeper understanding of the elements of reasoning, see *The Thinker's Guide to Analytic Thinking* by Linda Elder and Richard Paul, 2016, Dillon Beach: Foundation for Critical Thinking Press.

Sociocentrism: The Logic of Groupishness

Point of View
Seeing our group as the center of the world, and everything and everyone else as a means to getting what we want.

Purpose
To pursue group interests at the expense of the rights, needs, and desires of those outside the group.

Key Questions
How can we as a group achieve our group purposes (without having to examine our beliefs or change in any fundamental way)?

Implications and Consequences
By deliberately pursuing group agendas and ignoring the effects of our actions on others, we are most likely to get what we want.

Elements of Reasoning

Assumptions
Our group should be so placed in the world as to get what we want without having to change in any fundamental way, or to consider the rights and needs of others.

Information
Information that enables the group to achieve its purposes and get what it wants.

Essential Concepts
The concept of group superiority and group privilege.

Inferences
The group continually comes to conclusions that serve, or seem to serve, its agenda.

Sociocentrism: The Logic of Group Validation

Point of View
Looking at our beliefs as correct and good and true, without regard to objective reality.

Purpose
To maintain the beliefs and ideologies of the group to which one is a member.

Key Questions
How can we assimilate all information so as to maintain our group's beliefs? How can we best rationalize our position so we don't have to consider other viewpoints?

Implications and Consequences
By constantly validating group beliefs, we can believe anything we want and are justified in judging everyone outside the group according to whether they agree with us.

Elements of Reasoning

Information
Information selectively chosen that enables us to maintain our views; ignoring information that goes against our views.

Assumptions
Our group should never have to consider views it doesn't want to consider; we are justified in maintaining our beliefs, even if they are unreasonable.

Essential Concepts
The concept of telling one another within our group that our views are the best.

Inferences
Interpreting the information so as to maintain the views already held by the group, or the views that appeal to the group.

Sociocentrism: The Logic of Group Control

Point of View
Seeing group control as a necessity for survival, and group acceptance of rules a requirement.

Purpose
To maintain order and control within groups.

Key Questions
How can we ensure that people in the group conform to the group's beliefs, rules, customs, and taboos? How will we deal with group members who violate group rules?

Implications and Consequences
If people abide by the rules, taboos, and conventions of the group, the group will survive and prosper. If they don't, the group will suffer.

Elements of Reasoning

Assumptions
For the group to prosper, order must be maintained. Group members must follow the rules of the group. Group members who dissent are a threat to our groups.

Information
Information that enables us to maintain control over the group — includes information about group members, human nature, rules to be followed, punishment methods, etc.

Essential Concepts
Humans as group animals in need of control by those who know how to maintain law and order.

Inferences
Judgments about (1) which behaviors will be rewarded in the group, which will be punished, which will be allowed; (2) how to deal with those who "violate" the rules; (3) who gets power and who doesn't.

Sociocentrism: The Logic of Conformity

Point of View
Seeing conformity as necessary for survival; seeing groups as hierarchical in nature, requiring conformity to rules and conventions.

Purpose
To survive and be accepted within groups; to be validated by those in control.

Key Questions
How can I survive and be accepted within this group? What rules must I follow? What beliefs must I accept? If I disagree with the rules, how far can I bend them before getting into trouble?

Implications and Consequences
As long as I follow the rules of the group, I can survive in the group. If I go against group beliefs and rules, I will be punished.

Elements of Reasoning

Assumptions
To survive, I must learn to fit into groups; I will get into trouble if I question certain rules, taboos, or customs of the group.

Information
Information and knowledge about how the group functions—about its rules, taboos, and customs which will enable me to survive and be accepted in the group.

Essential Concepts
Conformity as necessary for survival and acceptance; humans as existing in hierarchies with beliefs and rules with which group members are expected to adhere.

Inferences
Judgments about group beliefs, rules, conventions, and taboos that help me understand the group so as to be accepted in it and not get into trouble.

INDEX

About the Author

Dr. Linda Elder is an educational psychologist and
internationally recognized authority on critical thinking who has
taught both psychology and critical thinking at the college level.
She has been president of the Foundation for Critical Thinking
and the executive director of the Center for Critical Thinking for
25 years. She has a special interest in the relation of thought and
emotion, as well as the cognitive and affective and has developed
an original theory of the stages of critical thinking development.
Elder has coauthored four books on critical thinking, as well as all
23 titles found in the Thinker's Guide Library.

The Foundation for Critical Thinking seeks to promote essential change in education and society through the cultivation of fairminded critical thinking—thinking committed to intellectual empathy, intellectual humility, intellectual perseverance, intellectual integrity, and intellectual responsibility. A rich intellectual environment is possible only with critical thinking at the foundation of learning. Why? Because only when we learn to think through the content we are learning in a deep and substantive way can we apply what we are learning in our lives. Moreover, in a world of accelerating change, intensifying complexity, and increasing interdependence, critical thinking is now a requirement for economic and social survival.

Contact us online at criticalthinking.org
to learn about our publications, videos, workshops, conferences, and professional development programs.

For More Information

(To order materials or to inquire about other resources)

Phone	707-878-9100
Toll-Free	800-833-3645
Fax	707-878-9111
E-mail	cct@criticalthinking.org
Web site	www.criticalthinking.org
Mail	Foundation for Critical Thinking
	PO Box 31080
	Santa Barbara, CA 93130